D1201376

WEALTH
OR
POVERTY

WEALTH
OR
POVERTY

Jane Austen's Novels Explored

STEPHEN MAHONY

ROBERT HALE · LONDON

LONDON PUBLIC LIBRARY

© Stephen Mahony
First published in Great Britain 2015

ISBN 978-0-7198-1439-6

Robert Hale Limited
Clerkenwell House
Clerkenwell Green
London EC1R 0HT

www.halebooks.com

The right of Stephen Mahony to be identified as
author of this work has been asserted by him
in accordance with the Copyright, Designs and
Patents Act 1988

A catalogue record for this book is available from the British Library

2 4 6 8 10 9 7 5 3 1

Typeset in Palatino
Printed in Great Britain by CPI Antony Rowe

Contents

For my wife Lucinda
who has no rival in my affections,
not even Jane Austen

Foreword

IN HIS 1937 POEM 'Letter to Byron', W.H. Auden wrote of Jane Austen:

> It makes me most uncomfortable to see
> An English spinster of the middle class
> Describe the amorous effects of 'brass',
> Reveal so frankly and with such sobriety
> The economic basis of society.

The 'economic basis of society' – of the society Jane Austen knew and worked within – is exactly what Stephen Mahony sets out to explore in this well-researched and very readable book. A glance at the chapter headings indicates the comprehensiveness of his investigation, covering subjects such as taxation, inheritance and speculation that lie beneath the surface of Austen's work.

The picture that emerges in these pages is one of flux, anxiety and financial insecurity at every level. Affluence existed, but was at all times precarious. Even wealthy landowners could find themselves deeply in debt, whether from their own extravagance or that of family members, or neglectful management on the part of trusted employees, or circumstances beyond their control like poor harvests, increases in taxation or lawsuits. Thus, Sir Thomas Bertram in *Mansfield Park* is beset on more than one side, with his West Indian estates making less good returns at the same time that his eldest son is incurring debts. And when that most financially

7

imprudent of all Austen's baronets, *Persuasion's* Sir Walter Elliot, is absolutely forced to retrench, Lady Russell comments that it is only what many of the first families have done, or should do. Many titled men let their houses and lived abroad, either because the cost of living was cheaper, or to escape their creditors. Indeed, it was the flight abroad of Lord Moira, owing a £6,000 unsecured debt to the bank of Jane's brother Henry Austen, which helped to bring about Henry's bankruptcy. Wealth may trickle down, but so does financial difficulty. From being a wealthy banker with a smart house and lifestyle in town, Henry became a curate on just over £50 a year.

Clerical incomes varied widely, and while those with good connections lived off the fat of the land, many a well-educated man with wife and family existed scarcely above the poverty level for want of powerful friends. Austen was to leave the portrayal of desperate country curates to Anthony Trollope in the next generation, but in *Sense and Sensibility*, Edward and Elinor Ferrars are not so much in love as to believe they can run even a modest family household on the tithes of Delaford Rectory without financial help from his mother; and in *Pride and Prejudice* Mr Collins' gratitude to Lady Catherine for his humble abode and living becomes perfectly understandable, if overdone. The point is that there was simply no career structure through which a diligent clergyman might hope to better his circumstances; everything depended on whom he knew.

Naval officers were in a slightly better position in that their own efforts made a difference, and fortunes could certainly be made at sea; but equally such men might find themselves without a vessel for possibly years, as officers were in greater supply than ships; and when unemployed or in peacetime they could be reduced to living on half-pay. One of Jane Austen's naval brothers, Charles, was poor for most of his life, never owning a home of his own. In his forties, desperate for a ship to command, he had to leave his second wife and innumerable small children at a few days' notice and be away at sea for four years. At least this prevented further increase of family, but it was hard on everyone concerned. Mahony calculates that when naval commander Frederick Wentworth first courts Anne Elliot he is on half-pay of about £118 a year, with no guarantee of more – no wonder Lady Russell considers this is not sufficient to wed the daughter of even a spendthrift baronet, and possibly bring a child a year into the world. Eight years later, with the boost of invested prize money and a step up in rank to captain, his income has risen to £1,440 a year, a huge increase.

Ranging over real-life examples in the shape of letters and diaries, this book is full of fascinating facts. Who could imagine that William Wordsworth would spend one Christmas Day writing to his brother about how best to avoid tax?

While regarded as a universal panacea for women, their 'pleasantest preservative from want' as Jane Austen terms it, marriage might solve a man's difficulties, or might augment them. Gentlewomen could not supplement their husbands' incomes by any kind of paid work, as that would be to lose caste. The only possibility of female contribution to living expenses was the bride who came with a dowry. Mr Elton in *Emma* is reviled for believing that if he cannot have Emma's thirty thousand pounds he will look for someone with twenty, or ten (and in Augusta Hawkins he secures such a woman in the marriage mart of Bath), but Mr John Knightley must also find the interest on his wife Isabella's own thirty thousand pounds (now or after her father's death) a very welcome addition to what he can earn as a lawyer. The average income of men in the legal profession, Mahony finds, was just £400 per annum, though John Knightley is said to be doing well and might be earning considerably more. An apothecary like Mr Perry averaged £300 per annum, and if *his* income is above average (enough even to think of setting up a carriage) it is because of his frequent visits to the richest man in town, the hypochondriac Mr Woodhouse. As for the plight of the unmarried woman of gentle birth and education but small or non-existent inherited fortune, like Jane Fairfax and Jane Austen herself, she had no hope of earning the means to establish a comfortable home of her own. The choice was between accepting charity as a poor relation, or going out as a governess. Austen was uncomfortably aware that she herself fell into the first category, until her novels began to bring in a little money, but even then she spent none of it, hoarding against an envisaged penurious old age. She knew all too many impoverished spinsters and widows. Her brothers were kind, but had their own large families and their own financial ups and downs. In her short adult life, Austen became very clear-sighted about money.

That the situation of the labouring classes was dire comes as no surprise to us, but from a relative scarcity of material at this level, Mahony extracts telling detail. In one example of a married couple with eventually eight children, though the husband works at three jobs, the wife has to undertake part-time work as a lace-maker in the home, supplementing the family income by a paltry £1. 6s a year – enough to provide for the cost of her lying-in, averaging 10s a year, and half a pound of butter a week – nothing more. There is a glimpse of this kind of rural poverty in *Emma*, with the heroine's visit of charity, the call on the parish system of relief of old John Abdy, crippled by rheumatic gout, and even lower down the scale of misery and want, the gipsies and the poultry thieves. Miss Bates has a very small income, likely to be eroded, as Mahony points out, by inflation (explaining Mr Knightley's pronouncement that she will become poorer still in her old age) and her niece Jane Fairfax faces the prospect of selling her intellect, time and health for £30 a year as a governess. Yet that this same novel can show families rising in prosperity through business or farming – Mr Weston, the Coles, the Martins, with their respective households acquiring the new consumer durables and increasing the number of their servants – is proof of the fluctuating fortunes, the ever-present possibility of rise and fall, that constitutes the economic basis of society which this book, with its statistics, tables, examples and interpretation, so admirably illuminates for us.

Preface

MONEY IS MENTIONED FREQUENTLY in Jane Austen's novels – indeed, within the first sentences of three of them. One of the purposes of this book is to explain the significance of these monetary references.

In *Capital in the Twenty-First Century* (2014) the distinguished French economist Thomas Piketty drew a contrast between what he saw as the stability of monetary references in the inflation-free world of Jane Austen and the volatile modern world. Nevertheless, it is unlikely that many of Jane Austen's contemporaries felt that financial matters were stable. In 1800 retail price inflation was 21.69 per cent, yet in 1802 retail prices deflated by 14.68 per cent. The price of government securities halved between 1783 and 1798. In 1797 the Restriction Act allowed the Bank of England to dishonour its promise to pay the bearer of its notes in gold. The value of paper money of all sorts was questioned. It was an anxious and unstable time for all. This book explores these anxieties and instabilities and, by doing so, help us to understand better Austen's novels.

Jane Austen mentions money, as John Mullan has written, not so much for us to notice as for us to see her characters noticing.[1] Besides those who are very interested in money, there are those who say they are not at all interested. Some mean what they say. Guileless Catherine Morland imagines that General Tilney thinks as she does. Lucy Steele's claim to be willing to 'struggle with any poverty' is patently false – as is evident (if we need proof) when she steals her sister's money. There is a clear moral compass by

11

which characters are judged in relation to money and how they think about money: not ignoring it like Mrs Dashwood, who never saved a penny in her life; nor being preoccupied with it like John Dashwood and his wife, who think of everything in terms of money – whether Marianne's value in the marriage market or the value of the presentation to the Delaford living.

Above all, it is made clear that happiness does not depend on money alone. The good tend to get the chance to live their morality. Even so, they can end up with less. Indeed, in *Sense and Sensibility* the most deplorable characters end up being the wealthiest.

> The whole of Lucy's behaviour in the affair, and the prosperity which crowned it ... may be held forth as a most encouraging instance of what an earnest, an unceasing attention to self-interest, however its progress may be apparently obstructed, will do in securing every advantage of fortune, with no other sacrifice than that of time and conscience.[2]

It is well known that the period of the novels saw increasing social change, derived from the economic effects of industrial developments and the growth in international trade. Jane Austen would have been informed about these economic and social things, not least through her active, intelligent brothers – a landowner, a clergyman, two sailors and a banker, later clergyman. She was also informed by her reading. One book we know she read was Robert Southey's *Letters from England by Don Manuel Alvarez Espriella translated from the Spanish* (1807). Southey wrote in the persona of a devoutly Catholic visitor to England. It is not a book to take completely seriously but it is still a valuable, and very well written, view of England. Jane Austen commented to Cassandra 'The Man describes well but is horribly anti-English. He deserves to be the foreigner he assumes.'[3]

She wrote those words while reading volume two aloud by candlelight. Her opinion cannot have been improved when she read in volume three:

> Literature is, like everything else, a trade in England, — I might

almost call it a manufactory. One main article is that of Novels; —
take the word in its English sense, and understand it as extending
to four volumes of one continued tale of love. These are manufac-
tured chiefly for women and soldier-officers. To the latter they can
do no harm; to the former a great deal.... these books represent
ordinary and contemporary manners, and make love the main
business of life, which both sexes at a certain age are sufficiently
disposed to believe it. They are doubtless the cause of many rash
engagements and unhappy marriages.... And there is as much
time wasted in talking of them as in reading them. I have heard a
party of ladies discuss the conduct of the characters in a new novel,
just as if they were real personages of their acquaintance.[4]

Southey (1774–1843) began as a radical but ended as an establishment figure and Poet Laureate. In *Espriella* he describes the
prosperity of England and also its price:

A happy country indeed it is for the higher orders; nowhere have
the rich so many enjoyments, nowhere have the ambitious so fair
a field, nowhere have the ingenious such encouragement, nowhere
have the intellectual such advantages; but to talk of English happiness is like talking of Spartan freedom, the Helots are overlooked.
In no other country can such riches be acquired by commerce, but
it is the one who grows rich by the labour of the hundred. The
hundred human beings like himself, as wonderfully fashioned
by Nature, gifted with the like capacities, and equally made for
immortality, are sacrificed body and soul.[5]

Jane Austen read about the social cost of the new industries as
described by Southey.

I cannot pretend to say, what is the consumption here of the two-
legged beasts of labour; commerce sends in no returns of its killed
and wounded. Neither can I say that the people look sickly, having
seen no other complexion in the place than what is composed of oil
and dust smoke-dried. Every man whom I meet stinks of train-oil
and emery. Some I have seen with red eyes and green hair; the eyes

affected by the fires to which they are exposed, and the hair turned green by the brass works.[6]

She knew also of the terrible exploitation of children in some factories of which Southey wrote 'I thought that if Dante had peopled one of his hells with children, here was a scene worthy to have supplied him with new images of torment.'[7]

Jane Austen's was a time, too, of considerable social unrest. In *Northanger Abbey* Henry Tilney teases his sister for misunderstanding Catherine Morland's reference to a forthcoming horrible and shocking Gothic novel. Henry says of his sister:

> ... she immediately pictured to herself a mob of three thousand men assembling in St. George's Fields; the Bank attacked, the Tower threatened, the streets of London flowing with blood, a detachment of the Twelfth Light Dragoons (the hopes of the nation) called up from Northampton to quell the insurgents, and the gallant Captain Frederick Tilney, in the moment of charging at the head of his troop, knocked off his horse by a brickbat from an upper window.

This is intended as a joke but in fact riots were frequent in the 1790s. Eliza de Feuillide, Jane Austen's cousin who married a Frenchman, wrote to Philadelphia Walter on 7 June 1792 about a riot in the middle of Mayfair in London.

> Tuesday last going thro' Mount Street in my Carriage I most unexpectedly found myself in the midst of an immense mob who were contending with a large party of Guards on Horseback, because these latter endeavored to disperse them & prevent their demolishing some Houses which they were determined, & had begun, to pull down. The noise of the populace, the drawn swords and pointed bayonets of the guards, the fragments of bricks and mortar thrown on every side, one of which had nearly killed my Coachman, the firing at one end of the street which was already begun, altogether in short alarmed me so much that I really have never been well since. The Confusion continued all that day &

Night & the following Day, & for these eight & forty Hours, I have seen nothing but large parties of Soldiers parading up and down.[8]

Besides the growing industrial revolution, another great overshadowing event was the war with France. Women as far apart as Mary Hardy in Norfolk and Elizabeth Grant in Inverness-shire recorded the fear of invasion and the plans being made for their safety. In *Pride and Prejudice* the young men dressing up in militia uniforms (and Chamberlayne being dressed up as a girl) may not seem very warlike to us but the threat of invasion was real.

It is less often remembered that economic changes, taxation and inflation also caused downward social mobility. Robert Southey described a process which terrified Jane Austen's class and of which we will see examples.

The gentry of small fortune have also disappeared. The colonial war bore hard upon them, but the last has crushed them. Inheriting what to their forefathers had been an ample subsistence, they have found themselves step by step curtailed of the luxuries and at last of the comforts of life, without a possibility of helping themselves. For those who were arrived at manhood it was too late to enter into any profession; and to embark what they possessed in trade was hazarding all, and putting themselves at the mercy of a partner. Meantime year after year the price of every article of necessary consumption has increased with accelerating rapidity: education has become more costly, and at the same time more indispensable; and taxation year after year falls heavier, while the means of payment become less. In vain does he whose father has lived in opulence, and whom the villagers with hereditary respect still address hat in hand, or bow to as they pass, – in vain does he put down the carriage, dismiss the footman, and block up windows even in the house front. There is no escape. Wine disappears from his side-board; there is no longer a table ready for his friend; the priest is no longer invited after service; – all will not do: his boys must out to sea, or seek their fortune in trade; his girls sink lower, and become dependents on the rich, or maintain themselves by the needle, while he mortgages the land, for immediate subsistence, deeper and deeper as the burthen of the times presses heavier and heavier; – and happy is he if it lasts long enough to keep him from absolute want before he sinks into the grave.[9]

Such anxiety was experienced personally by Jane Austen both when her father died and again in 1816, an 'annus horibilis' for her family. Henry Austen's bankruptcy caused losses particularly to his brother Edward Knight and to James Leigh Perrot. Charles Austen's ship was wrecked. Edward Knight was troubled by a law suit that might have deprived him of his Chawton estate. The Austen ladies faced a probable reduction in their income and possible homelessness, too. This was the anxious time after which *Sanditon* was written.

The collision between old and new is exemplified by a story which, if not true, still tells us a lot about the attitudes of this period. In Darlington, Co. Durham, in the early 1800s a leading Quaker banker called Jonathan Backhouse helped to finance the Stockton to Darlington railway, and thereby incurred the enmity of the Earl of Darlington (later Duke of Cleveland) whose fox hunting was disrupted by the railway. The enmity was mutual and long lasting. The Duke tried to engineer a run on Backhouse's bank. Backhouse, who was solvent but had insufficient money to hand, dashed to London to obtain enough gold coins to meet the crisis.

One day, it is said, the two men began to argue about who was the richer. Mr Backhouse challenged the Duke to a competition. They would sit at a table in a public house and would, in turn, tear up five pound notes. The first to stop would clearly be the poorer. The Earl agreed but did not understand that Mr Backhouse would be tearing up the notes issued by his own bank, which did not cost very much to print. Mr Backhouse won the competition.

The background to the novels, and the subject of this book, is a time of financial uncertainty and social change. *Wealth or Poverty* tries to show the financial and social experiences of a variety of people to add resonance to the novels. They include not only Jane Austen herself, her family and connections, bishops, admirals, and landowners, but also Richard Walker, a farmworker of Roade in Northamptonshire, George Watson, a seaman, Agnes Porter, a governess, Mary Hardy, the wife of a Norfolk brewer, Abraham Goldsmith, a leading figure in the City, William Jones, a curate at Broxbourne, Mary Berry, a society lady with literary interests, Philip Godsal, one of the most successful London coach-builders of his day, the Reverend Sydney Smith, preacher and wit, Matthew Flinders, an apothecary of Donington in Lincolnshire, Edward Gibbon, the historian, Percy Bysshe Shelley, the poet, and John Byng, later Lord Torrington, a great traveller around England. *Wealth and Poverty* is not just a reading of Jane Austen's novels; it also describes the experiences of contemporary people, which help us to understand better the resonances and references of Austen's novels.

Given the economic changes in Jane Austen's life we should ask whether the sums mentioned in *Sense and Sensibility* are comparable with those mentioned in *Mansfield Park* or *Persuasion*. Beyond saying that agricultural incomes had risen in the intervening years, it is very hard to conjecture a suitable adjustment. Later chapters deal with incomes from land – never very straightforward, even with proper management and accounting – incomes from tithes (which, we will see, in different places rose by widely different amounts), and incomes from investment in government and other securities where capital values fluctuated but income was stable. Writing to her sister Cassandra in April 1811 when revising *Sense and Sensibility*, Jane Austen was aware of the point that 'the incomes remain as they were, but I will get them altered if I can'. Alas, we do not know if she did alter them and, if so, in what direction. The most important comparisons are between the wealth and incomes of characters within a novel. Comparisons between novels are difficult.

One recurring question is what the amounts of money mentioned in the novels would mean today. Information about relative levels of wealth and income is probably more important than any attempt at calculating modern equivalents. But it is still tempting to ask 'What are the modern equivalents of sums of money in Jane Austen's novels?' This is a question to which there is no one, right answer.[10] Two useful measures, which produce very different results, are equivalent purchasing power and equivalent social position. The former gives us a multiplier of below 100 and the latter a multiplier above 1,000.

If we start with retail price inflation we must acknowledge that modern goods and spending are so different from spending in 1800 that a comparison of retail prices is difficult. Statisticians might describe this as a giant problem in hedonics – the task of adjusting for the changing quality of goods. However we should make an attempt. Over the past 200 years prices have risen over 72 times.[11] So, adjusting Mr Bingley's annual income of £5,000 for inflation gives us a figure of £360,000.

But tax rates have changed. Since this is a broad-brush exercise, let us assume that Mr Bingley spent 10 per cent of his £5,000 income on taxes of all sorts. Adjusting for inflation and modern tax rates Mr Bingley's gross income today might be about £540,000.[12]

An alternative approach is to look at his income relative to average earnings. This is not a question of purchasing power but of relative position in society.[13] To have an income today with the same relationship to the average income means that Mr Bingley's annual income of £5,000 would become about £5,300,000 – a startlingly different figure.

In summary, we might say that Bingley's gross income was the purchasing equivalent of something above £500,000 today but that in terms of social position it was much higher, equivalent to something above £5 million. It is no wonder that Mrs Bennet was so pleased to have him as a son-in-law.

'Seldom, very seldom, does complete truth belong to any human disclosure; seldom can it be happy that something is not a little disguised, or a little mistaken.'[14] We should not take the monetary amounts in the novels as being absolutely precise; nor can we be sure, at a time of such changes, of interpreting them with accuracy – and this book certainly does not propose a simplistic economic explanation of Austen's novels. But, once we have an idea of how much a character is worth in terms of their income or capital, we can begin to understand what might otherwise be hidden from us. And that, essentially, is the premise of this book.

Acknowledgements

THIS BOOK ORIGINATED IN a talk given to the Jane Austen Society conference at Sidmouth, Devon, in September 2012. I would like to thank Patrick Stokes for that invitation and Hazel Jones, Maggie Lane and Penny Townsend who together persuaded me to accept it, and who have been so helpful and encouraging since then as the talk grew into a book. I am also most grateful to Maggie Lane for writing the foreword to this book when she had so many other demands on her time.

Anyone writing about Jane Austen owes a great debt to a number of outstanding scholars. Pre-eminent among them is Deirdre Le Faye whose distinguished books include her editions of *Jane Austen's Letters*.

I am grateful to Roy and Lesley Adkins for their generous help with sources and references.

I owe particular gratitude to the London Library and its able staff, especially Amanda Corp and Guy Penman.

Others to whom I am indebted are Vivian Bairstow, Nikolas Barnes, Dr Nicholas Bennett, Honorary General Editor of the Lincoln Record Society, Professor Emma Clery, John Ford, Dr G.A. Metters, Honorary Secretary of the Norfolk Record Society, Christophe and Melissa Stourton, Samuel H. Williamson, and Dr Mike Wood, Vice-Chairman of the St Marylebone Society.

I am grateful to Gill Jackson, Managing Director of Robert Hale Ltd. for agreeing to publish this book and to her colleagues, Lavinia Porter and Esther Lee, for all their hard work.

My wife Lucinda has been very supportive and tolerant of a frequently preoccupied husband. For that, and much else, I am very grateful.

Text Credits

A Governess in the Age of Jane Austen: The Journals and Letters of Agnes Porter, Joanna Martin (Hambledon, 1998). Extract © Joanna Martin, 1988, Hambledon Continuum UK. Extracts reproduced by permission of Bloomsbury Publishing plc.

Jane Austen's Outlandish Cousin: The Life and Letters of Eliza de Feuillide, Deirdre Le Faye (British Library, 2002). Extracts reproduced courtesy of the British Library Board.

High Society in the Regency Period: 1788–1830, Venetia Murray (Viking, 1999). Extract reproduced by permission of the Jane C. Judd Literary Agency.

Coachmaker: The Life and Times of Philip Godsal 1747–1826, John Ford (Quiller, 2005). Extracts reproduced courtesy of John Ford.

The Diary of William Tayler, Footman 1837, edited by Dorothy Wise (The St Marylebone Society, 1987). Extracts reproduced courtesy of The St Marylebone Society.

Gratefull to Providence: The Diary and Accounts of Matthew Flinders, 1775–1802, edited by M. Beardsley and N. Bennett (Boydell, 2007–09). Extracts reproduced by permission of The Lincoln Record Society.

Jane Austen's Letters, 4th edition, Deirdre Le Faye (Oxford University Press, 2011). Extracts reproduced by permission of Oxford University Press.

Measuring Worth website (www.measuringworth.com). Extracts reproduced by permission of Samuel H. Williamson.

Mary Hardy's Diary, edited by B. Cozens-Hardy (Norfolk Records Society, 1968). Extracts reproduced by permission of The Norfolk Records Society.

Letters to William Godwin, dated 25 January 1816 and 24 November 1816, in *The Letters of Percy Bysshe Shelley*, edited by F.L. Jones (Oxford University Press, 1964), Vol. I. Extracts reproduced by permission of Oxford University Press.

The Letters of Sydney Smith, edited by Nowell C. Smith (Oxford University Press, 1953). Extracts reproduced by permission of Oxford University Press.

Extracts from *The Letters of William and Dorothy Wordsworth*, 2nd edition, edited by Ernest de Selincourt (Oxford University Press, 1967), Vol. I. Extracts reproduced by permission of Oxford University Press.

A Social History of the Navy 1793–1815, Michael Lewis (Allen & Unwin, 1960). Extracts reproduced by permission of Chatham Publishing, an imprint of Pen & Sword Books.

A Country House at Work: Three Centuries of Dunham Massey, Pamela Sambrook (National Trust, 2003). Extracts reproduced with the kind permission of the National Trust.

Extract from 'Letter to Lord Byron', in Auden, W.H. and MacNeice, L. (1937), *Letters from Iceland*. London: Faber and Faber.

Chapter 1

Social Change

JANE AUSTEN'S CHARACTERS ARE, for the most part, very fortunate and belong to a tiny top slice of society. Society was changing and it was easy, particularly for women, to fall out of that comfortable position.

One contemporary view of that society was provided by Dr Patrick Colquhoun, a most indefatigable collector of information and compiler of statistics. His *Treatise on the Wealth, Power and Resources of the British Empire* (first published in 1814) gives us an interesting picture of England in about 1812,[1] extracts of which are given in the appendix.

Jane Austen's England was still a largely rural country. Soon that would change, but for now, in 1811, England's population was numbered at about 9.5 million, of which 5.3 million lived in the countryside. In Jane Austen's own county, Hampshire, of a population of 245,000, 128,000 lived in the country.[2]

By far the largest city was London, with a population of just over 1 million in 1811. The next two largest cities in Britain were one tenth of London's size: Edinburgh (102,987) and Glasgow (100,749). Manchester, Liverpool and Birmingham followed. In the whole country only 20 towns and cities had populations of over 20,000.[3]

There was through the first half of the nineteenth century a large movement of population to the cities. The first two censuses in 1801 and 1811 show the population of England growing quickly – from 10.8 million in 1801 to 12.4 million in 1811. The population of Manchester, for example, rose by 20 per cent from 81,020 in 1801 to 98,573 in 1811 and would more than treble by 1851. Growth in rural areas was often less: Basingstoke rose hardly at all from 2,589 to 2,656 in the same period.

There was a feeling that cities were vicious places. 'Agricultural occupations are certainly more favourable to good morals among the labouring people than mechanical and handicraft pursuits, which are generally prosecuted in great towns where vice and misery prevail in a much greater degree than in the country.'[4]

Britain had an empire. In 1812 the population of the British Empire was estimated to be 61 million people. Of these some 16.5 million lived in Great Britain and Ireland. Around 40 million lived in what were termed the 'East India Company's territorial possessions' (supervised by about 25,000 Europeans), of whom 14.6 million (36.5 per cent) lived 'in a state of indigence'. The balance was made up of 2 million in Australia and the Pacific, about 1.1 million in the West Indies, and just under half a million in modern Canada, with others in the Channel Islands, Malta and Africa.[5]

The growth of manufacturing was the most significant economic change. Colquhoun wrote, 'It is impossible to contemplate the progress of manufactures in Great Britain within the last thirty years without wonder and astonishment.'[6] Southey, on the other hand, writing as Don Manuel Alvarez Espriella took a different view:

> In no other age or country was there ever so astonishing a display of human ingenuity: but watch-chains, necklaces, and bracelets, buttons, buckles, and snuff-boxes, are dearly purchased at the expence [sic] of health and morality; and if it be considered how large a proportion of that ingenuity is employed in making what is hurtful as well as what is useless, it must be confessed that human reason has more cause at present for humiliation than for triumph at Birmingham.[7]

Southey's own view was that:

If the manufacturing system continues to be extended, increasing as it necessarily does increase the number, the misery and the depravity of the poor, I believe that revolution inevitably must come, and in its most fearful shape.[8]

Different views of this progress are seen in the novels. When Elizabeth Bennet goes on a tour with the Gardiners in *Pride and Prejudice* their itinerary includes Oxford, Blenheim, Warwick, Kenilworth and Birmingham – all sights to see. The upstart Mrs Elton in *Emma* has, she says, a horror of upstarts, particularly a family called Tupman, 'encumbered with many low connections' who we are told came from Birmingham, 'not a place to promise much you know, Mr Weston. One has no great hopes from Birmingham. I always say there is something direful in the sound.'[9]

A much more rational account of Birmingham some years earlier can be found in John Byng's diaries:

Birmingham is a large town and daily increasing ... we spent this morning in visiting Clays and Boltons manufactories; the latter at Soho, two miles from the town ... an inspection of their different professions affords great pleasure, and an happy idea of the improvements of my countrymen.[10]

The inventiveness of the age was remarkable. Southey wrote in 1807 about 'rail roads' involving stationary engines:

It has been recommended by speculative men that they should be universally introduced, and a hope held out that at some future time this will be done, and all carriages drawn along by the action of steam-engines erected at proper distances. If this be at present one of the dreams of philosophy, it is a philosophy by which trade and manufactures would be benefited and money saved; and the dream therefore may probably one day be accomplished.[11]

One inhabitant of Birmingham, James Bisset, published, in 1800, an unusual book, which was partly an illustrated trade directory with handsome engravings and partly an encomium in verse. He imagines the gods on a ramble through Birmingham:

In BIRMINGHAM alone, — amaz'd THEY stood,
And ev'ry pile, with admiration, view'd.
They next, attracted by the vivid gleams,
Saw Marcasites dissolve in liquid streams,
And stubborn ORES expand, and smelting, flow
By strength of Calefaction, from below.

To see the PIN-WORKS then, the Gods repair,
Nor wonder'd less at what they met with there,
To find it was in any mortal's pow'r,
To POINT, and CUT, twelve thousand PINS an hour;
And fifty thousand HEADS their shapes acquire,
In half that time, spun round elastic wire.[12]

It was a time when hard work and mechanical ingenuity could be richly rewarded. The size and profitability of the largest manufacturing concerns made agricultural incomes seem small. Sir Robert Peel's father employed 7,000 people in his cotton mills and was thought to have an income of £70,000 a year.

One example from thousands of families on the rise is that of John Broadwood.[13] A cabinet-maker born in Berwickshire in 1732, he is said to have walked to London in search of work and persuaded the Swiss harpsichord-maker Burkat Schudi to take him into his workshop. He married his master's daughter Barbara, eventually inherited the business and revolutionized the making of pianos. His firm became the largest manufacturer of pianos in the world.

He had three sons who became a magistrate, a high sheriff and an MP who was also gentleman of the bedchamber to the Prince Regent. Two of them bought estates and the third lived in bachelor quarters in Albany, off Piccadilly.

Another more famous example was Sir Richard Arkwright, the son of a tailor, who invented a water-powered spinning frame, the spinning jenny. He became very rich. He built himself a castle which was not universally admired. When he died his son inherited all his business interests and his daughter was left £100,000. The contrast between the generations is seen in their obituaries in *The Gentleman's Magazine*, as Linda Slothouber observes.[14] Sir Richard's was an entry under *Obituary of Considerable Persons* in 1792.

> He has died immensely rich, and has left manufactories the income of which is greater than that of most German principalities.... Sir Richard, we are informed, with the qualities necessary for the accumulation of wealth, possessed, in an eminent degree, the art of keeping it. His economy and frugality bordered very nearly on parsimony. He was, however, if not a great, a very useful character.[15]

His son, however, had his own obituary in 1843 in which he was described as 'this highly respected and deeply lamented gentleman'.[16] He was 'a perfect gentleman', which usually meant 'not quite perfect'. He left more than a million pounds. He had five daughters and six sons who between them were an MP, several magistrates, a Deputy Lieutenant, a High Sheriff, and a clergyman. One son lived on an estate bought from the Earl of Essex; another on an estate bought from the Marquess of Ormonde.

In *Pride and Prejudice* we see Mr Bingley midway through the same process – he has inherited money (nearly £100,000, we are told) made in trade (possibly in cotton), been well educated though he's not at all bookish, and he is 'good looking and gentlemanlike'. He ought to purchase an estate (his sisters are very anxious that he should) to complete the family's rise, but Bingley's friends think he may be too lazy! Already the energy that made the family fortune seems to be seeping away!

Darcy is a good friend to Bingley but not utterly indifferent to his origins, saying that the Bennet family's 'want of connection could not be so great an evil to my friend as to me'.

It was, too, perhaps slightly harder for the daughters of trade fortunes. Bingley's sisters have faulty manners – Georgiana Darcy's companion Mrs Annesley appears better bred.

Jane Austen's contemporaries drew an important distinction between being in trade and being a manufacturer. The former was the more genteel. We see numerous Austen characters connected to trade but not one connected to manufacturing. Among those who have been engaged in trade in *Pride and Prejudice* (besides Bingley's father) are Sir William Lucas and Mr Gardiner. In *Sense and Sensibility* it is the late husband of Mrs Jennings. In *Emma*, we have Mr Weston, Mr Coles, Mrs Elton's father and probably also Mr Elton's family. He is 'without alliances but in trade'. Of the living, only Mr Gardiner, and possibly Mr Cole, are still active in trade. Many of the others are engaged in leaving trade behind. Of Mr and Mrs Coles we are told through Emma's eyes:

> The Coles had been settled some years in Highbury, and were very good sort of people – friendly, liberal and unpretending; but, on the other hand, they were of low origin, in trade, and only moderately genteel. On their first coming into the country, they had lived in proportion to their income, quietly, keeping little company, and that little unexpensively; but the last year or two had brought them a considerable increase of means – the house in town had yielded greater profits, and fortune in general had smiled on them. With their wealth, their views increased; their want of a larger house, the inclination for more company. They added to their house, to their number of servants, to their expenses of every sort; and by this time were, in fortune and style of living, second only to the family at Hartfield.[17]

Emma, a young lady from a genteel background, is displeased at what she sees as the presumption of the Coles, who are in trade, in inviting her to dinner. However, she is advised by the Westons to accept the invitation. Here is social mobility in action. We may note that although Mrs and Miss Bates are poorer than the Coles, their social standing is higher.

In *Mansfield Park* we find the word 'trade' used in two different but negative contexts. The first is a comment on the 'marriage market'. Fanny 'had not been brought up to the trade of coming out; and had she known in what light this ball was, in general, considered respecting her, it would very much have lessened her comfort'.[18]

The second use is in relation to the play being rehearsed. Edmund disapproves of the project and his sister Julia remonstrates:

Nobody loves a play better than you do, or can have gone much farther to see one. ... True, to see real acting, good hardened real acting; but I would hardly walk from this room to the next to look at the raw efforts of those who have not been bred to the trade: a set of gentleman and ladies, who have all the disadvantages of educa- tion and decorum to struggle through.[19]

Again, trade is used in a derogatory sense. Jane Austen is clear, however, that while trade itself may be unpleasant, not all those engaged in it are so. The obvious example is Mr Gardiner. 'The Netherfield ladies would have had difficulty in believing that a man who lived by trade, and within view of his own warehouses, could have been so well-bred and agreeable.' His wife, too, is 'an amiable, intelligent, elegant woman'.[20] It is interesting to note Elizabeth's belief, before introducing them, that the appearance of her aunt and uncle would lead Darcy to mistake them for 'people of fashion'.

Manufacturing, by contrast, is hardly mentioned. The only case is when General Tilney is talking about his breakfast china, which he finds neat and simple. He thinks it right to encourage the manu- facture of his country but 'this was quite an old set, purchased two years ago. The manufacture was much improved since that time'.[21] This passage is mostly about the General's poor taste in talking about his things, but it is also an acknowledgement of progress in manufacturing.

Jane Austen did know at least one family engaged in manufac- turing – the Portals who owned a paper mill, established in 1712, which had been making paper for the Bank of England since 1724. The Portals owned Ashe Park and were therefore also a landed family that gained a baronetcy and then a peerage in the twentieth century. They were of Huguenot descent, as were the Lefroys, three of whom were successive rectors of Ashe. Benjamin Portal visited the Austens at Steventon. In a letter Jane joked to Cassandra about his handsome eyes.[22]

A more recently successful man, Samuel Whitbread, the brewer, gradually built up his Southill estate in Bedfordshire to over 10,000 acres in the period from 1760 to 1795. But the stereotype of a newly successful man trying to join the landed gentry can be misleading: many prosperous businessmen did not buy estates but preferred to buy country villas, with only a small amount of land, within easy reach of their work. One might imagine that Mrs Elton's brother-in-law Mr Suckling – he of the recently acquired barouche-landau – had a house of this sort, despite the mention of Maple Grove's 'extensive grounds'.

There were some strange results as the newly rich made their way through society. In 1812 the Lord Chief Justice, Lord Ellenborough, complained about the amount of litigation arising from challenges to duels by merchants and tradesmen. He thought it was 'high time to stop this spurious chivalry of the counting house and the counter'.[23]

The collision of old money and new money is exemplified by Emma's thoughts about Mrs Elton: 'A little upstart, vulgar being, with her Mr E. and her *caro sposo*, and her resources, and all her air of pert pretension and under-bred finery. Actually to discover that Mr Knightley is a gentleman! I doubt whether he will return the compliment, and discover her to be a lady.'[24]

Jane Austen met such people. There was Mrs Britton who called at Godmersham in October 1813, 'a large, ungenteel Woman, with self-satisfied and would-be elegant manners'. A month or so later Jane Austen was writing to Cassandra saying that Mrs Britton 'amuses me very much with her affected refinement and elegance'. There was Miss Murden 'who talks so loud', Miss Armstrong, who was 'considerably genteeler than her Parents', one of the Miss Coxes who was 'a vulgar, broad featured girl' and the whole Jervoise family, who at a ball Jane Austen thought were 'apt to be vulgar'.[25] These extracts, taken from several letters over many years, may make Jane Austen seem arrogant and we should make allowances for the manners of another time.

There is in the novels a most interesting response to the question of what constituted gentility. The use of the word 'gentlemanlike' is particularly significant, as in Elizabeth's acerbic comment to Mr Darcy: 'You are mistaken, Mr Darcy, if you suppose that the mode of your declaration affected me in any other way, than as it spared me the concern which I might have felt in refusing you, had you behaved in a more gentlemanlike manner.'[26]

This famously withering response tortured Mr Darcy, by his own admission. 'Your reproof, so well applied, I shall never forget.'[27]

In this fluid society, with people rising and falling, what are we to understand by the terms 'gentleman' and 'gentlemanlike'? The traditional view of a gentleman is set out by one group of characters in the novels, which considers it to be a matter of family, of birth. Most famously perhaps, Lady Catherine de Bourgh takes this view. She says to Elizabeth Bennet, whom she considers 'a young woman of inferior birth, of no importance in the world', 'My daughter and my nephew are formed for each other. They are descended, on the maternal side, from the same noble line; and, on their fathers' from respectable, honourable, and ancient, though untitled families.'

Lady Catherine acknowledges that Elizabeth's father is a gentleman but exclaims: 'But who was your mother? Who are your uncles and aunts? Do not imagine me ignorant of their condition.'

And then she turns to Lydia's 'patched up' marriage to Wickham, saying, 'And is such a girl to be my nephew's sister? Is her husband, who is the son of his late father's steward, to be his brother?'[28]

An important part of the traditional view was that a gentleman should own land. A 'threat' to the stability of landed society came from money made in business, and the apparently disruptive power it represented.

The opening pages of *Persuasion* show Sir Walter Elliot enjoying the Baronetage, in which he can read of the creation of his own baronetcy in 1660, and look down on all the subsequent creations. When asked to recall 'the gentleman who lived a few years back at Monkford', he eventually says, 'Oh! Ay, – Mr Wentworth, the curate of Monkford. You misled me by the term *gentleman*. I thought you were speaking of some man of property. Mr Wentworth was nobody, I remember; quite unconnected; nothing to do with the

Strafford family. One wonders how the names of our nobility become so common.'[29]

Sir Walter also dislikes having to give precedence to people of inferior birth, particularly if their youth and vigour are cut up. He dislikes the navy as 'being the means of bringing persons of obscure birth into undue distinction, and raising men to honours which their grandfathers never dreamt of … a man is in greater danger in the navy of being insulted by the rise of one whose father, his father might have distained [sic] to speak to.'[30]

When in London he had to give place to Lord St Ives, 'whose father we all know to have been a country curate' and to an Admiral Baldwin, 'the most deplorable personage you can imagine'.

Sir Walter would have agreed with the correspondent who signed himself ' A Constant Reader' in the *Gentleman's Magazine* of July 1810 who wrote that those:

> who say that Naval and Military Officers, Doctors of Law, Physic and Divinity, should take precedence of Gentlemen, are not to be regarded, because we see that such ideas proceed from persons of no good extraction, who are always anxious that those who have sprung, like mushrooms, from the lowest stations into the appearance of gentlemen, should take precedence of those whose birth entitles them strictly to that appellation. How should we like to see a man, perhaps the son of a tailor, a stonemason, or a lodging-house keeper, merely because he had attained a high commission in the army or navy, rank before a man whose forefathers had been independently seated for many generations on an hereditary estate, and which forefathers may perhaps have partaken of the noblest blood.[31]

He went on to say that 'No wealth, no learning, can make a man a gentleman who is not born so. Wealth and learning are the ornaments, not the constituents, of a gentleman.'

But then he turned a little more liberal:

> I readily grant that a man, however low his station, after he has acquired a fortune, received a liberal education, and associated

with the enlightened, may be the *stock* from which *future gentlemen* may in the course of time spring, because his descendants, by dint of education, by separation from the pursuits of their founder, and by living for some generations on an hereditary property, grow gradually into, and finally become gentlemen.[32]

Shortly after, there was a response signed 'Miles Trim':

It appears to me very rational and just, that a Captain in the Navy, or a Colonel in the Army, should have considerable rank in that State, in whose defence he exposes his life in every quarter of the Globe, and to whom is entrusted the charge of a ship or a fort, and the constant superintending management of a thousand of our fellow countrymen.

When the active worth and weighty responsibility attached to these gentlemen is duly considered, it is very possible that the publick will allow them the Precedence of the Hidalgo breed of mere Country Squires, whose greatest exertion has most probably been in promoting a Turnpike Bill; or a florid display of Elocution at a Parish Vestry.[33]

And then as if to complete the foreshadowing of *Persuasion* in this exchange:

As for Hereditary worth ... daily instances occur of the woeful degeneracy of families; nor do I know of a more execrable wretch than he, who born with every advantage of family and wealth cannot preserve his fame and respectability; nor a more contempt-ible man than he who piques himself on his consequence, because he possesses what belonged to his family ten centuries ago.[34]

So the traditional and excluding view of a gentleman is based upon family, connections and the ownership of land. That it is espoused by two of Jane Austen's least sensible characters suggests that she was not sympathetic to it. She preferred a definition that would have included good manners, taste, and (if possible) intel-ligence. Such a definition opened up the description of gentleman to a much wider field. In *Emma* the sensible Mr Knightley describes his tenant Robert Martin as 'a respectable, intelligent gentleman-farmer' – a concept Sir Walter would hardly have understood.

But it is also clear that for a character to appear gentlemanlike is no guarantee of good behaviour. The term 'gentlemanlike' is applied to more than twenty individuals in the novels and what a mixed bunch they are. There are men who by background and behaviour seem to justify the term, such as Mr Darcy, Edward Ferrars, Colonel Brandon, Colonel Fitzwilliam, Sir Thomas Bertram, Edmund Bertram, both Knightleys, and Henry Tilney. There are those who are (more or less) gentlemen by background whose behaviour is ungentlemanly: Mr Wickham, Mr Crawford, Mr Elliot and General Tilney. Last, there are men who are gentlemen by manner and action if not by breeding. Bingley is 'good looking and gentlemanlike; he had a pleasant countenance, and easy, unaffected manners' even though his fortune was made in trade by his father. It is applied to Mr Gardiner, 'a sensible, gentlemanlike man, greatly superior to his sister, as well by nature as education', though he lives in Gracechurch Street in the City of London 'within sight of his own warehouses'. Some of the things that made up a gentlemanlike air are named when Elizabeth takes pleasure in hearing 'every sentence of her uncle, which marked his intelligence, his taste, or his good manners' in his conversation with Darcy. Mr Perry, Mr Woodhouse's apothecary is also termed 'an intelligent, gentlemanlike man'. None is of ancient family or owns land.

In a time of social change a significant and nuanced character is Mr Weston in *Emma*, 'a man of unexceptional character, easy fortune ... pleasant manners' who moved back and forth between the two worlds. He 'was a native of Highbury, and born of a respectable family, which for the last two or three generations had been rising into gentility and property. He had received a good education, but on succeeding early in life to a small independence, had become indisposed for any of the more homely pursuits in which his brothers were engaged'[35] and joined the county militia.

Captain Weston married a Miss Churchill 'of a great Yorkshire family' who missed the luxuries of her former home and spent too much. She died after three years. He had to leave the militia and engage in trade to repair his fortunes. He had 'brothers already established in a good way in London, which afforded him a favourable opening'. Having realized an 'easy competence' after eighteen or twenty years, he was able to buy a little estate adjoining Highbury and to marry the portionless Miss Taylor, Emma's former governess. Yet he was not quite a perfect gentleman. His manners were a little faulty. We read that his son Frank Churchill was 'too well bred' to hear Mr Weston's hint that Frank could stay behind with Emma.

The short biography of Mr Weston summarizes the fluidity of society and reflects Austen's own position which could have so easily fallen out of the gentle world for lack of money. But equally Jane Austen is clearly disapproving of those with money but without taste or manners. Mrs Elton provokes in Emma surprisingly vitriolic thoughts.

Another socially marginal character is Charles Hayter in *Persuasion*:

> Mr Hayter had some property of his own but it was insignificant compared with Mr Musgrove's; and while the Musgroves were in the first class of society in the country, the young Hayters would, from their parents' inferior, retired, and unpolished way of living and their own defective education, have been hardly in any class at all but for their connexion with Uppercross; this eldest son of course excepted *who had chosen to be a scholar and a gentleman*, and who was very superior in cultivation and manners to all the rest.[36]

The italics in the above extract are added to highlight an interesting idea utterly at variance with the Elliot point of view. This sentence expresses a quite different concept of a gentleman. It stresses the importance of 'cultivation and manners' and allows characters possessed of these qualities to be described as 'gentlemanlike'.

In the case of Charles Hayter, Charles Musgrove still relies on the ownership of property as crucial in defending Hayter's social position. It may be noted that besides owning property there is, in Charles Musgrove's mind, also a question of style. Charles Hayter will live in a very different sort of way from his parents. What we see is an evolution in the use of the word gentleman from a long-established landowner to a man, perhaps of modest property, who is a gentleman by manner and education but not a member of the landed gentry. Jane Austen's subtle use of the word 'gentlemanlike' reflects this ambiguity.

Mr Gardiner is a representative almost of another world – the commercial world in London – and while we know he is a keen fisherman, his interests and pleasures may be supposed to be largely metropolitan. One indicator of the growing wealth in the City is what counted as poverty there. An alderman could decline to stand for mayor if he could plead 'insufficiency of wealth'. What was thought insufficient was a fortune in 'Land, Goods and Separate Debts' of less than £20,000 in 1799 which had risen to £30,000 in 1813.[37] Another indicator is that the premium demanded by a merchant to take on an apprentice had grown during the eighteenth century to the point that 'parish gentry', yeomen and lesser tradesmen were priced out of providing for sons in that way.[38]

Richard Rush, in effect the American ambassador in London, noted in 1818 the prosperity of this commercial world after a dinner at the Guildhall where he heard 'of riches among mechanics, artisans and others engaged in the common walks of business in this great city ... I heard of a haberdasher who cleared thirty thousand pounds sterling a-year, by retail shop-keeping; of brewers whose buildings and fixtures necessary to carry on business, cost four hundred and fifty thousand pounds; of silversmiths worth half a million; of a person in Exeter Change, who made a fortune of a hundred thousand pounds, chiefly by making and selling razors' as well as the fortunes made by confectioners, woollen drapers and others.[39]

Charles Greville recorded in his memoirs one quite exceptional fortune.

Old Rundell (of the house of Rundell and Bridge, the great silversmiths and jewellers) ... died worth between £1,400,000 and £1,500,000, the greater part of which is vested in the funds ... The old man began the world without a guinea, became in the course of time partner in that house during its most flourishing period, and by steady gains and continual parsimony amassed this enormous wealth. He never spent anything and lived wretchedly.[40]

Robarts the banker, one of the executors, told Greville that when the executors went to prove the will at Doctors' Commons they were told that it was the largest sum that ever had been registered there.

At the top of the commercial world one could achieve high social status but probably not while continuing in business. The only new British peer from commerce was Robert Smith who became Lord Carrington, but he was no longer active in his bank and had acquired estates in Buckinghamshire and Lincolnshire.

Further down the scale a family might achieve a temporary social elevation such as Sir William Lucas' knighthood. Having made a tolerable fortune in trade and being mayor, he was knighted on making an address to the King. This was the sort of honour which provoked Southey:

Knighthood is here bestowed indiscriminately upon the greatest and the meanest occasions: it was conferred upon Sir Sidney Smith, who stopt the progress of Bonaparte in Syria and drove him from Acre; and it is lavished upon every provincial merchant who comes up with an address from his native city to the King upon any subject of public congratulation.[41]

During the eighteenth century notions of gentility were modified. Since early in the eighteenth century it had been argued that 'to become a Merchant of Foreign Commerce hath been allowed no Disparagement to a Gentleman born, especially to a younger brother'. Through the century the development of an urban genteel culture brought the manners of the commercial elite closer to those of 'polite society'.

In the public schools the sons of City men mingled with the sons of landed gentlemen. About half of London aldermen in the mid-eighteenth century gave their sons an education identical to that of a landed gentleman's son. This was expensive. Sydney Smith wrote to Francis Horner, his boy's godfather:

> I went in search of schools for Douglas. At Ripon I found an insignificant man, in melancholy premises, and boys two in a bed. At Richmond I was extremely pleased with Mr Tate, who takes thirty boys, and appears to be a very enlightened man. Westminster costs about £150 or £200 per annum. I have little to do and am extremely poor. Why not keep Douglas at home until he is sixteen, send him for three years to Mr Tate, then to Cambridge?[42]
>
> (from *The Letters of Sydney Smith*, edited by Nowell C. Smith (OUP, 1953). Reproduced by permission of Oxford University Press.)

Smith was glad when his brother paid £100 a year towards Douglas's education and his son went to Westminster.

Marriage between families in business and country families was facilitated by the development of the Season, which brought the latter to London. But many great City families were not obviously anxious to enter the world of landed society. The sophisticated pleasures of London, the widening range of their 'investable world' and closeness to parliament must often have outweighed the charms of the quite different style of country life.

Typically merchants bought houses within easy reach of London or other cities and with a relatively small amount of land attached. Nor did these properties have the significance for their families that would have been characteristic of landed families. They were often sold on a death.

There has been a long discussion between historians about how much businessmen bought land and about what proportion of their personal wealth that land represented. There is better information available for the second half of the nineteenth century than for the first. One may speculate, also, on the reasons for such purchases. Motives might include pleasure and sport, diversification of investments or political or social advancement. Not everyone wanted to be a country gentleman.

The prosperity of England was remarkable. We might, for example, consider what the rich ate, as described by Southey.

All parts of the world are ransacked for an Englishman's table. Turtle are brought alive from the West Indies, and their arrival is of so much consequence that notices are immediately sent to the newspapers, particularly stating that they are in fine order and lively. Wherever you dine since peace has been concluded you see a Perigord pye. India supplies sauces and curry-powder; they have hams from Portugal and Westphalia; reindeers' tongues from Lapland; caviar from Russia; sausages from Bologna; maccaroni from Naples; oil from Florence; olives from France, Italy, or Spain, and choice cheese from Parma and Switzerland. Fish come packed up in ice from Scotland for the London market, and the epicures here will not eat any mutton but what is killed in Wales. There is in this very morning's newspaper a notice from a shopkeeper in the Strand, offering to contract with any person who will send him game regularly from France, Norway, or Russia.[43]

This prosperity was not shared by many of the gentry and their connections. Mr Knightley in *Emma*, for example, has little spare cash. Elizabeth Grant, of a long-established but newly impoverished Scottish land-owning family and proud of her 'old Highland blood', wrote of her encounters with the newly rich in the north of England (the 'mercantile aristocracy of England'):

> The profusion of money among all these people amazed poor me; guineas were thrown about as *we* would not have dreamed of dealing with shillings. There was no ostentation, no great show anywhere, but such plenty, such an affluence of comforts, servants well dressed, well fed; eating, indeed, went on all day upstairs and downstairs, six meals a day the rule. Well-appointed stables, delightful gardens, lights everywhere, fires everywhere, nothing wanting, everything wished for was got.[44]

Elizabeth Grant goes on:

> Generally speaking, the generation which had made the money in the mills was more agreeable than the generation which had left the mills and was spending the well-earned money. The younger

people were well educated – so-called – the men school and college bred, gentlemanly, up to the times; but there was a something wanting, and there was too much vivacity, too much noise, no repose. The young women were inferior to the young men; they were accomplished, in the boarding-school acceptation of the word, but *mind* there was not, and manners were defective – no ease. They were good, charitable, and highly pleased with their surroundings and with one another, and extremely proud of their brothers.[45]

We see in the novels both those rising up in society – the Bingleys and the Eltons, for example – as well as those falling downwards – the Dashwood women and the Elliots. Neither group is all good or all bad. Jane Austen was too acute an observer of the social movements which so entertain us in the novels.

Chapter 2

Incomes and Taxation

INCOMES OR FORTUNES ARE often specified in Jane Austen's novels. This chapter will try to set those incomes in a contemporary context. References to tax are few in the novels – a blessing, perhaps – but taxation during the Napoleonic War with France was comparatively heavy and a matter of great concern. Laconic references to incomes 'clear' of taxes and so on carried more significance to Jane Austen's contemporaries than they may to the modern reader.

Patrick Colquhoun, Jane Austen's contemporary, set out what he believed to be the average incomes of each class in society.[1] Modern historians generally believe that average incomes were lower than Colquhoun thought. On balance I have thought it better to use the information that was in the public domain in Jane Austen's lifetime and which indirectly might have helped to form her world view. Modern estimates reduce the incomes of baronets and of knights and esquires by £500 per year and those of gentlemen by £100. Colquhoun began at the top. The average income of 516 noblemen was £10,000 a year. In this class averages are particularly misleading – some families had incomes greater than the sovereigns of the lesser European states, others 'got by' on perhaps £5,000 a year. Until the creations of Pitt the Younger, the nobility was a group of about 170 families – fairly homogeneous and exclusive. By the end of the eighteenth century the nobility consisted of some 300 families with a further 200 Irish peers – still a small group, though differing widely in their economic circumstances. Mr Rushworth (£12,000) and Mr Darcy (£10,000) are the only two characters with this level of income.

Colquhoun estimated that 861 baronets had on average £3,510. Charles Bingley's income is between £4,000 and £5,000. Henry Crawford has an income of £4,000 a year. Both are very rich young men. John Dashwood's income may be larger – perhaps £5,000–£6,000.

The gentry formed a much larger, more diverse and less exclusive group – a group nearly a hundred times larger than the nobility. An important identifier was the ability to live a life more or less of leisure on an income derived from rents, mortgages and investments – the life of a gentleman. Colquhoun estimated that 11,000 knights and esquires had an average income of £2,000. Colonel Brandon has such an income. Below this level, Captain Wentworth's income would have been about £1,440 – a combination of a captain's half-pay and interest on his capital of £25,000 – still quite modest on which to marry the daughter of a baronet.

Willoughby's income after marriage could not be more than £3,100 and is likely to be less, depending on how much of Miss Grey's fortune is required to settle his debts.

Colquhoun estimated that there were some 35,000 'Gentlemen and Ladies living on incomes' who on average had incomes of £800. Edward Ferrars would have had this or a little more after his marriage, as rector of Delaford. The Reverend Mr Norris enjoyed an income of just under £1,000, made up of his wife's income (about £350) and his living, which (we may assume) was a little less than £650. Edmund Bertram had about £700 at Thornton Lacey, which would have risen to about £1,350 or so, when he took on the parish of Mansfield in addition.

These figures give us a context also for women's incomes. However, as we will see later, the assumption that incomes were 5 per cent of capital needs to be treated with care. It was not always so.

Miss Grey has a fortune of £50,000. She, or her husband, would have been thought to enjoy an income of £2,500 per year from it. Three women have fortunes of £30,000 – Emma Woodhouse, Georgiana Darcy and Miss Morton – which would each have been assumed to produce £1,500 a year. Four women had fortunes of £20,000 – Mary Crawford, Bingley's sisters and General Tilney's late wife – which conventionally were thought to represent incomes of £1,000 a year. Then we have women with fortunes of £10,000–£12,000 or £500–£600 a year: Miss Campbell, Mrs Dashwood, Mary King, and Augusta Elton, who was once thought to have a fortune of £20,000. We can only speculate on whether it was her social ambition or Mr Elton's self-consequence that gave rise to that mis-understanding. Then we descend past Lady Bertram (£350 a year), Mrs Grant (£250), Mrs Bennet (£200), possibly Anne Elliot (£167 – being the income on a third of £10,000, if her father can afford to give it to her), and Catherine Morland (£150) to the Dashwood sisters (£50) and the Bennet sisters (£40).

Besides land, gentlemen might hope to have income from government posts. Even better, after the 1810 Act entitling public servants to pensions, was retirement from a government post. In 1818, Sir Bellingham Graham from Yorkshire enjoyed pensions from four different offices, each of which he had retired from on grounds of ill health before taking up the next.

Amongst the professions, 19,000 lawyers averaged £400, 18,000 physicians and apothecaries £300 – a likely benchmark for Mr Woodhouse's favourite apothecary Mr Perry.

The idea of a 'competence' was an important one in the lives of gentlefolk. It was the amount of money that 'will allow you to live independently of your own exertions'.[2] A contemporary called it 'amongst the prime ingredients in the cup of human happiness'.[3]

Elinor and Marianne talk about this in Sense and Sensibility. While Marianne says that 'beyond a competence, it [money] can afford no real satisfaction as far as mere self is concerned' her competence is 'about eighteen hundred or two thousand a-year, not more than that'. Elinor laughed. 'Two thousand a-year! One is my wealth!' Marianne's response is: 'two thousand a-year is a very moderate income … a family cannot well be maintained on a smaller. I am sure I am not extravagant in my demands. A proper establishment of servants, a carriage, perhaps two, and hunters, cannot be supported on less.'[4]

We should remember that while Marianne appears absurd, she was a young girl who had until lately lived in a family with at least double her 'competence'. Generally something between £500 and £600 seems to have been the minimum for a family competence, both in the novels and in Jane Austen's own life.

Think, too, of the consequences of not having a competence. Poor Jane Fairfax in *Emma*, for example, has to put up with women like Mrs Elton in her search for a post as a governess which, when she found it, would have paid perhaps 20–30 guineas plus board and lodging. And Harriet Smith is even more vulnerable. This is why 'the yearly income is an obsessive motif in women's fiction at the turn of the eighteenth century.'[5]

Whatever you had, everybody thought they knew the particulars. Details of marriage settlements, for example, were repeated in private letters and conversation. John Dashwood tells Elinor about the proposed settlement if Edward Ferrars marries Miss Morton. Mrs Norris tries to find out how much money Mrs Grant had brought as her portion. 'Inquire where she would, she could not find out that Mrs Grant had ever had more than five thousand pounds'.[6]

Agriculture is the source of income of many characters in the novels, both the landowners and the clerics whose tithes derived from it. The composition of the nation's income was changing but agriculture was still the largest component – £217 million or just over half a total estimated by Colquhoun as £431 million, followed by manufacturing's £114 million, foreign commerce and shipping's £46 million, and inland trade's £31 million.[7]

This was the national income that Pitt had to tax in order to pay for the war against Napoleon. When the disagreeable John Dashwood complained in *Sense and Sensibility* about the demands on his purse, he would have been understood to be referring to the numerous new taxes.

In the period 1793–1815, government spending was 61 per cent on the wars, 30 per cent on interest payments and only 9 per cent on civil government.[8] In 1810, government tax revenue came in very roughly equal proportions from three sources: direct taxes on wealth and income, customs duties on retained imports and excises and stamps levied on domestic products and services.

Taxes were of four sorts: government, assessed or 'King's' taxes, indirect taxes in the form of excise duties, and local taxes levied by a town vestry or parish council.

The oldest government tax was window tax, based on the number of windows in a residential dwelling. Jane Austen may have known that her brother Edward paid tax on 61 windows at Chawton Great House[9] At Sotherton the party from Mansfield Park are shown over the house and visited 'many more rooms than could be supposed to be of any other use than to contribute to the window tax and find employment for housemaids'.[10] Philip Godsal, the leading coach-maker and a rich man, paid window tax of £28 6s. 6d. in 1807 on forty windows of his house at 243 Oxford Street.[11] We will use his tax records to illustrate how taxes worked.

Income tax was introduced in 1799 and repealed in 1816. Incomes below £60 were exempt. There was a sliding scale of tax on incomes from £60 to £200. Above that, all income was taxed at 10 per cent. In 1803 the tax was removed briefly after the Peace of Amiens but soon reintroduced as property and income tax. The top rate quickly returned to 10 per cent.

Each person had to complete a return – a form of self-assessment. They might then be summoned to explain themselves. The discussions with the assessor seem quite modern. Matthew Flinders, the Lincolnshire apothecary, recorded in his diary for Tuesday 28 May 1799:

> I was summoned to appear at Boston on my Statement on the Income Tax, which was a disagreeable business, tho' the Gentlemen behaved very Polite to me, and I think I profited by the journey, for tho' they disallowed 2 of my deductions, viz. the Assessed Taxes of last year & Parochial Assessments amounting to about £3, I was allowed for 5 Children, which I scarce expected.[12]

It was not until 1806 that the income of married couples was taxed as one. Before that, married women living with their husbands had their income accounted for separately and the tax was paid separately. It was possible for a married couple to arrange their affairs so as to reduce their total tax bill.

On Christmas Day 1805, William Wordsworth wrote to his brother Richard in London:

> I wrote to you some time ago about the Income tax wishing to know in what way ours could be given in to be the least burthensome. Persons under sixty Pounds a year I understand pay nothing could we not take advantage of this in some way; at least do tell me what is best to be done.[13]

> (from *The Letters of William and Dorothy Wordsworth*, 2nd edition, edited by Ernest de Selincourt (Clarendon Press, 1967). Reproduced by permission of Oxford University Press.)

Nobody knew very much about the incomes of the nation in the early nineteenth century. When Pitt introduced his income tax there were various estimates of what revenue it would raise. Pitt expected about £10 million; others from £12 to £15 million.[14] In fact, the tax raised less than £6 million. Contemporary estimates proposed a more equal distribution of incomes than seems to have been the case.

Deductions allowed in calculating taxable income included other tax payments, interest payments, and allowances made to one's family and others. There were allowances for children given as a percentage of the tax assessed. Total deductions were typically 30 per cent so that taxable incomes were about 70 per cent of gross incomes. What is remarkable is that, of the total income tax paid in 1799/1800 of £6.2 million, almost £0.5 million was in voluntary contributions. In 1800–1 there were just over 320,000 tax payers.

Land tax was charged at 4 per cent of a notional rental income. This was the largest government tax. In *Sense and Sensibility* we read that Mrs Ferrars, if Edward will give up Miss Steele and marry Miss Morton, is prepared to settle on him the Norfolk Estate, 'Which, clear of land tax, brings in a good thousand a-year'.[15]

House tax was assessed on the rental value of houses. Godsal paid £13 15s. on his house at 243 Oxford Street.

Carriage tax was a vehicle licence tax on any four- or two-wheeled vehicle – with the exception noted elsewhere of simple carts. Godsal paid £11 for one carriage in 1807. Horse tax was naturally closely related to carriage tax. In 1807 the rate was £5 0s. 6d. per horse. Servant tax was charged only on male indoor servants. The rate was £3 6s. in 1807 and rose later.

The most important local tax was the poor rate, paid on the value of a householder's property and collected by parish overseers who used the money raised to maintain workhouses and to make subsistence payments to the unemployed or to those whose earnings were too small for them to survive on. Godsal paid £13 6s. 8d. in poor rate on his house in Oxford Street. Other smaller taxes included the church rate, and the highway rate.

Thereafter the variety of taxes is bewildering. There was an armorial tax levied on those who displayed arms, whether or not entitled to such arms. The rate was £2 2s. and also rose later. Godsal paid this although his entitlement to arms was uncertain. Hair powder tax was one of the new taxes introduced by Pitt. It was set originally at one guinea and increased eventually to two guineas. Wigs were rarely worn after 1800 though powdering the hair continued. In 1812 more than 46,000 people paid this tax. There was even a dog tax at 12s. per year, later increased to 14s.

We know the assessed taxes Philip Godsal paid in 1807:[16]

Window tax (40)	£28–6–6
House tax	£13–15–0
Servant tax (3)	£9–18–0
Carriage tax (1 four-wheeled)	£11–0–0
Horse tax (3)	£15–2–6
Hair powder tax	£2–2–0
Armorial tax	£2–8–0
Property & Income tax	£178–14–3
Total	**£261–6–3**

In the period from 1791 to 1807 Philip Godsal's assessed taxes rose by 750 per cent from £39 18s. 4d. to £261 6s. 3d. While partly the result of his growing wealth, it also reflects the rise in the tax burden.

So much for direct assessed taxes. There were also indirect taxes applied to tea, coffee, sugar, wines, spirits, beer, candles, soap, glass, tobacco, snuff and other commodities. There was also an auction tax.

Women appear as considerable tax payers in their own right. In 1799/1800 in London women with large taxable incomes included Mrs Judy Levy (£12,440), the daughter of Moses Hart, a wealthy merchant, and two widows of Indian nabobs – a Lady Hughes (£14,730) and a Mrs Dupre (£16,420). A Lady Andover of Elford in Staffordshire paid tax on an income of £21,000 in 1799/1800.[17] In Bath female tax payers seem to have outnumbered male tax payers – at least among those paying directly to the Bank of England. The widowed Eliza de Feuillide, Jane Austen's first cousin, complained that she was:

> almost ruined by the hard times. These new taxes will drive me out of London, and make me give up my carriage for I cannot afford an increase of House Rent which my Landlord already talks of, Thirty two pounds a Year in addition to the present expence of a vehicle, and four Guineas more on my Man Servant Account.[18]

Eliza married Henry Austen three weeks later.

A Whig view of Pitt's taxes came from Sydney Smith.

> I cannot describe to you how disgusted I am by the set of canting rascals who have crept into all kinds of power during the profligate reign of Mr Pitt, who patronised hypocrisy, folly, fraud and anything else which contributed to his power ... he was one of the most luminous eloquent blunderers with which any people was ever afflicted. For 15 years I have found my income dwindling away under his eloquence, and regularly in every Session of Parliament he has charmed every classical feeling and stript me of every guinea I possess. At the close of every brilliant display an expedition failed or a Kingdom fell, and by the time his Style

had gained the summit of perfection Europe was degraded to the lowest abyss of Misery.[19]

(from *The Letters of Sydney Smith*, edited by Nowell C. Smith (Clarendon Press, 1953). Reproduced by permission of Oxford University Press.)

This chapter will have served to explain a little of the dreadful John Dashwood's concern about the 'perpetual demands upon his purse, which a man of any consequence in the world was beyond calculation exposed to', though nothing could make him a sympathetic character.

Chapter 3

Land and Settlements

IN *PERSUASION* CHARLES HAYTER is a young man in search of a curacy but he is also an eldest son who, according to another eldest son, Charles Musgrove, stands to inherit:

> the estate at Winthrop (which) is not less than two hundred and fifty acres besides the farm near Taunton, which is some of the best land in the country ... whenever Winthrop comes into his hands, he will make a very different sort of place of it, and live in a very different sort of way; and with that property he will never be a contemptible man. Good, freehold property.

Landed property was the foundation of eighteenth-century society. 'Income from land tended to confer a higher social status on its owner than an equivalent income from any other source.'[1] Land gave stability to the society that was based upon it. Part of the story of nineteenth-century politics, and of the novels, is the decay of the landed interest in relation to other wealth. But it was not a quick process. As late as 1865 it was said that thirty-one families supplied one quarter of the House of Commons.[2]

D'Archenholz (1741–1812), a Prussian officer and a historian touring England in 1789, wrote:

I was witness, at a contest for the town of Newcastle, to a very singular circumstance. Two candidates had offered themselves for this place: the one was the friend and relation of the late Duke of Northumberland, who went there on purpose to assist him, and engage the people in his interests: the other was patronized by a merchant of London, of the name of Smith, who had acquired a fortune of £100,000 in the coal-trade, and had a considerable interest among the inhabitants. The Duke of Northumberland, who, besides the advantages of his rank and fortune, had also occupied some of the most distinguished situations in the state, did not imagine that such a man could oppose him with any probability of success. However, on his arrival at Newcastle he was soon convinced of his mistake. In consequence of this he sent for Mr. Smith, who observed, that he had no business with the duke, and that his grace must wait upon him. The duke actually complied, and said, that if he would allow his relation to represent the borough, his friend should be returned for a town in the neighbourhood that was entirely at his own disposal. Smith upon this roughly refused his grace's proposition, saying, 'I have promised my friend that he shall represent this place, and no other; and I am not in the habits of breaking my word.' 'Very well,' replied the duke, 'it only remains that we should try our strength,' and immediately departed. In fine, each used his utmost efforts; but the coal-merchant's candidate was elected in spite of all the interest of the lord lieutenant of the county, whose little credit became the subject of ridicule.[3]

The sources of rental income from real property in the whole country can be summarized as follows. In 1810 rent from real property amounted to £53.8 million. Agricultural land yielded £33.4 million of this – some 62 per cent. Rental income from houses was £14.2 million and tithes £4.3 million. Other land and property contributed £2.1 million.[4]

It was also possible to own land abroad. Sir Thomas Bertram has an estate in the West Indies. Patrick Colquhoun, writing in 1815, estimated the capital value of the West Indies to be £175,234,864. At the same time he valued the United Kingdom and Ireland at £430,521,372. This gives us a sense of the importance of the West

Indies, being worth about 40 per cent of the Mother Country. Antigua, where Sir Thomas has his estate, was a relatively small part of this – about 2.5 per cent of the West Indies – being valued at £4,364,000. However Colquhoun valued the annual production of Antigua at £898,320, or just under 5 per cent of the total West Indies' production.

The population was made up of 3,200 white, 1,400 free persons of colour, and 36,000 negro labourers, though the population was falling as a result of a run of bad years. Colquhoun explained the difficulties.

> The casualties to which they are exposed, the great expences incurred, particularly in time of war, in transporting their produce to the Mother Country, the high duties imposed on the produce of the soil, the hazards to which the land-holders are liable by hurricanes and bad seasons producing deficient crops, and frequently bad markets have brought thousands of industrious individuals from a state of affluence to misery and want.[5]

Mrs Norris feared that 'Sir Thomas's means will be rather straitened, if the Antigua estate is to make such poor returns'[6] and indeed Sir Thomas sets off to arrange his affairs there.

Colquhoun noted that from 1807–11 sugar prices were on average below the cost of production, excluding duty and that as a result 'Estate after estate has passed into the hands of mortgagees and creditors absent from the islands, leaving large districts in which there is not a single proprietor of a sugar plantation resident!' Sir Thomas was one of these absentees. Probably his estate would have been a sugar plantation. Colquhoun reported of Antigua that 'besides Sugar and Rum it produces some cotton and tobacco, and in good years a considerable quantity of provisions are raised; but the seasons are very variable, and the island suffers greatly by droughts, by which the crops of sugar are often reduced to ¼ of the produce of the island in favourable years.'[7] Most of the sugar produced in Antigua was exported to England. During wartime that was expensive and uncertain.

Fanny asked Sir Thomas about the slave trade. There was a dead silence and her 'cousins were sitting by without speaking a word, or seeming at all interested in the subject'. Edmund tells her that Sir Thomas would have liked to have been inquired of further but the subject lapses. Jane Fairfax talks of the guilt of the slave trade, so I think we can accept the author's disapproval. However, abolishing the slave trade and abolishing slavery were two different things. Chillingly, Colquhoun noted that negro labourers were 'formerly valued at £50. Their value has, however, greatly increased, particularly since the abolition of the slave trade. Averaged, they cannot now be worth less than £55'.[8]

Jane Austen did not write as a member of the landed gentry – but as an observer, related to and often visiting them. Her life was lived between the poles of genteel poverty at Chawton and the luxury of two fires in the great rooms at Godmersham, between travelling in a donkey cart and riding in a barouche. Jane Austen was a member of what has been called 'the pseudo-gentry' though I prefer 'un-landed gentry' – those who by birth, manners and upbringing were very similar to the landed gentry. Many of them descended from land-owning families. The ruthless application of primogeniture excluded them from the comforts they or their parents had enjoyed as children. These 'un-landed gentry' were the younger sons and upper professional families living in the country – clergymen, barristers, army officers and so on. This position on the margin forms Jane Austen's view of the landed gentry – well informed but amused and critical.

In *Sanditon* Lady Denham makes the distinction clearly. Speaking of the families that visit the resort she says, 'as far as I can learn, it is not one in a hundred of them that have any real Property, Landed or Funded. An income, perhaps, but no property. Clergymen maybe, or Lawyers from Town, or Half-pay officers, or widows with only a jointure.'[9]

Landowners are among the important characters in the novels: Mr Darcy, Mr Bennet, Mr Knightley, Sir Thomas Bertram, Mr John Dashwood, Colonel Brandon, Sir Walter Elliot, and so on. However, several of them did not actually own the land that gave them their consequence. Mr Bennet and Sir Walter Elliot, for example, have only life interests in their estates. The trusts that determine the future of the Longbourn and Kellynch estates play important roles in *Pride and Prejudice* and *Persuasion* respectively.

Many estates were held in strict settlements – trusts of which the apparent owner was merely a life tenant. This served to protect family estates from reckless spendthrifts and to ensure their descent, usually to men who would continue the family name and influence. The amount of land held in settlements was large – perhaps between one half and two-thirds of the land in England.[10]

The use of trusts developed during the Interregnum in the seventeenth century when royalist landowners facing fines might lessen them if they could argue that they were only life tenants and not absolute owners of their estates. At its simplest it worked as follows: an arrangement was made when an eldest son came of age or married by which his father – the apparent owner of the estate – became a life tenant. After his death his son, too, would be a life tenant and after the son's death the estate would descend to *his* eldest son (as yet unborn) as 'tenant in tail'. When this last son came of age he might enter into a new settlement to repeat the process down through further generations. However, if the tenant in tail wished he could quite easily break the entail and become the absolute owner.

A settlement prescribed what could be done with an estate, particularly whether, and to what extent, it could be used as security for a mortgage or whether it could be charged with a jointure, an annual income for a widow, or portions for daughters or younger sons.[11]

The purpose of these arrangements was to preserve an estate as one entity and thus the standing of the family. It tended to create a feeling that what was inherited should be handed on intact. The middle classes, which tended to have much less wealth in land and much more in personal assets, did not feel such obligations and tended to provide for children more equally and usually not in the form of a settlement.

Having once settled an estate, a father lost an important means of controlling his eldest son and reduced that son's ability to limit the excesses of his own eldest son. A settlement made on a son's majority reduced the family's freedom to negotiate a subsequent marriage settlement as well as the father's influence over the choice of bride. Some families preferred to delay making such settlements until the eldest son was about to marry. Another solution to this problem was not to settle all one's land but to keep some back in personal ownership (known as a 'fee simple').

As to the remainder (backstop beneficiaries) of a settlement, in the absence of a direct male heir a settlor was likely to prefer to see his brothers or nephews inherit ahead of his own daughters or the daughters of his sons. Mrs Bennet's problem is the strict settlement that governs the future of Longbourn in *Pride and Prejudice*. The search for a male heir to an estate could lead to distant relatives, like Mr Collins. Thomas Knight II of Godmersham adopted as his heir Edward Austen, the great-grandson of his paternal grandmother's brother.

The use of such trusts was not universal. In *Pride and Prejudice*, Lady Catherine de Bourgh saw 'no occasion for entailing estates from the female line. It was not thought necessary in Sir Lewis de Bourgh's family.'

The preservation of the family estate and the local and sometimes national influence that it supported was the chief duty of a landowner and his trustees. It is the consequences of this intention that propel the four Dashwood ladies from a large estate where the family had long been settled and respected into a rented cottage in a different county. The beneficiary of this apparent injustice was John Dashwood, who was unpleasant but not irrational.

Failing a male heir, one turned to females. Sometimes this, too, proved difficult. Sir Thomas Wentworth, fifth and last baronet of Bretton, had a child, Diana, by his gamekeeper's daughter. He was a substantial landowner and had assumed the name of Blackett on inheriting Blackett estates in addition to his own. 'He took his daughter from the kitchens of his home at Bretton Park to make her his sole heiress.' Diana married Colonel Thomas Richard Beaumont (1758–1829). The Beaumonts had been landowners in Yorkshire since the thirteenth century and were among the wealthiest commoners in England, with property in Northumberland, Yorkshire and Durham.[12]

If a man got into financial trouble, the family settlement might be an obstacle to resolving it. Edward Gibbon recalled his father's difficulties. He remembered that:

> his graceful person, polite address, gentle manners, and unaffected chearfulness, recommended him to the favour of every company ... His labours were useful, his pleasures innocent, his wishes moderate: and my father seemed to enjoy the state of happiness which is celebrated by poets and philosophers ... but the last indispensable condition, the freedom from debt was wanting to my father's felicity: and the vanities of his youth were severely punished. The first mortgage on my return from Lausanne (1758) had afforded him a partial and transient relief: the annual demand of interest ... was a heavy deduction from his income: the militia was a source of expense: the farm in his hands was not a profitable adventure: he was loaded with the costs and damages of an obsolete law-suit; and each year multiplied the number, and exhausted the patience of his creditors.[13]

Gibbon consented to a further mortgage and the sale of a house in Putney, which had been his grandfather's property. But his father was 'no longer capable of a rational effort'. We are told that 'his constitution was broken, he lost his strength and his sight: the rapid progress of a dropsy admonished him of his end, and he sunk into the grave' in 1770.

Gibbon was not much more effective than his father, taking fifteen years to sell his estate at Lenborough near Buckingham to pay his father's debts. Nevertheless he noted that the 'remains of my patrimony have been always sufficient to support the rank of a Gentleman, and to satisfy the desires of a philosopher'. He was confident that 'the remnant of my estate affords an ample and honourable provision for my declining age'.[14] Remarkably unsentimental, he remarked of his five brothers and one sister who all died in infancy, 'the shares of fortune to which English children are reduced by our English laws, would have been sufficient however to oppress my inheritance'.[15]

Gibbon was a cooperative son. One who was not was the poet son of a substantial landowner in Sussex, Sir Timothy Shelley.

Sir Timothy's father, Sir Bysshe Shelley had tried, by settlement and will, to 'perpetuate a large mass of property' – indeed he left £240,000 to his heirs upon his death. The poet Shelley's inheritance under his grandfather's will was contingent on his giving up the right to bring the settlement to an end after his own father's death, when he could have sold the estates. The poet wrote that:

> ... the principles which pronounce on the injustice of my hereditary rights ... are far dearer to me than life. But these principles teach me to set a high value on the power with which their violation may one day entrust me.[16]

(from *The Letters of Percy Bysshe Shelley*, Vol. I, edited by F.L. Jones (OUP, 1964). Reproduced by permission of Oxford University Press.)

He refused to accept the inheritance on these terms.

Shelley's subsequent negotiations with his father were based, as he admitted, on his father's mistaken belief in the 'prudence and regularity of my conduct'.[17] In fact, he had pressing debts and was trying to raise money on annuity or on his reversionary interest as a last resort.

In *Pride and Prejudice* Wickham is careful to describe Darcy's income as 'a clear ten thousand per annum'. In other words Darcy's income was clear of the charges so often found on estates. This may be attributable to the diligence and 'active superintendence' of Wickham's father, whose 'good conduct' Darcy acknowledges.

There is a tendency among film-makers and others to think of Pemberley as being similar to Chatsworth, the Duke of Devonshire's house in Derbyshire. There is no evidence that Jane Austen ever visited Chatsworth, though some have proposed an unrecorded expedition from Hamstall Ridware and have detected similarities in the descriptions of park and house. It is also pointed out that Chatsworth was then a smaller house than now. The sixth Duke of Devonshire, a bachelor, later built the north wing and gilded the window frames after seeing houses in St Petersburg so decorated in 1825.[18] Chatsworth was clearly a large house, but not then a small palace.

Mr Darcy, with a clear income of £10,000 a year, has a park at

Pemberley which is ten miles round – a good 4,000 acres if roughly square in shape. Mr Rushworth's park at Sotherton is about 700 acres though his income is £12,000 a year. The difference is not necessarily an authorial mistake. It would depend on the use to which the park at Pemberley is put. A mixture of forestry and grazing might have been very productive.

Whether settled or not, debt became a burden on many estates in the early nineteenth century. In addition, the estate might be liable to pay annuities – so disliked by Mrs Ferrars. To take a rather grand example, the seventh Duke of Bedford, succeeding in 1839 after two prolific and extravagant predecessors, found he had inherited £551,940 of debts including £482,970 of mortgages. The largest part of the mortgages – £283,910 – was to secure portions for thirteen relatives. This debt cost £26,553 per annum on top of which were annuities of some £16,000. The Duke was somewhat comforted when comparing these costs with those of Earl Spencer. His interest and annuities cost him 42 per cent of his income, whereas Earl Spencer's were about 79 per cent.[19]

Whether in trust or not, debt crept up on many estates. In 1823, when the Bank of England offered to lend money on mortgages, there were fifty-seven applications for loans from landowners including the Duke of Devonshire, who asked for £130,000, the Duke of Newcastle (£160,000), the Marquess of Bath (£200,000), the Duke of Rutland (£300,000) and the Earl of Oxford (£350,000).[20] These were very large sums.

Other dukes were in better positions, usually as a result of careful management. The Duke of Northumberland owned almost 150,000 acres in Northumberland, let as 372 farms from which the total rent was £92,000.[21] The Duke's total income was thought to be about £150,000. The Dukes of Bedford owned some 80,000 acres spread through five counties but the most important were the 119 acres they owned in London – in Bloomsbury, Covent Garden and St Martin's. The net income from the London property was about £67,300; the income from all the other land was about £26,470.[22]

Accounting was not very advanced even on well-run estates and it would often have been hard for a borrower to know his exact position, taking into account unpaid bills, arrears of salary and so on. It was later said that mortgages amounted to half the value of the land in England. There were disasters among the great estates, of which the collapse of the Duke of Buckingham was the most notorious. Other families had similar difficulties. In 1804 bailiffs took possession of Warwick Castle and in 1817, on the death of the fourth Duke of Marlborough, bailiffs moved into Blenheim. It was to events like these that Lady Russell refers when discussing the possible retrenchments that Sir Walter Elliot might make. 'What will he be doing, in fact, but what many of our first families have done – or ought to do?' There was indeed nothing singular in his case. Nor was extravagance confined only to old-established aristocratic families. For example, several members of the Drummond banking family incurred heavy debts.[23]

One of the difficulties Sir Walter faces is a lack of room in which to manoeuvre. 'There was only a small part of his estate that Sir Walter could dispose of.' Lacking a cooperative son, Sir Walter would probably have had no way of 'letting in' debts (turning personal debts into debts of the settlement) or of creating another trust specifically to deal with his debts. In such cases hard-pressed gentlemen could try to negotiate the reduction of portions with relatives or delay the timing of the payments. The expenses of a big house were one obvious target and closing up a house for a number of years was a common step. Some went abroad to live cheaply and be out of the reach of their creditors.

The exposure of landowners to agricultural cycles was not symmetrical. They received no immediate benefit from an agricultural boom, because rents only changed at the end of a lease, but they suffered an immediate growth in rent arrears in an agricultural depression.

Land could come to have a non-agricultural value either because of what was beneath it or because of its development possibilities. Urban development and minerals helped some families. The five great London landlords, Grosvenor, Bedford, Cadogan, Portman and Portland, were in a special position.

As to minerals there was a great change, recorded, for example, in 1811 by Louis Simond (1767–1831), a Frenchman who lived safely in the American colonies during the French Revolution.

There are farms underground as well as on the surface, and leased separately. I know of a subterranean farm of this kind of 5000 acres, for which the rent of L. 3000 sterling a year is paid, and a percentage besides depending on the quantity of coals extracted, which may double that rent. It is remarkable enough, that when the estate in which this mine is situated was sold, thirty years ago, the purchaser, refusing to pay a trifling consideration for the right of mining, it was reserved by the proprietor, who receives now £3,000 a-year, possibly six (thousand) or more, for what was not deemed worth buying at any rate so few years ago. Not that either party were ignorant of the existence of coals, but the steam-engine was not then so generally applied to mining and the other branches of the art had not readied their present improved state; – the consumption, likewise, was much less.[24]

Darcy's income, though large, did not match that of the grandest aristocrats. The twelfth Duke of Norfolk, for example, had a gross income of £66,000 per annum when he succeeded in 1815. The largest incomes were very large indeed. The first Duke of Sutherland's income approached £200,000 towards the end of his life in 1833. The fifth Duke of Portland, a bachelor, had £180,000 per annum.

Besides extravagance or an inflated idea (such as Sir Walter Elliot's) of the state required by one's rank, the next cause of indebtedness was the provision of money for settlements on marriage or for jointures on widowhood. A typical portion for a girl, the daughter of a landed-gentry family, on marriage would be roughly equivalent to one year's gross income of her father. If a girl was marrying well it might be more and if marrying 'beneath her' possibly less. When Mr Collins is trying to persuade Elizabeth to marry him, he tells her that 'your portion is unhappily so small that it will in all likelihood undo the effects of your loveliness'. It seems that all Elizabeth will have is the interest on £800 (a fifth of her mother's £4,000) and only after her mother's death. A suitor might have expected about £2,000 to have been settled on her at marriage.

Settlements also made provision for what would happen after

the husband's death. A widow's jointure was often between 10 and 20 per cent of her portion. The attraction of jointures was that settlements made before marriage provided jointure in bar of dower. Dower had given widows larger amounts – typically one-third of her late husband's income.[25] Estates used to provide jointure income were notoriously badly managed for income alone.

There seems to have been an inflation in the portions of rich women. In the late eighteenth century the portions of the rich were typically about £20,000, as was that in *Northanger Abbey* of the Miss Drummond who married General Tilney with a fortune of £20,000 'and £500 to buy wedding clothes'. But the early nineteenth century saw higher amounts. In 1808 the Duke of Devonshire gave his daughter by Elizabeth Foster £30,000 on her marriage to George Lamb. Sir Robert Peel gave his daughter Harriet the same amount on her marriage in 1824. Willoughby's Miss Grey was indeed a good catch.

In the marriage market, daughters of the lesser gentry, such as the Bennet girls, might not be able to marry into landed families. Restricted to their locality and lacking sufficient portions, they often married a husband with an income from his own exertions, whether clergymen, lawyers, soldiers or sailors. Many of these professional men were also descended from gentry families. These husbands might not be very young either. Those who made their living in a trade or profession might not achieve financial success until close to middle age. Mr Weston and Captain Wentworth would be examples. *Emma* suggests that this will be so of Mr Robert Martin. Sons of landed families, on the other hand, might easily be in possession of a good income when young.

Wealthy brides, such as Colonel Fitzwilliam might have sought, could be daughters of landed families with unusually large portions, heiresses to land where the male line was extinguished, widows already enjoying jointures, or the daughters of the *nouveaux riches* who usually brought ready money or easily realizable assets handed over on marriage rather than a portion secured on a landed estate and perhaps not paid over until the death of the bride's father. Elizabeth jokes, 'And Pray, what is the usual price of an earl's younger son? Unless the elder brother is very sickly, I suppose you would not ask above fifty thousand pounds.' In *Sense and Sensibility* Miss Grey, who had £50,000, is described as being of age and beyond the control of her guardians and so free to marry Willoughby.

Love matches between people of very unequal circumstances – such as Darcy and Elizabeth – were uncommon. The history of such events in the eighteenth century includes the three actresses who married peers, all as second wives, and the beautiful daughters of Colonel John Gunning from Roscommon in Ireland, two of whom married peers. Unequal marriages of this sort were often made by men who had succeeded to their property and were without parental pressure. Mr Darcy is in this position. Perhaps there was a gradual loosening. In the first half of the nineteenth century seven actresses married peers, five of them as first wives.[26]

Because of the number of relatives who might have a portion or jointure dependent on the family estate, or might have expectations, however distant or unlikely, marriage among landowners was a matter of family concern. Lady Catherine's concern is a parody of a common interest. Established families were usually widely related and kept in touch on important matters. We remember that the Elliot failure to write to the Dalrymples was long-remembered. A wide number of relatives might have a personal interest in knowing whether a marriage represented a further burden on the family estate or an augmentation of wealth.

If we turn from the economics of landowning to the effects on the land itself, we will see that economic factors affected the appearance of the landscape, particularly hedges and trees. Enclosure gave rise to new straight hedges where old hedges were often not straight. New hedges were usually less varied in their composition. Some hedges were kept wide at the insistence of landowners to provide cover for game.[27] Others were narrowed to increase the amount of land that could be cultivated. The hedges in the novels include newly planted ones – perhaps related to recent enclosure – which Miss Bickerton in *Emma* could clear, and much larger ones, such as that in *Persuasion*, in which Anne Elliot hears Captain Wentworth and Louisa making their way through a 'a rough, wild sort of channel, down the centre'.

Timber was valuable. Jane Austen wrote to Cassandra after her brother Henry had brought a friend to Chawton to see the Great House, 'Mr Tilson admired the Trees very much but grieved that they should not be turned into money'.[28] Linda Slothouber's research into the Chawton estate records has shown that Edward Knight did sell wood but usually underwood from coppices.[29] Big trees were felled more rarely and really only in an emergency such as that in 1819 when Edward had to pay to settle a law suit. The potential value of timber can be illustrated by a single oak tree blown down in the park at Dunham Massey in January 1802, which was worth almost £134.[30]

Hard-pressed landowners felled timber to raise money. John Byng on his tour of the Midlands visited several houses where this had happened. At Ricot House, he recorded, 'everything bears the mark of desolation. Till within these few years, this park boasted of its fine timber, which is now nearly felled, and the noble trees near the house are prostrate; and these appear to have been its chief ornament: I think that lordly distress does not authorise such demolition.'[31] Lord Abingdon had retrenched to another house. Byng also saw a Mr Hewer's house at Shireoaks, where Derbyshire, Nottinghamshire and Yorkshire meet. It was 'a good old place, shaded and green, tho' he has lately fell'd a fine avenue.'[32]

In the novels we see a changing attitude to land. In the earlier novels a landed estate is a sort of haven, and marriage to the owner of such an estate is the object of several heroines. But in *Persuasion* we have a hero who does not offer the security of a landed estate. It is his company not his property that Anne Elliot values in Wentworth. Practical abilities are valued more than breeding: besides professional distinction, there are Wentworth's competence with unruly children and Captain Harville's 'ingenious contrivances'. At Lyme Anne finds 'a bewitching charm in a degree of hospitality so uncommon, so unlike the usual style of give-and-take invitations, and dinners of formality and display ... "These would all have been my friends," was her thought; and she had to struggle against a great tendency to lowness.'[33] The daughter of Sir Walter Elliot is rejecting a large part of his world.

Chapter 4

Poverty

WHEN, IN *PERSUASION*, SIR Walter Elliot leaves Kellynch Hall he is 'prepared with condescending bows for all the afflicted tenantry and cottagers'. The 'affliction' of the tenantry is not Sir Walter's departure for Bath. It is a reference to the terrible state of the rural poor.

We need to understand the nature and extent of this poverty to fully understand certain passages in the novels. It is also a corrective to have in mind when we read about heroines wondering how many thousand a year would constitute their happiness. This chapter will stray from a close reading of the texts in order to give a sense of the poverty that lay below incomes derived from land. This knowledge gives resonance to many passages in the novels.

Some contemporaries took a robust approach. 'The poor have nothing to stir them up to labour but their wants which it is wisdom to relieve, but folly to cure', wrote one. In *The State of the Poor*, Sir Frederic Morton Eden commented that 'the present age, whatever its characteristic vices may be, is an age of alms-giving. The evil, perhaps, most to be complained of, is, that benevolence is exercised without discrimination or selection, and that idleness is encouraged.'[1]

Certainly it was a time when many charitable organizations were formed, often with very specific objectives. Amongst those to be found in London were the Humane Society for the recovery of drowned and suffocated persons, the society for the relief of clergymen's widows, the society for the relief of widows and orphans of medical men, the society for the support of poor artists and their widows, the society for the support of widows of poor musicians, the society for the relief of sick and maimed seamen in the merchants' service, and the society for the relief of persons confined for small debts.

The attitude of certain characters to the poor and their actions to alleviate poverty are one of the means by which their moral worth is established in the novels. In *Pride and Prejudice* Darcy is held to be a liberal man active in relieving the poor, both by Wickham, who attributes his philanthropy to family pride, and by his housekeeper Mrs Reynolds, who describes him as always 'affable to the poor'. 'There is not one of his tenants or servants but will give him a good name', she says – praise that is in contrast to what we might imagine to be the case at Kellynch Hall in *Persuasion*, where Sir Walter had only 'condescending bows for all the afflicted tenantry and cottagers'. The inhabitants of Lambton, too, who thought Darcy proud, acknowledged that he was 'a liberal man, and did much good among the poor'. Even Mr Crawford in *Mansfield Park* knows what he ought to do as a good landlord at Everingham, and portrays himself as 'the friend of the poor and oppressed' to win Fanny's approval.

We see Emma making a charitable visit to a poor sick family, in a passage that does a great deal to establish her moral character.

Emma was very compassionate; and the distresses of the poor were as sure of relief from her personal attention and kindness, her counsel and her patience, as from her purse. She understood their ways, could allow for their ignorance and their temptations, had no romantic expectations of extraordinary virtue from those for whom education had done so little; entered into their troubles with ready sympathy, and always gave her assistance with as much intelligence as good-will.[2]

There is an echo of this emphasis on intelligence in *Sanditon*, where having discussed an unfortunate local family called Mullins for whom it is hoped to get up a subscription, Miss Diana Parker then tries to raise money for 'a poor woman in Worcestershire, whom some friends of mine are exceedingly interested about', for a 'Charitable Repository at Burton on Trent', and for 'the family of the poor man who was hanged last assizes at York'. There is a suggestion that personal intervention in one's own community is more praiseworthy than scattering donations at random.

Jane Austen herself certainly acted according to this principle. Writing to Cassandra in December 1798 she said:

> Of my charities to the poor since I came home you shall have a faithful account. – I have given a pr [pair] of Worstead Stockgs to Mary Hutchins, Dame Kew, Mary Steevens & Dame Sharples; a shift to Hannah Staples, & a shawl to Betty Dakins; amounting in all to about half a guinea.[3]

> (from Le Faye, D. (ed.), *Jane Austen's Letters*, 4th edition (OUP, 2011). Reproduced by permission of Oxford University Press.)

In 1807 Jane Austen, then living at Southampton, spent £3 10s 3 ½d on alms-giving out of total spending of £44 10s 6d.[4]

Of course, personal intervention might not be very pleasant for the recipients. One feels that the coachman who was nursed all winter by Mrs Norris was not the most fortunate of patients. Of Lady Catherine de Bourgh we read that 'whenever any of the cottagers were disposed to be quarrelsome, discontented, or too poor, she sallied forth into the village to settle their differences, silence their complaints, and scold them into harmony and plenty.'[5]

This is intended to be ridiculous, with practical help replaced by arrogance. In *Sanditon*, Lady Denham seems to share Lady Catherine's robust approach. She dislikes the idea of a doctor being engaged for the resort. 'Why, what should we do with a Doctor here? It would be only encouraging our Servants and the Poor to fancy themselves ill if there was a Doctor at hand.'

Among other female characters even Fanny Price, out of very small resources, tries to help the especially poor. Of Miss Bates Emma says that 'I really believe, if she had only a shilling in the world, she would be very likely to give away sixpence of it'.[6] The invalid Mrs Smith in Bath still tries to do good 'to one or two very poor families in this neighbourhood', by selling the thread-cases, pin-cushions and card-racks that she makes. The author's moral view is that right-thinking people will try to do something for the less fortunate whatever their means. The implicit duty on the rich is much greater.

This is a point made in *Persuasion* when Anne says about leaving Kellynch: 'and one thing I have had to do, Mary, of a more trying nature; going to almost every house in the parish, as a sort of take-leave. I was told that they wished it'. The passage shows just how far the Elliot family has strayed from a proper way of thinking. Apart from the incongruous formality of 'a sort of take-leave', the visits should have been made because the Elliots wished it, so that they might be sure of the parish's well-being in their absence. The parish's wish for take-leave visits may have been only an imagining of Sir Walter. It is mere luck that the Crofts give the poor 'the best attention and relief', which makes Anne feel 'that Kellynch has passed into better hands than its owners'. Jane Austen would have seen similar circumstances at Chawton when her brother let the Great House to various tenants.

Mrs Norris in *Mansfield Park* is thoroughly unsympathetic. She remembers grudgingly that:

> a great many things were due from poor Mr Norris, as clergyman of the parish, that cannot be expected from me. It is unknown how much was consumed in our kitchen by odd comers and goers. At the White House, matters must be better looked after.

This adds to the picture of her miserly, selfish character.

All these references to poverty had their effect because contemporaries knew so much about it. The force of Jane Austen's moral view reflects the severity of the problem.

One of the most important works on this subject was Sir Frederic Morton Eden's three volumes entitled *The State of the Poor*, published in 1797. Of many similar reports from different parts of the country, at Clyst St George in Devon, for example, it was recorded that:

no labourer can, at present, maintain himself, wife, and two children, on his earnings: they all have relief from the parish, either in money, or in corn at a reduced price. Before the present war, wheaten bread, and cheese, and, about twice a week, meat, were their usual food: it is now barley bread and no meat: they have, however, of late, made great use of potatoes. Their common earnings are 6s a week, and liquor. An industrious healthy man, however, can earn 8s a week, by task work, on an average, throughout the year. Labourers' children, here, are often bound out apprentices, at 8 years of age, to the farmers by the parish; a labourer, prior to the present scarcity, if his wife was healthy, could maintain two young children on his 6s a week, and liquor, without any parochial relief. A very few years ago, labourers thought themselves disgraced by receiving aid from the parish; but this sense of shame is now totally extinguished.[7]

In the mid-1790s an industrious, healthy man could make as a farm labourer £20 a year, on which a family of four tried to live. It is salutary to make an agricultural wage our unit of account in the discussion of the 'competences' of gentlefolk. The Prince Regent's extravagance is well known. It extended to his family. Eliza de Feuillide was told that when the Princess Royal married the Duke of Württemburg on 18 May 1797 her wedding night-cap cost eighty guineas.

While there is much detailed information in *The State of the Poor*, we often cannot identify the people who are described. One example where Sir Frederic Morton Eden's information can be combined with other sources is the family of Richard and Mary Walker from Roade in Northamptonshire. The combination shows us that for even the most hard-working it was almost impossible to make ends meet but that the key to survival was an extended family. It was the kin-poor who were most unfortunate and who were in the greatest danger of having to go to the workhouse when infirm.

In 1795 Richard Walker was thirty-six and married with five children aged from one to nine. Richard was a labourer, with 'the character of an honest, industrious man'. He earned £20 per year but the total family income was £26 8s. To earn more than he could as a labourer Richard rang the church-bells twice a day, for which he was paid £1 6s. a year. He earned a little as a barber and dug graves at the dissenting chapel (about a fifth of the parish were Baptists). His wife, Mary, was a part-time lace worker earning £1 6s. a year. Two of the children were at the lace school where together they earned 6d. a week. The family also collected corn by gleaning at harvest time. But despite all their efforts there was an annual deficiency of about £3 18s. Richard did not receive any parochial assistance but his neighbours who knew him to be industrious and careful were kind to him and gave him old clothes and so on. His landlord, the Duke of Grafton, also sometimes assisted him.[8]

This is how the Walkers spent their money in 1795:

	£.	s.	d.
Bread – 7s or 8s a week. It formerly cost 5s	13	0	0
Butcher's meat – 2s 6d a week. Formerly 2s a week	5	4	0
Beer, about a gallon a week, at 4d*		17	4
Butter, ½ pound a week at 8d per pound		17	4
Tea & Sugar, about 11d per week	2	7	6
Cheese, potatoes & milk (of which very little is used) annually	1	10	0
Soap, candles etc, annually		15	0
Shoes, 25s, Shirts, about 12s, other clothes about 10s	2	7	0
House rent (the cottage was one of about 30 owned by the Duke of Grafton in the village)		8	0
Wife's Lyings-in (say once in two years) cost annually about**		10	0
Fuel (wood)	2	10	0
Total	**30**	**6**	**2**

*Richard earned about 1s per day with his breakfast and beer when working by the day or 10s 6d a week with beer in hay time but when working by the piece 1s 6d or 2s a day presumably without beer.

**Lydia, William, Sarah, John and Thomas had been born by 1795 when this account was made. Ann (1797), Joseph (1799) and Richard (about 1805) followed.

Richard married Mary Caves in Roade on 13 May 1784. The Caves had lived in Roade since the seventeenth century. Mary's mother Judith (who lived to be ninety-four) and her father John had two other surviving children who lived in Roade. Richard and Mary had three more children after 1795 and had twenty-one grand-children. The men of the family were generally labourers and the women lace-makers – particularly pillow-lace-makers. When he died in 1841 Richard had his eldest daughter Lydia and his son Joseph living with him, along with Lydia's daughter Mary. The family survived. There are Walkers still living in Roade.

When Jane Austen described Sir Walter Elliot's tenants in Somerset as 'afflicted' she was very accurate. Farm wages were much influenced by the alternative job opportunities. Farmworkers were therefore often better paid near industrial areas. Somerset was not such an area.

Exact calculations are impossible[9] but it seems likely that, measured in pence per day, the national average farm wage rose from 14.3d. in 1790–94 to 23.2d. in 1810–14.[10] Farmworkers worked a six-day week so in 1810–14 the average weekly wage was just over 12s. 6d. – about £31 5s. per year. In the Midlands the average wage was higher at 26.4d. per day – just over 13s. a week, and in the South-West – including Somerset – it was lower at 19.3d. per day or about 9s. 6d. a week (£23 15s. a year).

Turning these nominal figures into inflation-adjusted values[11] suggests that, across the country as a whole, farmworkers suf-fered a fall in real wages from 1790 to 1809. During this period the problem of poverty worsened. The regional differences are stark. Farmworkers in the South-East and South-West of England saw a substantial fall in the real value of their earnings in 1810–19 to 91 per cent of their 1770–1779 value while those in the Midlands, and to a lesser extent the North, achieved increases in real wages – the Midlands to 127 per cent of the earlier level.

While the details do not change the grim overall picture it is difficult to know exactly what farmworkers earned. They might receive board and lodging as well as customary benefits such as the 'largeses' described by Mary Hardy in Norfolk in 1774[12] – after the harvest labourers visited neighbouring farms for gratuities.

The other contrast to draw is between richer families, such as those we see in the novels, where not many worked, and labouring families in which almost everyone worked. It is likely that many women, like Mrs Walker in Northamptonshire, had a number of wage-earning activities. The effect of the depression that followed the end of the Napoleonic Wars was felt across all occupations. In low-wage agricultural areas it seems that women and children's participation in work remained high out of necessity. Indeed, they typically contributed about 20 per cent to the family income. In high-wage areas, that contribution was about 10 per cent.[13] In families engaged in outwork – work done at home for an employer – the women and children's contribution was much higher – typically 35 to 40 per cent. The contribution of children to a family's income might equal or exceed that of their mother.

Women were paid less than men. While there is some evidence that where markets were not competitive women's wages were set by custom rather than by any market-related process, in general it is thought that productivity rather than discrimination accounts for much of this difference. Estimates vary but suggest that in some circumstances women earned between one-third and two-thirds of male earnings.[14] This seems to have been so in agricultural work, industrial work and even school-teaching. There is one widely quoted example of such discrimination in pottery-painting. A Mrs Wilcox, a skilled flower-painter in Wedgwood's London workrooms, earned 3s. 6d. a day, exactly two-thirds the top rate for male painters who received 5s. 3d. a day.

Some of the apparent discrimination may be a result of different hours worked – women often had other duties. When paid by piece rate for a unit of output, average earnings are simply the piece rate times the output. Often the apparent gap in earnings will be a result of a difference in output, not in piece rates. There is evidence that in weaving, for example, men and women often received the same rate of wages.[15]

Some difference, too, may be attributable to differences in human capital arising from discrimination in access to education and training. Men tended to be better-educated and have more skills than women – apprentices were more often boys than girls.

Physical strength, too, was important. Overall it is at least not a clear picture of injustice and it seems likely that wages broadly matched productivity in some if not all fields.

We now turn to the formal support of the poor. In *Emma* Harriet and another parlour boarder, Miss Bickerton, when out for a walk, encounter a party of gipsies. 'Miss Bickerton, excessively frightened, gave a great scream, and calling on Harriet to follow her, ran up a steep bank, cleared a slight hedge at the top, and made the best of her way by a short cut back to Highbury.' But Harriet is suffering from cramp and 'soon assailed by half a dozen children, headed by a stout woman and a great boy, all clamorous and impertinent'. She gives them a shilling and is then surrounded by the whole gang which demands more until Frank Churchill rescues her. We are later told that the 'gipsies did not wait for the operations of justice; they took themselves off in a hurry.'[16]

Early readers would have understood why the girls were frightened in a way that we may not. Contemporaries thought that there were probably more than a million paupers out of a population of just over 9 million and that there were a further 175,000 vagrants, most of whom would not have qualified for Poor Law relief, the only social safety net.

The nineteenth-century Poor Law was deeply unpopular but in the period of the old Poor Law the picture is more nuanced. The old Poor Law had a wide influence over parish life, affecting not just the allocation of relief and treatment of the elderly, but also employment, apprenticeships, the grain market, and rights of settlement.

English poor relief was better-organized in the country than in the towns. It was funded by a local tax on property. Men and women could expect relief in a number of circumstances including illness, seasonal unemployment, old age or widowhood. Aid from the parish was only available to those who had the right to reside in that place, but the right of settlement need not always be a barrier to aid. Some parishes gave casual relief to those without entitlements, or might seek to recover the cost from the person's own parish. While there were dreadful workhouses, much aid was given to people who continued to live in their own homes. It has been estimated that by the end of the eighteenth century spending on the Poor Law amounted to about 2 per cent of national income. Poor relief could be an important part of a family's income. For low-waged agricultural families in the period 1816–35 it was about 13 per cent and for casual workers' families about 21 per cent.[17]

It is perhaps not surprising that, given the importance of settlement rights in being eligible for Poor Law relief, there seems to have been a national trend for marriages increasingly to be between people from the same village.[18] Accompanying this was a growing distrust of outsiders or 'foreigners', whether Irish harvesters, beggars or gipsies who were outside the system and could be expected to be desperate, which is why Miss Bickerton ran away.

More fortunate in the same novel is old John Abdy who was clerk to Miss Bates's father for twenty-seven years but now is very poorly, bed-ridden 'with the rheumatic gout in his joints'. His son, who is head ostler at The Crown, asks Mr Elton for some relief from the parish to help him look after his father. There would have been no doubt about his right to reside.

The greatest threat to those living on small fixed incomes was inflation. In *Emma*, when Mr Knightley reproaches Emma for her bad behaviour towards Miss Bates, he says, 'She is poor; she has sunk from the comforts she was born to; and, if she live to old age, must probably sink more. Her situation should secure your compassion.'[19]

He is referring to the effects of inflation on a small fixed income. In the twenty-nine-year period 1790–1819 inflation in the United Kingdom averaged only 1.58 per cent, an average we can calculate but which was lost to contemporaries in the violent annual fluctuations in prices. The period was very volatile and the average figure includes annual inflation figures of 21.69 per cent (1800) and 11.2 per cent (1795) as well as annual deflation figures of 14.68 per cent (1802) and -5.56 per cent (1815).[20] These dry numbers represent a frightening time of shortages and economic uncertainty. Nor do averages reflect the large rises in certain basic commodities, which affected everyone.

Inflation in the early 1790s was particularly severe in certain food prices. Since the cost of food was a larger share of the spending of the poor than it was for the richer classes, the working class suffered most.

In the Hundreds of Colneis and Carlford (an area of some twenty-eight parishes between Ipswich and the coast) in Suffolk, for example, Sir Frederic Morton Eden recorded the following price increases in the three years 1792–5.[21]

Item	%	Item	%
Candles	4.20	Hops	46.70
Malt	7.10	Flour	54.80
Beef	19.40	Potatoes	140.00
Butter	22.20		

For the poor the increase in flour and potatoes were the most significant. While exact prices differed from place to place, the picture was broadly the same across the agricultural parts of the country. It is no wonder that there were comers and goers at the kitchen door of the Mansfield parsonage, despite Mrs Norris. In many communities an increase in the poor rate was used to subsidise the price of corn. Mary Hardy recorded one such example in Norfolk in 1789.

It is often said that the miserable condition of the poor was made worse by the enclosure of common land.

In *Sense and Sensibility* John Dashwood is engaged in the enclosure of Norland Common. It is typical that this meanest of men is so engaged. In the last forty years of the eighteenth century (1761–1801) parliament approved some 2,000 acts of enclosure that deprived the poor of access to over 3 million acres of land. These enclosures were of common land and waste land. Yorkshire and Lincolnshire accounted for about a quarter of the total. Sussex, where John Dashwood is enclosing land, did not see much enclosure – there were four acts in respect of 1,450 acres during the period from 1702 to 1797.

Contemporaries were particularly concerned at the impact of bad harvests and the uncertainty of imports in a time of war. Increasing domestic production seemed prudent. The total of waste and common land was estimated at 6,259, 670 acres in England, 1,629,307 in Wales and 14,218,224 in Scotland. It was felt that if a good proportion of this land could be well farmed it would be to the benefit of the country.

Acts of Enclosure were expensive to arrange so there needed to be a prospective benefit for those undertaking such projects. There were great variations in cost – from say 12 shillings and six pence an acre up to £5 an acre if there was opposition. More typical would have been £4 an acre. One clergyman wrote of his parish Wolsingham in County Durham:

> It has been a general observation, applicable to every division of common in this parish, that the resources of the small proprietors (and they are principally here of that description) have been for the most part so entirely exhausted &c. that they have been inca-pacitated for cultivating their allotments in a proper manner. The mischief has gone farther; for it has rendered them less adequate to cultivate the ancient lands, for which such shares of common were allotted. It is believed, that had the proprietors come to the cultivation of their allotments in their full strength, unimpaired by the above causes, that the quantity of produce, both in the new and ancient lands, might have been increased to an inconceivable degree in this parish.[22]

Closely connected both to landowners and to a church that had benefited from enclosure, it would be too much to expect Jane Austen to have been a vociferous critic, but there is a degree of ambivalence towards enclosure.

The view of the enclosers of land was that:

> There are thousands and thousands of acres in the kingdom, now the sorry pastures of geese, hogs, asses, half-grown horses and half-starved cattle, which want but to be enclosed and taken care of, to be as rich and as valuable, as any lands now in tillage.[23]

We can imagine John Dashwood being enthused by such senti-ments. The argument in favour of enclosure continued loftily:

> the advantages which cottagers and poor people derive from

commons and wastes are rather apparent than real: instead of sticking regularly to any such labour as might enable them to purchase good fuel, they waste their time ... in picking up a few dry sticks or in grubbing up, on some bleak moor, a little furze or heath. Their starved pig or two, together with a few wandering goslings, besides involving them in perpetual altercations with their neighbours, and almost driving them to become trespassers, are dearly paid for, by the care and time, and bought food which are necessary to rear them.[24]

Clergymen might be vociferous advocates of enclosure. The Minister of Westwell in Oxfordshire wrote:

There is a large tract of land in this neighbourhood, I should think, consisting of from eight to ten thousand acres, in an useless state; but of much better quality than any upon the Cotswold-hills: I mean the Forest of Whichwood, at present the best nursery for idleness and thieves in this kingdom. What a pity, that so valuable a piece of land, and so easily converted into tillage, should be suffered to remain in its present state, when it is acknowledged that the land under cultivation at present, in this kingdom, is insufficient to produce a proper quantity of food for its inhabitants.[25]

There was concern at the social cost that might follow an enclosure. Charles Wray Haddelsey, curate of Tetney in Lincolnshire, wrote to the Board of Agriculture:

I cannot close these answers without remarking the very laudable conduct of a principal land-owner in this parish, Col. Sibthorpe, MP for Lincoln, who has rendered many of his inferior tenants comfortable, by permitting them to rent small parcels of ground: they are now enabled to keep a milch cow, bring up a few young sheep, and kill one or two large pigs. Were this plan universally adopted, the labourers in villages would never be heard to murmur; our poor-rates would be considerably diminished, and our markets would be better supplied with articles of food — cheese, butter, &c, &c.[26]

Whether the presentation of Mr Haddelsey to be vicar of Holton Le Clay by the Lord Chancellor was brought about by Colonel Sibthorpe I do not know, but this sounds like a curate sucking up.

One effect of enclosure was on the landscape. Enclosure acts required the planting of new hedges – an expensive business offset by a seven-year holiday from tithes on newly enclosed land. Southey described the results in one place in Devon:

> The vale of Honiton, which we overlooked on the way, is considered as one of the richest landscapes in the kingdom: it is indeed a prodigious extent of highly cultivated country, set thickly with hedges and hedge-row trees.[27]

There is debate about the wider effects of enclosure, and particularly whether it eroded the economic independence of agricultural workers.

> Poor inhabitants who live on the borders of the forests and other wastes, and who may not possess any one of the real and defined rights; yet frequently exercise an undenied privilege of pasturing a cow, horse, or ass which assists them in their means of obtaining a livelihood. Waste lands have been occupied in some sort, as the common estate of those who have no other; they are spaces of the earth on which every man walks in freedom, and imagines he is committing no trespass.[28]

Only owning a cow grazed on common land could be sufficiently profitable to make a significant difference to independence – the produce of a cow might amount to as much as half the wage of a male agricultural labourer. The Board of Agriculture's 1808 report mentioned many places where the poor found it much harder to get milk after enclosure. The impact of enclosure was felt only by those with common-right cottages. In some villages those owning or renting such property might be 20 per cent of the population[29] and in general, though with regional variations, the proportion of those affected seems to have been of this order of magnitude. These suffered most unjustly from enclosure but the whole rural population did not necessarily do so, though enclosure also made life harder for all gipsies and travellers. William Howitt in *The Rural Life of England* commented that 'the rapid enclosure of waste lands during the war, tended greatly to break up their haunts, and put them into great straits.'[30]

What of the most unfortunate, and contemporary attitudes to beggars and gypsies? Beggars went on seasonal visits to Bath following the rich. Their base was Holloway, to the west of the city. The Reverend Richard Warner wrote in 1802 about the cost of their accommodation there.

> the poor beggar who has been unfortunate in his avocation, and cannot afford the luxury of a bed, pays one penny per night for the privilege of sitting up in a room, the common dormitory of this lowest order of mendicants; the sum of two-pence entitles the lodger to a pallet and a blanket; whilst the luxurious, jolly, and successful beggar reposes his remaining limbs in a pair of sheets, at the increased charge of four-pence.[31]

Mr Warner was not that sympathetic to their plight, writing:

> The exposition of maimed limbs and chronic sores in the streets is a tax upon the feelings of the public, which in a country so amply providing for the poor and the distressed as that in which we live, should not be endured.[32]

Besides poverty, inequality would increase in the middle years of the nineteenth century. Economists calculate a thing called the Gini Coefficient to express inequality in incomes where 0 is perfect equality and 1 is perfect inequality. One study suggests that England's Gini Coefficient rose from 0.4 in 1823 to 0.63 in 1871. The Gini coefficients of the USA and the UK today are about 0.4.

Chapter 5

Servants

Towards the end of *Pride and Prejudice* Mr Bennet says to Jane on her engagement to Bingley, 'You are each of you so complying, that nothing will ever be resolved on; so easy, that every servant will cheat you; and so generous, that you will always exceed your income.'[1] Jane Austen's contemporaries would have had a good idea of the sort of household that would be typical for a family living on different incomes, including Mr Bingley's handsome income of £5,000 a year.

Few things made more difference to a gentlewoman's comfort and quality of life than having good servants. Without the machinery that we now take for granted, almost any everyday task was laborious. Without the array of consumer products available to us, many more things had to be made at home. Without modern plumbing even keeping clean was hard work. In 1804 Jane Austen was at Lyme Regis and had an excellent manservant:

> James is the delight of our lives ... My Mother's shoes were never so well blacked before, and our plate never looked so clean. – He waits extremely well, is attentive, handy, quick, & quiet.[2]

(Le Faye, D. (ed.), *Jane Austen's Letters*, 4th edition (OUP, 2011). Reproduced by permission of Oxford University Press.)

At Christmas 1802 Mary Hardy in Norfolk recorded that:

> all our labourers and families amounting to between 60 and 70, our
> own family included, dined here. 32 lbs mutton, 16 lbs pork, 16 lbs
> beef, 2 stone flour, about 12½ (lbs) plumbs, 5 lbs suet about 20 pints
> milk.[3]

Mary went to church both before and after this feast, something
she could not have done without servants.

One could also look at a household's numbers of servants as a
measure of the social cost of 'genteel' life – the number of those
employed on low wages to make so-called 'civilized life' possible.
On the other hand, domestic service offered food and lodging and
sometimes security. It could be a good career. Samuel Adams, the
author, with his wife Sarah, of *The Complete Servant* wrote that he
was:

> educated in a foundation school, entered service as a footboy,
> in 1770, and during fifty years he served successively as groom,
> footman, valet, butler, and house-steward. His Wife began the
> world as maid of all work, then served as house-maid, laundry-
> maid, under-cook, housekeeper and lady's maid, and, finally, for
> above twenty years, as housekeeper in a very large establishment.[4]

People on very modest incomes tried to have at least one servant,
even if only a part-time 'maid of all work'. It is a measure of the
poverty of Mrs Smith in *Persuasion*, living in lodgings in Bath,
that she is 'unable even to afford herself the comfort of a servant'.[5]
In *Emma* Jane Fairfax has to do her own hair for want of a maid,
unlike Emma. At the other end of the social scale, the Duke of
Marlborough had at Blenheim 'eighty house-servants; one hundred
out of doors, of whom thirty are for the pleasure-grounds.'[6]

When the Austens were moving to Bath with an income of
about £600 a year, Jane wrote to Cassandra in January 1801:

> My mother looks forward to our keeping two maids – my father is
> the only one not in on the secret. We plan having a steady cook and

a young, giddy housemaid, with a sedate, middle-aged man who is to undertake the double office of Husband to the former and sweetheart to the latter. No children of course to be allowed on either side.[7]

(Le Faye, D. (ed.), *Jane Austen's Letters*, 4th edition (OUP, 2011). Reproduced by permission of Oxford University Press.)

Jane Austen jokes about the pregnancy of servants but pregnancy was a justification for instant dismissal. Rare were employers who acted differently, such as the Reverend John Murgatroyd of Slaithwaite near Huddersfield in Yorkshire. When his servant Phoebe Beatson became pregnant he did not dismiss her. After great but unsuccessful efforts to make the father of the child, a George Thorp, marry Phoebe, he allowed her to stay in his house and have her child there on 29 August 1802. Murgatroyd became fond of the baby, Elizabeth, leaving mother and daughter £300 and furniture in his will. Murgatroyd, aged 83 when Elizabeth was born, was the son of a blacksmith and a quite unusual clergyman in not having been to university. Being a widower without children made his charitable behaviour possible, if still controversial.[8]

The other topic with which this chapter will deal is that of the right treatment of servants. Qualities that are praiseworthy in the novels include the correct management and care of servants both during and after their working lives. Several characters are illustrated by their behaviour in this respect and it is clearly something about which Jane Austen felt strongly.

The misery of having a bad servant is made clear in *Mansfield Park*. Fanny's mother has 'a trollopy-looking maid-servant' who has to be 'prevailed upon to carry away the tea things' and whose failings engross Mrs Price. Fanny finds it a noisy household. 'Whatever was wanted was halloo'd for, and the servants halloo'd out their excuses from the kitchen.' But the fault is not the maidservant Rebecca's alone as Jane Austen makes clear when she describes Mrs Price: 'her days were spent in a kind of slow bustle; always busy without getting on, always behindhand and lamenting it, without altering her ways, wishing to be an economist, without contrivance or regularity, dissatisfied with her servants, without skill to make them better, and whether helping, or reprimanding, or indulging them, without any power of engaging their respect.'[9]

By contrast, Mrs Price's sister, Lady Bertram, has a large household of servants at Mansfield Park. They include a bailiff, a steward, the butler Baddeley, a cook, a lady's maid Chapman, a dairy-maid, the old coachman Wilcox, John Groom and two other grooms, Stephen and Charles, a gamekeeper and carpenters including 'my friend Christopher Jackson' as Sir Thomas calls him, whose son Dick is treated so harshly by Mrs Norris. There would have been other servants, including underservants, five of whom were made 'idle and dissatisfied' by the scene-painter hired for *Lovers' Vows*.

Jane Austen would have seen a similar household at Godmersham, staying with her brother Edward. Later, in 1820, Mrs George Austen, her mother, noted that Edward's household at Chawton Great House included the governess and nineteen servants.[10]

Criticizing other people's servants was a popular pastime. Mrs Elton thinks that the Donwell servants:

> are all, I have often observed, extremely awkward and remiss. – I am sure I would not have such a creature as his Harry stand at our sideboard for any consideration. And as for Mrs Hodges, Wright holds her very cheap indeed.[11]

In *Persuasion* Anne finds herself in a cross-fire of criticisms between her sister Mary and Mrs Musgrove. Mary blames Mrs Musgrove's upper housemaid and laundry-maid for gadding about the village and distracting her nursery-maid, Jemima. Mrs Musgrove however thinks that it is Jemima who is 'always upon the gad' and 'such a fine-dressing lady, that she is enough to ruin any servants she comes near'.[12]

'Fine dressing' seems to have been considered almost a threat to the social order. The housekeeper at Sotherton turns away two housemaids for wearing white gowns. Mrs Price is 'discomposed' on her Sunday walk to see her maid Rebecca with a flower in her hat.

In the novels gentlewomen contend with a wide variety of

circumstances, ranging from Mrs Smith with no servants, to the indolent Lady Bertram, or the future mistress of Pemberley with many of them. Jane Austen's contemporaries would have had in their minds a rough framework relating incomes to numbers of servants.

£100 a year might just afford you one low-waged servant – probably a part-time char for £3 a year, 'A stout girl of all works' as Mrs Jennings says when contemplating the possibility of Edward Ferrars and Lucy Steele marrying on such an income. Mrs and Miss Bates have Patty, which suggests that their income was perhaps at this level. One contemporary thought that a widow or other unmarried lady with this income might keep a young maidservant, at a low salary: say from 5 to 10 guineas a year. As one's income rose above £100 one might have a better servant on a higher wage, but only one.

Elinor Dashwood and Edward Ferrars 'were neither of them quite enough in love to think that three hundred and fifty pounds a-year would supply them with the comforts of life'.[13] £300–£350 would still have been below the borderline of gentility for a couple. A household on such an income, perhaps with children, could afford two maidservants – one at £12 and one at £8. Fanny Price's mother has two maids in Portsmouth and that household is not a model of gentility. James Austen, Jane Austen's eldest brother, married his first wife, Anne Mathew, on £300. Ann was a granddaughter of the second Duke of Ancaster and kept her own closed carriage. James had a pack of harriers. Unsurprisingly, their income was inadequate.[14] £300 a year could make you 'Comfortable as a bachelor' but supposedly it was not enough to marry, according to Colonel Brandon.

£400 a year is the income which, when well-managed, approached closer to the comforts of genteel life. Isabella Thorpe doesn't think much of James Morland's prospective income in *Northanger Abbey*. Fanny Price's mother has as much but manages badly in *Mansfield Park*. One could afford two maidservants, costing £24, and either a third servant with a gardener occasionally or a horse with occasional groom costing about £42.

£500 a year is the income on which the Dashwood ladies must

live in *Sense and Sensibility* and roughly what the Austen ladies lived on, too. Mrs John Dashwood's view of it was:

> what on earth can four women want for more than that? They will live so cheap! Their housekeeping will be nothing at all. They will have no carriage, no horses, and hardly any servants; they will keep no company, and can have no expenses of any kind! Only conceive how comfortable they will be! Five hundred a year! I am sure I cannot imagine how they will spend half of it.[15]

At this level of income a manservant can be afforded, at £31 4s. per annum including duty, and two maids. Alternatively one might have had a third female servant and a boy.

There is a strange echo of Mrs John Dashwood's comment in a letter from Henry Austen to his brother Frank about their mother's position on an income of £450 after their father's death, though Henry's intentions were benevolent if optimistic.

With £600 a year a married couple could afford three females: a cook, a housemaid and a nursery-maid, or other female servant, plus one man: a livery-servant, as groom, footman and occasional gardener. So when Mrs Norris plans her retirement on £600 a year and speaks of retrenchments it is because she enjoys economy not because she has an inadequate income. It is certainly not true that she has 'hardly enough to support me in the rank of a gentlewoman'.[16]

£750 a year is not enough for Willoughby to be 'dashing about with his curricle and his hunters'[17] and Mary Crawford doesn't think much of £700 for Henry. A family might afford three maids and a man who doubled as both groom and footman, plus a gig or other two-wheeled carriage and two horses.

£800 a year was, according to Colquhoun, an average gentleman's income. It is also the cost of Lady Catherine de Bourgh's chimney-piece!

£1,000 a year is Elinor Dashwood's competence – she and Edward have about £850 a year in the end. Her ideal household would be made up of a coachman and a footman/groom, a cook, a housemaid and a nursery-maid. Wages for these five servants, and liveries and duty for the men, would have cost about £220 per annum in all. This is the level at which a carriage – as opposed to something like a gig – might be afforded. When, in *Emma*, Mr Perry is said to be thinking of setting up his carriage, the improbability is that it would require an income perhaps three times that of a typical physician or apothecary (say £300).

We are now approaching the income level of Captain Wentworth (perhaps £1,250 from his capital with his naval half-pay of perhaps £200 on top) and Emma herself who is heiress to an income of about £1,500.

£2,000 a year was Marianne's competence. It is also Colonel Brandon's income. Marianne's household would have ten servants compared to Elinor's five or fewer. Marianne would have a coachman, two grooms, a footman and a kitchen gardener. In the house there would be a cook/housekeeper, two housemaids, a kitchenmaid and a nurse. Colonel Brandon could afford a coach, a gig and five horses. Mr Bennet's income is about this level. It is sufficiently high for contemporaries to have appreciated his imprudence in not putting anything by. Mr Collins, who is generally well informed about the Bennet family's money, annoys Mrs Bennet by implying that her daughters have to cook.

£5,000 a year is Bingley's income and probably John Dashwood's. We will ignore the possible diminution in the Bingleys' income that might have resulted from buying 'an estate in a neighbouring county to Derbyshire'. This was a plentiful income. It was said that to spend more a man would have to go into 'horse-racing or illegitimate pleasures'!

So what sort of household might the mild-mannered Jane Bingley have had to run? 'It was the remark of an old domestic, that the worst mistresses a servant can live with are young married women – "They are unreasonable," she said, "in their commands; they expect too much; nor do they rightly know when to commend, or when to blame."'[18] It is hard to imagine Jane being unreasonable or inclined to blame.

A household of twenty-two servants would have been typical: thirteen men including a coachman, four grooms to look after ten horses, two footmen, a valet, a butler (the best paid on £50 a year) and three gardeners and a kitchen gardener. The nine female servants would have included a housekeeper (the best-paid female on £26 a year), a lady's maid, a nurse, a cook, and five maids. The total bill for wages, liveries and tax might have been about £642 or about one eighth of Bingley's income. The bill for their food, drink and heat would be in addition. The details are set out in the appendix. Jane's nine female servants would have cost a total of £152 10s. each year. What did they all do?

THE HOUSEKEEPER

In *Mansfield Park* Mrs Norris is glad to be closeted with 'good old Mrs Whittaker', the housekeeper at Sotherton who, 'after a great many courtesies on the subject of pheasants, had taken her to the dairy, told her all about their cows and given her the receipt [recipe] for a famous cream cheese'. Mrs Whittaker is a disciplinarian, being 'quite shocked when I asked her whether wine was allowed at the second table'.[19]

The housekeeper might be the public representative of the house and family. Mrs Whittaker knows more than Mrs Rushworth about Sotherton and its contents. In *Pride and Prejudice* Mrs Reynolds is the housekeeper at Pemberley, 'a respectable-looking elderly woman, much less fine and more civil than she [Elizabeth] had any notion of finding her.' She praises her master and engenders a 'more gentle sensation' towards him in Elizabeth's heart. She felt that 'the commendation bestowed on [Mr Darcy] by Mrs Reynolds was of no trifling nature. What praise is more valuable than the praise of an intelligent servant?'

Certainly the housekeeper would have known most of the family secrets. In *Pride and Prejudice* it is Mrs Hill 'whom they could trust the most' when Mrs Bennet is hysterical and likely to be indiscreet about Lydia's elopement.

In *The Complete Servant* Samuel and Sarah Adams wrote:

the situation of a housekeeper, in almost every family, is of great importance. — She superintends nearly the whole of the domestic establishment, — has generally the control and direction of the servants, particularly of the female servants — has the care of the household furniture and linen — of all the grocery — dried and other fruits, spices, condiments, soap, candles, and stores of all kinds, for culinary and other domestic uses. She makes all the pickles, preserves, and sometimes the best pastry. She generally distils and prepares all the compound and simple waters, and spirits, essential and other oils, perfumery, cosmetics, and similar articles.[20]

She might also be responsible for keeping accounts and for keeping an inventory of all the furniture, linen and china.

One notices the large number of things that were made at home rather than bought from an external supplier. *The Complete Servant* includes a great number of recipes, some of which seem eccentric. One is for 'cheap and wholesome claret':

Take a quart of fine draft Devonshire cider, and an equal quantity of good port. Mix them, and shake them. Bottle them, and let them stand for a month. The best judge will not be able to distinguish them from good Bordeaux.[21]

I have not found this to be true.

Reflecting a housekeeper's seniority among staff, the contemporary estimate set average salaries at £26 per year but it could be anything up to twice that amount. She could also expect better accommodation than other staff. At Dunham Massey in 1819, the housekeeper, Mrs Princep, had a bedroom 'with a fireplace, four-poster bed, wall paper of a pretty blue and white floral design and good furniture'. Her main workroom 'was fitted up with a cast iron hob-grate, carpet, hearth rug and good mahogany furniture, a writing desk with drawers, two tables, a clock, a bookcase, [and] fifteen chairs.'[22]

THE LADY'S MAID
In *Mansfield Park* Lady Bertram sends her own lady's maid to help Fanny Price dress for the ball. She attributes Fanny's beauty

to this, repeating complacently that she had sent Chapman to her. The job of Chapman and other lady's maids was relatively straightforward:

> She is generally to be near the person of her lady; and to be properly qualified for her situation, her education should be superior to that of the ordinary class of females, particularly in needle work.[23]

Her job was to dress, re-dress, and undress her lady. I have not found any reference to warming her mistress's pearls as described by the poet laureate. Her wages were typically £21 per annum, with tea and washing. By custom a lady's maid was also entitled to the cast-off clothes of her mistress. Ladies' maids were often quite grand in manner. Miss Bingley and Mrs Hurst are waited on by 'two elegant ladies'.

The range of duties of a lady's maid can be illustrated by the recipes that the authors of *The Complete Servant* felt might be useful. These include Roman balsam for freckles of the skin, preventive wash for sunburn, Darwin's ointment for pimples, pomade for removing wrinkles, balsam for chapped lips, wash for the teeth and gums, lotion for toothache, draught for bad breath with costiveness, *palma christi* oil for thickening the hair, infallible corn-plaster, varnish for old straw or chip hats, as well as many techniques for cleaning clothes and stockings.

The Head Nurse

Nurses became dear to their charges and often stayed with their employers after children were grown. Mrs Harville had a nursery-maid 'who had lived with her long and gone about with her everywhere'. Frank Churchill walked in quest of an old nurse from one end of the main street in Highbury to the other.

> This important Servant, ought to be of a lively and cheerful disposition, perfectly good tempered, and clean and neat in her habits and person. She ought also to have been accustomed to the care and management of young children, as all the junior branches of the family are intrusted to her care and superintendence, confiding

in her skill, experience, and attention. She usually takes the sole charge of the infant from its birth.[24]

THE COOK

Jane Austen knew the value of a good cook, writing to Cassandra, 'I am very glad the new Cook begins so well. Good apple pies are a considerable part of our domestic happiness'.[25] General Tilney is proud of the renovated kitchens at Northanger Abbey with 'every modern invention to facilitate the labour of the cooks'. It was one of Mrs Norris's grudges against Mrs Grant that she 'was scarcely ever seen in her offices' so that her cook was not supervised. Mrs Norris complained, too, of the high wage paid to the parsonage cook, 'as high as they did at Mansfield Park' and of 'the quantity of butter and eggs that were regularly consumed in the house'. The only cook named in the novels is Serle, who has such a way of boiling an egg for Mr Woodhouse in *Emma,* and who must have been driven to despair to see dishes returned uneaten because of an employer's nervousness. Serle's gender is not specified but it seems less likely that a more expensive male cook would have been employed to boil eggs for a fussy hypochondriac.

The Complete Servant described what was required of a cook and emphasized regular accounting:

> To be well qualified for every situation, the Cook must not only understand the business of the kitchen, but must be a good judge of provisions, as in many families, where there is no housekeeper, she will be required to go to market. She must also be able to keep an account of the current expenses of the family; and to examine, check, and pay the tradesmen's bills, which she will have to settle with her mistress weekly, or when required.[26]

HOUSEMAIDS

The most exhausting job seems to have been that of the housemaid, which began at five o'clock in the morning. It was said that 'Those who would thrive must rise by five'. This is the time at which Marianne Dashwood, on a cold gloomy morning in January and only half-dressed, was writing in tears to Willoughby.

Her daily work before breakfast included cleaning the stoves, fireplaces, and hearths in the principal rooms, lighting fires, sweeping carpets, and dusting rooms, window curtains and hangings. In bedrooms she emptied the slops, replenished the ewers and filled the kettles for warm water. Having done these tasks, she swept down the principal staircase and only then went to her breakfast.

Once they were free she went to the bedrooms, opened the windows, aired and made the beds, and cleaned out the rooms. After that she cleaned the staircases, landings, and passages. She had her dinner at one and then probably did needlework until four.

> In most families she has the care of all the household linen, bed
> and table linen, napkins, towels, &c. which she also makes and
> keeps in repair.

Her evening work was generally a repeat of the morning and preparing all the bedrooms for the night. But if there was a dinner party the housemaid washed up the plate and china. For all this, her wages were typically 18 guineas a year.

Knowing how much work was required, we can understand why, when staying with her brother Henry at 23 Hans Place in London, Jane Austen noted in a letter to Cassandra that there was 'one maidservant only', though 'a very creditable, cleanlooking young Woman'.[27]

Maids seem to have been the most troublesome of servants. In Norfolk, Mary Hardy recorded regular incidents in her diary. One entry reads 'our two maids quarrelled and fought in the morn'. She turned away two other maids for 'raking with Fellows', and sacked a third for becoming pregnant.[28]

THE LAUNDRY MAID

Maids are only shadows in the novels, referred to indirectly (if at all). In real life, and in an era before washing-machines, when every piece of cloth had to be washed by hand, laundry maids were very important to one's personal comfort and cleanliness. The frail, pale muslins loved by Catherine Morland and others must have been the dread of laundresses. The job of a laundry maid was described as follows:

> This Servant washes all the household and other linen belonging to her employers, and is assisted, generally, by the housemaids; or the housemaids, kitchen maids, and scullery maids wash for themselves. All the men servants find their own washing, except the footmen's aprons and jackets. The foul linen is given out to her on Monday morning, and returned clean, on Friday night or Saturday morning.[29]

Her wages were typically 12 guineas a year.

THE KITCHEN MAID

The Complete Servant thought that 'This servant has, in many families, the hardest place in the house.' She cooked all plain joints and dishes, fish and vegetables. In the absence of a scullion, she cleaned the kitchen, scullery, larder and everything in them. Early in the morning she had to light the kitchen fire and prepare hot water. She prepared the breakfasts in the housekeeper's room, and the servants' hall and all the rest of the day's meals for family and servants. Her wages were about £10 per annum.

THE STILL-ROOM MAID

The still-room maid worked under the housekeeper in the distillation of aromatic waters, spirits, and oils, in the making of essences, perfumery, etc. and in the making of pickles, preserves, pastry, and confectionery; also in making coffee, etc., to go upstairs. She washed up the china and managed the storeroom. Her wages were typically £10 a year.

Having looked at the work of the indoor servants, we should pause for a moment to think how much a single maid of all work – like Mrs Bates' Patty – had to do each day.

What of male servants during this period? Jane Bingley would have had four indoor male servants out of a total of thirteen male servants, costing a total of £495 18s. These were more expensive than female servants for three reasons. Male servants were paid more, they often had livery provided for them, and they were taxed. The tax on male servants lasted from 1777 until 1937. There was a tax on female servants for just seven years in the eighteenth century.

THE BUTLER

The butler was responsible for overseeing the meals of the family, often helped by under-butlers and footmen. In *Mansfield Park* we catch glimpses of Baddeley, the butler, half-smiling at Mrs Norris' self-important misunderstanding and, later, heading 'the solemn procession … of tea-board, urn and cake bearers'. The division of duties involved in evening tea was well known:

> The tea tray is carried up by the Butler, assisted by the footman; and in waiting at tea, the Butler hands round the cups on the tray, the footman assisting with the eatables. The Butler removes the tea-tray, and the footman the urn, etc. The footman carries in coals, but the Butler manages the candles.[30]

The butler controlled the wine and beer. Wine often came in casks and the butler would oversee its bottling and sealing. Here lay temptation. In a house where no steward was kept (unlike Mansfield Park) the butler would pay the bills for wine, spirits, ale, malt, coals, and in general all bills not in the departments of the housekeeper or the kitchen.

The Adamses described the butler's role in the ritual of dinner:

> He sets and displays the dinner on the table, carrying in the first dish, waits at the sideboard, hands wine round or when called for; removes every course, and sets and arranges every fresh course on the table according to his bill of fare, which is placed on the sideboard for reference; and does not leave the dinner room till the dessert and wine have been placed on the table by him or under his direction. It is then his business to see that the plate, glasses, &c.

are carried to the pantry, cleaned, and wiped by the under butler and footman, and the whole carefully put in their proper places.[31]

A division of cleaning by gender may be observed. Male servants usually cleaned silver and valuable objects, while other cleaning was women's work.

The American Mrs Stevenson found the number of servants at dinner could be unpleasant. 'At dinner you must be looked at by a dozen [servants] if there are as many in the house each one with a napkin over their right thumb – poor Scott [her American servant] makes a sad figure among them as yet – but I hope he will improve.'[32]

John Cam Hobhouse recorded in his diary going to dinner at Devonshire House in London. There were 'thirty-eight at table and a scene of magnificence which I have never seen before. More than twenty servants of whom about twelve in full dress with ruffles, white gloves and swords, so that the guests looked very shabby in comparison with the attendants.'[33]

Butlers received wages and certain other benefits. A butler's salary would be typically £50 per annum. His perquisites were 'the pieces of wax candles, the second hand cards, compliments on paying tradesman's bills, or Christmas boxes and wine for his own use'.[34]

Good butlers were to be treasured and sometimes indulged. Thomas Moore, in his *Life of Byron*, recorded that while dining with Murray (his butler, not his publisher) standing behind his chair, Byron would pass a glass of wine over his shoulder to him.

In 1788 John Byng made a brief visit to Battle Abbey in Sussex with a companion.

We were permitted, till the family assemblage, to run into the house, catching a glimpse of the lofty old hall, and one old chamber; and saw, yet a greater curiosity, the family butler, Mr Ingall, 103 years of age, who had been a post boy in York, in Queen Anne's reign; and now, frequently in a passion, gives warning, and threatens to quit his place: he was very deaf, else I would have spoken to him; but we both bowed to him; and his age bowed him to us.[35]

At Dunham Massey each week two bottles of second-quality port and two bottles of Lisbon wine were issued to the steward's room to be drunk by senior servants. In the second half of 1822 thirty-three bottles of brandy and four of sherry went to the housekeeper's room, again probably for the enjoyment of senior servants.[36]

Not every household followed accepted practices. Sydney Smith at his Yorkshire parsonage found 'A man servant was too expensive; so I caught up a little garden-girl, made like a milestone, christened her Bunch, put a napkin in her hand, and made her my butler. The girls taught her to read, Mrs Sydney to wait, and I undertook her morals; Bunch became the best butler in the county.'[37]

THE VALET
The valet waited on his master when dressing and undressing, had the care of his wardrobe and kept his clothes in good order.

The Adamses remarked that:

> As the valet is much about his master's person, and has the opportunity of hearing his off-at-hand opinions on many subjects, he should endeavour to have as short a memory as possible, and, above all, keep his master's council.[38]

A typical salary was £29 a year but might often be more. Perquisites were his master's cast-off clothes.

Servants could become very grand. Mrs Lybbe Powys recorded that on 31 December 1785 Mr Pratt, the rich only son of Lord Camden, married a Miss Molesworth with a fortune of nearly £40,000. The happy couple set out in two post-chaises, 'the bride and bridegroom dressed with the utmost plainness in one carriage, and in the other that followed the lady's maid and valet fine to a degree'.[39]

THE FOOTMAN
The footman's responsibilities included cleaning the knives, shoes, plate and furniture; answering the door, going on errands, waiting at table, and answering the parlour bell. The footman paid for

his own linen, stockings, shoes and washing; but silk stockings, or any extra articles were paid for by his employer. A footman's wages were typically £27 a year, with two suits of livery and two undress suits.

Livery was often unpopular with those who had to wear it, but it was a mark of the status of the employer and often easily recognized. In one letter Jane Austen noted that a man called John Binns had refused to work for her aunt Mrs Leigh Perrot because he was supposed to be unwilling to wear a livery. At the inn at Lambton Elizabeth Bennet recognizes the livery of Darcy's servants. Livery was usually colourful at a time when gentlemen's clothes were generally quite plain. Sir Walter Elliot's livery had orange cuffs and capes. Byron as a young man followed his family tradition in his servants' livery – claret coats and breeches with scarlet waistcoats and silver lace (in fact, metallic braid). Livery was adopted, too, by the newly rich – in *The Watsons*, Mr Edwards has a man in livery with a powdered head (both man and powder were taxed).

Footmen were often chosen for being handsome, and perhaps their liveries had some effect, also. Elizabeth Grant of Rothiemurchus recorded that the Duchess of Manchester, having had eight children by the Duke, eloped with one of her footmen in 1812.[40]

THE UNDER-FOOTMAN
In families where two or more footmen were kept, the under-footman was expected to do the most laborious tasks: cleaning knives and forks, boots and shoes; carrying up the coals and attending all the fires above stairs during the day. He carried out cards and messages, and assisted in carrying up and waiting at dinner. Wages were typically £20 per annum with liveries.

Turning to the Bingleys' probable outdoor servants, they might typically have been five men in the stables and three in the gardens. For transport the Bingleys would have had a four-wheeled coach, a curricle – drawn by two horses – and a gig – drawn by one horse. All of this would have been in the care of the head coachman. *The Coachman* commented:

On the sobriety, steady conduct, and respectable appearance of this important servant, depends the exterior appearance of the family with which he resides. Every genuine Coach man has his characteristic costume. His flaxen curls or wig, his low cocked hat, his plush breeches, and his benjamin surtout, his clothes being also well brushed, and the lace and buttons in a state of high polish.[41]

Fanny Price was accompanied by a 'steady old coachman', Wilcox, when she rode without her cousins. This was the same coachman who, according to Mrs Norris, complained 'bitterly of the narrow lanes scratching his carriage' on the road to Sotherton, who suffered from rheumatism and had all his sponges ruined by the scene-painter hired to make the set for *Lovers' Vows*. Mr Woodhouse's coachman James is a great comfort to him on the journeys to and from dinner parties. Coachmen seem to have been the subject of what must have been unwelcome attention when ill or injured. Mrs Norris has been nursing the Mansfield Park coachman since Michaelmas for his rheumatism. Mrs Diana Parker in *Sanditon* writes of visiting a friend, Mrs Sheldon, whose coachman had sprained his foot cleaning the carriage. She took it upon herself to rub the ankle with her own hand for six hours without intermission. It took the unfortunate coachman three days to recover.

Besides the obvious work of driving a coach, the coachman was responsible for the care of the horses, harness and coaches, dealing with farriers, coach-makers and horse-dealers. In Mr Bingley's household he would have had several grooms under him.

The wages of a coachman might be £33 per annum, with, generally, two suits of livery – a box coat once in two or three years, two hats, and two pair of boots; also one or two stable dresses, consisting of overalls, jackets, waistcoats, and undress frock coat.

GROOMS
The Adamses felt that grooms, and indeed everyone in the stable department, should rise at about five in summer and six in winter. When a groom had two or more horses under his care, with a chaise or other vehicles, he was generally allowed a boy to assist him in the stables. Wages for grooms might be from £21 to £26 a

year with, generally, two livery suits and two stable dresses a year.

One groom, who worked for Sir George Cayley in Yorkshire, had a shock when told to fly in one of the earliest gliders. Sir George had set out the principles of fixed-winged flight in his treatise *On Aerial Navigation* (1809–10) and thereafter set about testing gliders at Brompton Dale. The groom, on landing, cried out, 'Please Sir George, I wish to give notice, I was hired to drive and not to fly.'[42]

Servants in a large house might have other sources of income besides their pay and perquisites. Showing a house, its gardens and parks to visitors would usually earn a tip. John Byng remarked on how expensive it had been to visit Blenheim in 1781, 'the servants of the poor Duke of Marlborough being very attentive in gleaning money from the rich travellers'.[43] Another visitor to Blenheim noted that it cost him a total of 19s. to tip the seven people involved in showing him round. The seventh guide was a 'coxcomb of an upper servant, who hurried us through the house'.[44] When Elizabeth visits Pemberley with her aunt and uncle they are shown round by just two people – Mrs Reynolds the housekeeper and the gardener.

Servants knew almost all of what was going on in a family. Some wrote down what they saw. One footman, William Tayler, worked for an elderly lady, a Mrs Prinsep and her family in London and for a year kept a diary. One Sunday after a period during which Mrs Prinsep had been ill, William wrote:

> Our old Lady is got quite well, thinks of little elce but playing cards and paying visets all the time. was takeing in breakfast to the drawing room – she was talking about cards and who was good players and who was bad ones and choosing the people she should have to her next party and when it should be. When I went to take the breakfast away, she was fretting because her violets were all withered and had lost their smell. When I went to take lunch up, she was making matches or candlelights. When I took lunch away, she was reading a novel with the Bible laying by her, ready to take up if any body came in.[45]

There were two circumstances in which having servants was either no help or an absolute hindrance: entertaining royalty and committing adultery.

Mrs Philip Lybbe Powys recorded how in October 1785 a widow, Mrs Freeman, was confined to her house, Henley Park, with a violent cold. One morning her butler came running up to her dressing-room saying, 'The King and Queen, M'am'. She replied, 'Don't alarm me William, they are not coming here.' However, another footman followed immediately, saying the carriages were just driving up, and he had got a good fire in the drawing-room. 'She had only time to say, "A smart breakfast, William", and to throw on a huge cloak, and was down just as the King, Queen, two Princesses, Lady Louisa Clayton and two gentlemen entered.' We are told that, 'The worst of these great visitors are that no servants must appear, and you are obliged to wait on them yourself; this, ill as she then felt, was very fatiguing: besides not knowing the art, one must do it awkwardly.' Mrs Freeman managed to make tea but forgot that the King was to be served first. The people in waiting could not have breakfast in the presence of their Majesties and Mrs Freeman had not had notice to prepare a second breakfast in another room. The party stayed for two and a half hours and talked incessantly. The lady in waiting apologized and whispered that the King and Queen loved to take people by surprise. They left and Mrs Freeman went back to bed.[46]

The second circumstance was adultery. It was very hard indeed to carry on an affair without the servants knowing and they might not be discreet. In *Mansfield Park*, for example, 'the maid-servant of Mrs Rushworth, senior, threatened alarmingly' to publicize Maria and Henry's elopement. A cautionary tale is that of Lady Cadogan, the much younger second wife of the third Lord Cadogan. In 1792 she fell in love with an impoverished clergyman, the Reverend William Henry Cooper, a married man with four children and twenty-two years her junior. Her loyal maid smuggled him in and out of her bedroom. The affair was discovered by a housemaid. The story became common knowledge in the servants' hall. In time the story reached the butler of one of Lord Cadogan's sons by his first marriage. He told his master's wife, Lady Jane Cadogan, who told her husband. He refused to act without proof. In March 1794 the servants were able to report that the Reverend Mr Cooper had spent the whole night with Lady Cadogan and disaster followed. Lady Cadogan was sent home to her father and subsequently divorced. A suit for criminal conversation was launched against Cooper who went to jail for non-payment of the resulting damages.[47]

English servants were thought to be very good. Some years later Sallie Coles Stevenson, the Virginian wife to a former Speaker of the United States House of Representatives appointed as Envoy Extraordinary and Minister Plenipotentiary to Great Britain in 1836, wrote 'I am sensible of the folly of bringing American servants to this country. They are in every way inferior and an incumbrance rather than "helps".'[48]

Just as in gentle society, so among servants there was a hierarchy in the servants' hall:

In large establishments, the housekeeper, the lady's maid, and the men servants out of livery, usually take their meals by themselves, in the housekeeper's or steward's room; but when they take their dinner together, they preserve an order at table like the following: — The housekeeper usually takes her seat at the head, and the butler at the lower end of the table; the cook at the right of the housekeeper, and the lady's maid on her left; the under butler on the right, and the coachman on the left of the butler; the house-maid next to the cook, and the kitchen-maid next to the lady's-maid; and the men servants always occupying the lower end of the table.[49]

The servants of a Duke might be rather grand and numerous. At Devonshire House – one of the Duke's two houses in Piccadilly – in 1811 there were thirty-one male and twelve female senior servants, with many helpers. At Chatsworth there were eighty gardeners. When, in 1811, the sixth Duke inherited he increased many of their wages. At Devonshire House, for example, the butler's pay was increased from £60 to £80, the footmen's from £25 to £35 and the junior housemaids' from £11 to £16.[50]

Naturally, servants also had their disagreements. Jane Austen wrote to Anna Austen that:

> Your Aunt Frank's Housemaid has just given her warning, but whether she is worth your having, or wd take your place I know not. – She was Mrs. Webb's maid before she went to the Gt. House. She leaves your Aunt, because she cannot agree with her fellow servants. She is in love with the Man – & her head seems rather turned; he returns her affection, but she fancies that every body else is wanting to get him too, & envying her.[51]

(*Jane Austen's Letters*, 4th edition, Deirdre Le Faye (Oxford University Press, 2011). Reproduced by permission of Oxford University Press.)

There is implicit in the novels a strong view about the right conduct and duties of the rich. If you were wealthy, ownership of land or riches brought with it responsibilities to those who worked for you, and to wider society. The attitude to those duties is used to define some of the characters.

There were some appalling masters. Charles Apperley (Nimrod) wrote of his father, 'He had some strange fancies respecting domestic servants, some of which were not exactly in unison with a liberal and highly cultivated mind. It would almost appear, indeed, that he associated their situation more than he should have done with that of slaves.' Apperley's father caught an apprentice footman 'in the act of stealing some guineas out of a drawer, when summary punishment was inflicted upon him; he was stripped to the waist, hoisted over the servants' hall door and very well flogged.'[52]

The unstable third Earl of Portsmouth, who had been a pupil of Mr Austen and whom Jane Austen met at balls, beat his servants and his animals. His coachman broke his leg and after it had been set, the Earl went into his room and broke it again, telling him it served him right.[53] The Earl's solicitor, Hanson (who also acted for Byron), arranged for him to be married in 1814 to Hanson's daughter Mary Ann, who also proved to be a sadist, horsewhipping her husband severely.

In *Pride and Prejudice* Elizabeth comes to realize 'that to be mistress of Pemberley might be something'. Not the least of Darcy's qualities, as described by his fond housekeeper, is that he is, like his father, 'very affable to the poor' and a good master. 'There is not one of his tenants or servants but what will give him a good name.' In *Emma*, on the other hand, Mrs Elton claims not even to be able to remember the names of her male servants.

Equally it might be possible to be overfamiliar – as, for example, is Lydia Bennet when she goes 'after dinner to shew her ring and boast of being married, to Mrs Hill and the two housemaids', who we may assume know the whole story of her elopement.

'Next to the care and attention due to your husband and children,' says another female writer, 'your servants claim, as your nearest dependents; and to promote their good, both spiritual and temporal, is your indispensable duty. — Let them join your family devotions, and endeavour to make them spend their Sabbath properly.' In *Mansfield Park* Mary Crawford laughs at this idea and makes Edmund angry. She notes, 'It must do the heads of the family a great deal of good to force all the poor housemaids and footmen to leave business and pleasure, and say their prayers here twice a day, while they are inventing excuses themselves for staying away.'[54]

Byron's care for his elderly servant Joe Murray is a good example of a patriarchal but caring relationship between master and servant. Murray was born about 1737 and entered the fifth Lord Byron's service in 1763 or 1764. Byron acquired him with Newstead as his butler. Washington Irving was told by an old servant that Murray was very neat in his dress but given to singing ribald and profane songs in the most unsuitable company.[55] His portrait, commissioned by Byron, still hangs at Newstead.

Murray's welfare was of interest to the Byron family. Byron wrote to Augusta Leigh from Newstead Abbey on 14 December 1808: 'Joseph Murray is at the head of my household, poor honest fellow! I should be a great Brute, if I had not provided for him in the manner most congenial to his own feelings, and to mine.'[56] Writing again to Augusta from Newstead on 30 August 1811, he said, 'Joe has been getting well of a disease that would have killed a troop of horse, he promises to bear away the palm of longevity from old Parr.'[57] Byron wrote to Charles Hanson from Venice on 31 May 1818, 'For old Murray I leave you Carte blanche – & request you to deduct from remittances any sum for his comfort and well doing – & the same half yearly.'[58] Murray died in 1820.

Some female servants, too, became friends and family confidants. Sydney Smith's daughter remembered the faithful Annie Kay, who entered service at nineteen, worked for the Smiths for thirty years, was called into consultation on every family event and nursed Smith at his death. She was 'the most faithful of servants and friends'.[59]

Other women had a quite different experience. The author of *The Duties of a Lady's Maid* wrote: 'unfortunately for the character of our country, it is considered to be a matter of little moment for a gentleman to ruin an unsuspecting and confiding girl' and warned her readers against the dangers of overfamiliarity.[60] The conduct of Charles Fothergill towards a servant girl at The White Swan at Middleham in the Yorkshire Dales recorded in his diary of 1805 is typical of such behaviour.[61]

There is a mausoleum at Seton Delaval, built by Sir John (later Lord) Delaval, in memory of his only son John, who died 'as a result of being kicked in a vital organ by a laundry maid to whom he was paying his addresses'. To my regret, I have been unable to discover the name of the determined laundry maid. The boy's father also had form with women. Educated at Westminster and Eton, he went up to Pembroke College, Cambridge in 1746. 'His academic career was curtailed when the "Captain Hargreaves" living with him proved to be female.'[62]

The public account of young John Delaval's death was, of course, rather different. On 14 July 1775, *The Morning Post* reported:

> On Friday last died at Bristol, in the twentieth year of his age, after a severe illness of several months continuance, which he bore with a truly Christian Patience, John Delaval, Esq; son of Sir John Hussey Delaval, Bart. whose death is grievously lamented by his most afflicted Parents, and by all who had the happiness of being acquainted with him: His Manners were so pure, unaffected and amiable, and his Behaviour so engaging and irresistible, that he

captivated the affections, and was the delight of all who knew him. He spent a precious Life of Innocence and Goodness in this world, by which he prepared himself for the perpetual Felicity in the next; to which he has been called.

Even allowing for the customs of another time, this chasm between what was presumably attempted rape and the eulogy for the would-be rapist is breathtaking.

Chapter 6

Investment and Speculation

THERE WAS NO SAFE place for one's money in Jane Austen's time. It was indeed an age of anxiety. Even what was money could be uncertain. There were bank notes issued by private banks as well as by the Bank of England. These might be payable in gold on demand or they might not. Coins were uncertain, too. They might be domestic or foreign in origin. For example, captured Spanish silver dollars were stamped with King George's head and issued by the Bank of England. Coins might be of precious or base metal or they might not be coins at all but tokens issued by the Bank of England and, in profusion, by businesses and other entities.

Bank notes might be forgeries. Coaching inns could be used by forgers to spread notes widely. *The London Guide and Stranger's Safeguard Against the Cheats, Swindlers, and Pickpockets* (1818) warned that 'the New comer [must] be upon his guard against bad-money' and gave an account of a prosecution for passing forged bank notes at the Swan with Two Necks inn. It was reported that:

> John Lees, inspector of bank notes at the Bank of England, stated to the magistrates, 'that there was scarcely a coach-office in town but forged notes [similar to that now produced from The Swan] had been passed at, and afterwards brought into the bank.[1]

Coins also were forged. In *The Watsons* Robert Watson is described as 'pondering over a doubtful half-crown'. It was thought to be a by-product of advances in manufacturing according to Colquhoun:

One of the greatest sources of these multiplied and increasing frauds is to be traced to the various ingenious improvements which have taken place of late years in Birmingham in mixing metals, and in stamping and colouring ornamental buttons. The same ingenious process is so easily applied to the coinage and colouring of false money, and also to the mixing of the metals of which it is composed, that it is not to be wondered that the avarice of man urged by the prospects of immense profit, has occasioned that vast increase of counterfeit money of every description with which the country is at present deluged.[2]

If one were inclined to anxiety about the money in one's pocket the following passage from Colquhoun in a book published in 1797 would have caused alarm.

So dexterous and skilful have these criminal people become, that by mixing a certain proportion of pure gold with a compound of base metal, they can fabricate guineas that shall be full weight, and of such perfect workmanship as to elude the possibility of a discovery, except by persons of skill; while the intrinsic value does not exceed thirteen or fourteen shillings, and in some instances not above eight or nine. Of this coinage considerable quantities were circulated some years ago, bearing the impression of George the Second: and at the present period another coinage of counterfeit guineas of the year 1793 bearing the impression of his present Majesty, is actually in circulation, finished in a masterly manner and nearly full weight, although the intrinsic value is not above eight shillings.[3]

Colquhoun claimed to know a great deal about the number of forgers and their activities. He said that people working for forgers could earn two guineas a day making coins and that there were between forty and fifty 'private mints' in existence.

Forgers might be hard to catch, not least because they were almost always executed if convicted. Southey told the following story:

> Information of a set of forgers had been obtained, and the officers entered the house: they found no person on any of the lower floors; but when they reached the garret, one man was at work upon the plates in the farthest room, who could see them as soon as they had ascended the stairs. Immediately he opened a trap-door, and descended to the floor below; before they could reach the spot to follow him, he had opened a second, and the descent was impracticable for them on account of its depth: there they stood and beheld him drop from floor to floor till he reached the cellar, and effected his escape by a subterranean passage.[4]

The value of a promise even by the Bank of England was shown to be uncertain by the 1797 Restriction Act, which suspended the rights of holders of Bank of England notes to exchange them for gold. At the end of February 1797 £100,000 a day was being withdrawn in gold from the Bank and its reserves were so small as to leave it 'one panicky mob away from collapse'.[5] Paper money, by whomever it was issued, was now thought to be destabilizing the economy. This uncertainty is echoed in jest by Henry Tilney. 'I am come, young ladies, in a very moralizing strain, to observe that our pleasures in this world are always to be paid for, and that we often purchase them at a great disadvantage, giving ready-monied actual happiness for a draft on the future, that may not be honoured.'[6]

One of the measures taken to aid trade and liquidity was to introduce bank notes of smaller value. There were both Bank of England notes and notes issued by private banks. Southey commented:

> I can plainly see that every person dislikes these small notes; they are less convenient than guineas in the purse, and more liable to accidents. You are also always in danger of receiving forged ones; and if you do, the loss lies at your own door, for the Bank refuses to indemnify the holder. This injustice the directors can safely

commit: they know their own strength with Government, and care little for the people; but the country bankers, whose credit depends upon fair dealing, pay their forged notes, and therefore provincial bills are always preferred in the country to those of the Bank of England. The inconvenience in travelling is excessive: you receive nothing but these bills; and if you carry them a stage beyond their sphere of circulation they become useless.[7]

If money was invested there was uncertainty there, too. The prices of investments fluctuated widely. Events in or rumours concerning the war were some of the greatest influences on changes in investment values. Besides large rises and falls in the value of investments there were large changes in the prices of goods, so that it was sometimes hard to know either the value of capital or the purchasing power it represented.

The increasing number of possible investments reflected both rising prosperity and a more general increase in willingness to take risk. Investment and gambling were, then as now, closely related. The government arranged issues of bonds and also of lottery tickets. That there were popular card games called speculation and lottery – both played in the novels – is a sign of the extent to which the ideas they represent had penetrated society.

While references to investments are not frequent in the novels, the speculative climate and the possibilities of sudden large profits or disastrous losses are in the background. In the unfinished *Sanditon* they take centre stage. In *Emma* Mr Weston had to go to work in London to repair the losses he suffered with his expensive first wife and after some eighteen or twenty years has realized an easy competence. Sir Thomas Bertram has to leave Mansfield Park on a trip to Antigua to supervise his estates where there have been recent losses. Sudden financial shocks occurred in Jane Austen's own life too. Her brother Henry's bankruptcy is well known. Caroline Austen wrote in her *Reminiscences* of the difficulties of the Harwood family, good friends of the Austens. In 1813 'on the death of the old man sad disclosures came to light. Old Mr Harwood had contracted debts quite unsuspected by his family. He had borrowed and mortgaged so freely that it seemed as if the estate itself could scarcely pay its own liabilities'. His son 'found himself a ruined man on his father's death, blighted in all his hopes and prospects of life'.[8] Jane Austen hoped that he would marry Mrs Heathcote, a widow to whom he was attached, but he felt unable in his new circumstances.

There is a moral and political context to this subject. The behaviour of the fashionable gamblers of the late eighteenth century – examples would be Charles James Fox and Georgiana, Duchess of Devonshire – had been much criticized. Certain ladies of fashion who themselves ran illegal faro banks were brought to court and fined in 1797. The affair inspired many caricatures. Quite frequently the faro bank money was said by its proprietress to have been stolen from her. Such entrepreneurial behaviour was at variance with traditional ideas of modest conduct in women. The ladies were threatened with being put in the pillory and with other punishments of a sort applied also to those convicted of prostitution. Caricaturists, including Gilray, were inspired by the possibilities.

More widely, excessive gambling was thought of as undermining the moral authority of the aristocracy at a time of crisis. In the year of 1797, the Bank of England suspended the conversion of its bank notes into gold 'on demand'.[9] The association of the Bank of England with a faro bank and the portrayal of its activities as a form of gambling might be thought to undermine the stability of public credit in a time of war.

Lydia Bennet is very fond of the card game known as lottery. 'She grew too much interested in the game, too eager in making bets and exclaiming after prizes to have attention for anyone in particular.'[10] It was just the game for Lydia being a game that involved little or no skill. It needs only a brief description in Hoyle's book of the rules of the most popular card games.[11] It is a game involving two packs of cards, one dealt as prizes, one as tickets and 'Each person deposits a fixed sum, either in money or counters, to which a value is fixed, forming a fund for the lottery.'[12] It was in effect an imitation of the real lotteries.

The government arranged lotteries for cash prizes.[13] Lotteries provided the Treasury with an annual income of, typically, between £300,000 and £500,000. The prize fund was usually equivalent to £10 a ticket and tickets were sold at a higher value to contractors who resold to the public. Tickets were issued by the Bank of England and sometimes even signed by the chief cashier, though the Bank employees involved were paid separately by the lottery commissioners.

The price paid by the public was not fixed. Lotteries might be drawn over a number of days. If a day passed with no big prize won, the price of tickets would increase. Prices might also fall and contractors might lose money after costs.

In 1810 there were eighteen licensed lottery offices in London which sold tickets or fractions of tickets to the public. These fractions, known as shares, ranged down to one sixty-fourth of a ticket. Lottery office-keepers were often stockbrokers also. They then had agencies throughout the country. Branscombe & Co., for example, had thirty-nine provincial agents.

Other ways of participating (often illegally) included buying 'chances' which paid only if the ticket won a big prize but did not share in smaller prizes, hiring a ticket for a period of hours during which it might win a prize, or paying a premium to insure a ticket for the purchase price. Financial engineering has a long history.

The top prize was usually £20,000 with many small prizes. After 1808 there was an annual limit of 60,000 lottery tickets a year in one or more lotteries with the same prize fund of £10 a ticket.

From 1815 lottery prizes could be paid in the form of government stock – usually 3 per cent Consols – but these were bought in the market so the government did not benefit. However, it allowed prizes to be advertised at the nominal value of the stock when the market price might be only 60 per cent.

More fun was the 1817 lottery where the prizes included two chances of £30,000, two of £2,000, and two of £1,000 in gold sovereigns 'with the addition of four pipes of port or madeira or four hogsheads of claret'.[14]

People of every sort bought tickets, reflecting a widespread enthusiasm for gambling. There is a reference in one of Jane Austen's letters to Martha Lloyd owning one-sixteenth of a lottery ticket.[15] The lottery for 1792 made the government just over £300,000. The lottery was drawn in 1793 and one lottery office published the ownership of ticket 12087 which won a prize of £30,000. The firm had sold it in sixteenths – now worth £1,875 each – as follows:[16]

A clergyman near Brigg, Lincolnshire
A tradesman at Dartford, Kent
A gentleman in Scotland Yard, Westminster
A housekeeper in a Gentleman's family, King Street, Grosvenor Square
A tradesman in Long Acre
A servant at Newbury, Berks
A Gentleman and Lady in St Martin's Lane
An innkeeper at Gillingham, Kent
A Gentleman at Malverton [Milverton?], Somersetshire
A Gentleman at Hazlemere, Surrey
Two Gentlemen's Servants, in Hamilton Street, Hyde Park Road
Two Gentlemen at Newmarket
Two young ladies (sisters), Bloomsbury
Two servants to a Widow Lady at Epsom
Six servants at a Merchant's, St Mary-at-Hill
Twelve tradesmen in King's Gate Street, Holborn

There were also private lotteries, each established by Act of Parliament. In 1774 the Adams brothers held a lottery to finance the completion of the Adelphi off the Strand. Prizes included properties, cash, pictures and statues. In 1775 James Cox, who owned a museum of mechanical art and who had run into difficulties, held a lottery in which the prizes were jewellery, art and mechanical toys. In 1786 Sir Ashton Lever held a lottery in which there was a single prize – his natural history museum. Some 8,000 tickets were sold. A Fleet Street print-seller held a lottery to dispose of seventy-six paintings in 1799 and several more picture collections were disposed of in the same way. In 1803 John Boydell held the Shakespeare Lottery to dispose of his collection of paintings, drawings and engravings. There were 22,000 tickets sold at 3 guineas a ticket. The first twenty-six prizes were paintings by Poussin, Titian, Teniers, Rubens, Caracci, Vernet, Hogarth and others. Unsuccessful tickets won the original cost of the ticket in engravings. Pigot's diamond lottery in 1801 is self-explanatory.[17] Unsuccessful speculative building gave rise to the City Lottery with freehold houses as prizes. In 1816 the Sunderland Bridge was refinanced by a lottery when the original lender collapsed.

Stories of gamblers ruined by their addiction to lotteries were common. More uncommon was the story told by Dr Thomas Trotter: 'A naval officer, while abroad in the late war, received a letter from his sister, telling him, that his ticket in the lottery had come up a prize of £20,000. He was so elated with the news, that he became instantly delirious; leaped from a wardroom window into the sea, and was drowned.'[18]

In 1808 a Committee of the House of Commons had commented that 'the foundation of the lottery system is so radically vicious, that your Committee feel convinced that under no system of regulations which can be devised will it be possible for Parliament to adopt it as an efficacious source of revenue and, at the same time, divest it of all the evils of which it has, hitherto, proved so baneful a source.'[19] The last state lottery was held on 18 October 1826.

The other popular card game was speculation. Speculation is a word which appears in two contexts in the novels. It appears with reference to the card game of that name in which players buy and sell cards of the trump suit. The player with the highest trump wins the pot. We know from her letters that Jane Austen enjoyed the game. However it has been observed that in *Mansfield Park* the Crawfords – representatives of London values – are very good at speculation while Fanny Price – the representative of more rural values and good morality – is hopeless. Speculation in *The Watsons* is 'the only round game at Croydon' but much less smart than the vingt-un played at Osborne Castle.

The name of the card game reflected the increasing appetite for financial speculation which reached even the most dour and prudent. The Reverend Thomas Somerville (1773–1830), a Doctor of Divinity and Minister of Jedburgh in Scotland, admitted to a speculation in his memoirs:

After the commencement of the American war, the price of tobacco had been gradually advancing, and in the year 1781 it reached the unprecedented rate of two shillings per pound. Dr. Jackson, a gentleman who possessed a small estate in the vicinity of Kelso, had, for two years preceding, laid out a few acres in the culture of tobacco, which he perfectly understood, having resided several years in America, and given particular attention to that branch of agriculture. If I rightly recollect, he mentioned to me his having sold the whole of his crop at the rate of two shillings and sixpence per pound.[20]

Following Dr Jackson's example:

many thousand acres were planted with tobacco in the spring of 1782. I did not escape the epidemical mania, and, in partnership with Dr. Lindesay and Mr. Fair, two of my intimate acquaintances, I set apart five acres of the glebe for a tobacco plantation.[21]

It was a disaster. The weather was terrible and very little of the crop survived. Worse, a tax was imposed. To save the growers, the Commissioners of the Customs were authorized to purchase such tobacco as remained at a price not above fourpence per pound 'upon the condition of its being carried to Leith, where it was to be weighed and consigned to the flames'. Poor Dr Somerville continued:

About this time pecuniary embarrassments, arising from a variety of causes into which I need not enter, first suggested to me the idea of becoming an author.[22]

Somerville went on to become a well-known historian.

In *Sanditon* a speculation is described. Mr Parker, a man of 'easy, though not large, fortune' has invested his all in developing the village as a seaside resort. He is a rather ridiculous figure. Supporting Sanditon, he is loud against every other seaside resort, saying, 'those good people who are trying to add to their number are, in my opinion, excessively absurd and must soon find themselves the Dupes of their own fallacious Calculations.'[23]

He is particularly hostile to the two or three speculators trying to bring 'that paltry hamlet' Brinshore into fashion. But he is an enthusiast for Sanditon:

> the success of Sanditon as a small fashionable Bathing Place, was the object for which he seemed to live. A very few years ago, and it had been a quiet Village of no pretensions; but some natural advantages in its position and some accidental circumstances having suggested to himself and the other principal Land Holder the probability of its becoming a profitable Speculation, they had engaged in it, and planned and built, and praised and puffed, and raised it to Something of young Renown, and Mr Parker could now think of very little besides.[24]

Sanditon is 'his Mine, his Lottery, his Speculation and his Hobby Horse; his Occupation, his Hope and his Futurity'. Interestingly, his 'Colleague in Speculation' is a woman, a very rich old lady with a fine active mind but miserly.

The comfort of Mr Parker's old home, a 'very snug-looking place' with an excellent garden is contrasted with the windswept, exposed site of his new home, Trafalgar House. Besides his house there is the Terrace, with a milliner's shop, a library, a hotel and a billiard room. A Waterloo Crescent is planned. There are bathing machines on the beach.

To his credit he is aware of the risks facing others drawn into his project and is anxious to support them. Other elements include the library, where one might buy parasols, gloves and brooches, and old Stringer and his son, whom Mr Parker encouraged to set up as market gardeners and who are not doing well.

It is impossible to know how the story might have developed but the author's tone of detached, sceptical amusement is established. There is explicit doubt of Mr Parker's wisdom. He has abandoned his old home and invested his fortune – which was enough to live on – in this speculation which is not going very well.

Jane Austen was describing a well-known phenomenon. In the late eighteenth century Brighton and Hastings were the leading seaside resorts in Sussex. Others included Margate and Ramsgate in Kent and Exmouth and Teignmouth in Devon. A host of others followed including Sidmouth, Dawlish, Torquay, Minehead, Ilfracombe, Tenby and Weymouth (thanks to George III). In the North, Scarborough was popular. One writer identified the basic features of a successful seaside resort as 'comfortable access to a clean sandy beach, a straight shore with gently sloping cliffs and a lack of steep gradients.'[25]

Early seaside holiday accommodation was in small houses. In *Sanditon* we are told that in the village lodgings in cottages were available and a harp could be heard from the window above the baker's shop. There were, for example, 108 lodging houses in Weymouth in 1800 – about one house in seven. Most lodging-house-keepers had other economic activities. At Exmouth small cot-houses with four or five rooms let at a guinea a week in 1782.

As in *Sanditon*, landowners were key in the development of more sophisticated resorts. Very few were created out of nothing – mostly one sees established towns increasing piecemeal. Speculation developed in the early-nineteenth century. Brighton's Royal Crescent (1798–1807) was financed by J.B. Otto, a West Indian planter. It contained fourteen elegant lodging houses. A larger scale of speculation followed, including Bedford Square (forty-two houses) and Regency Square (seventy buildings).[26]

There was a real resort called Sandgate in Kent, quite similar to the fictional Sanditon, described in a guide of 1813 as follows:

> This is a pretty little village, exactly halfway between Folkestone and Hythe, and which has suddenly started into notice. Here are six or eight bathing-machines, besides hot and cold baths. Lodgings may be obtained here on reasonable terms; and of late there have been erected some very good houses. Purday keeps a small circulating library, adjoining to which is a billiard-room. There is another billiard-table, kept by Woore.
>
> The beach consists entirely of shingles, so that the water is very clear, and by shelving gently from the shore it presents any depth that may be desired … The New Inn is the usual place of entertainment, but there is neither a ball nor assembly-room.[27]

The guide did not mention the Shorncliffe army camp established in 1794 just above the village and which may have been a reason it did not prosper.

But what of the developing financial markets and particularly the market in government bonds? In some ways this did not seem a great deal better than the lottery. The newspapers reported frequently on the operations and scandals in the market. In 1810 Abraham Goldsmith, who acted as an important bill-broker for the government, had to admit to a Select Committee of the House of Commons that he had given £5,000 of stock to the clerks of the Exchequer Bill Office at the Bank of England to obtain favoured treatment for his bill-broking transactions.[28] No one lost his job as a result of the revelation.

This was long before the days of best execution rules. Economic author Charles Hales warned that:

> No person must ever expect, from a Jobbing Broker, fair and open advice when to buy or sell. It is a pity that these men should have such a controul [sic] over the property of others; they practise such tricks in Stock-jobbing, as not only alarm people, but materially affect both the trade and credit of the country.[29]

It is interesting to see that some terms in present-day use are more than 200 years old. Then as now private investors were at the mercy of professional speculators holding investments for only short periods of time.

> A Stock-jobber is called a bull; and he is also called a bear. The bull contracts for the purchase of stock but, probably, being unable to pay for it, he sells it again, at the chance of gain or loss, before the settling-day arrives. The bear is the animal that contracts to sell stock; but he sells, perhaps, more than he is possessed of (perhaps possesses none at all), and is yet obliged to fulfil his contract by the time agreed on.[30]

A bull who had bought stock not for cash settlement but for settlement at the end of the six-week account might find it expensive to roll his position into the next account period. Stock-jobbers might charge continuation rates equivalent to 16 per cent or more. So a jobber with a speculative position needed a quick result.

> It is to Stock-jobbing that we are indebted for the various rumours of victories, of defeats, &c. without a syllable of truth in them. Dreadful news comes from abroad, conveyed by some foreign jobber to the jobber at home: the latter knows what is meant; the object is, to depress stock; he therefore spreads the news. The Funds tumble; the proprietors tremble, — at least the credulous and timid part. They sell their stock, and soon repent; for, in a few days, some capital intelligence arrives, contradicting former reports, and raising the stocks to a higher price than that at which the proprietors sold.[31]

The newspapers reported frequent attempts to move market prices. Indeed, newspapers were sometimes *involved* in these efforts. In February 1796 an edition of the French newspaper, *L'Eclair* was forged and circulated in London to spread a rumour of a treaty between France and Austria.[32] In September 1813 copies of the French newspapers containing news of French successes near Dresden were suppressed in London to give those in the know a day in which to trade on the knowledge.[33]

Forgery and impersonation were also used. *The Morning Chronicle* reported on Thursday 5 May 1803:

> A pretended letter from Lord Hawkesbury to the Lord Mayor, was delivered at the Mansion-house, informing his Lordship the dispute with France was amicably adjusted. About nine o'clock yesterday morning the pretended messenger arrived at the Mansion-house with the fabricated letter. He was booted and spurred, and had all the appearance of one who had just finished a long journey. Having enquired for the Lord Mayor, he declared himself a messenger belonging to the Foreign Office, who was charged to give a letter to his Lordship.[34]

The letter was sealed with Lord Hawkesbury's seal. The Lord Mayor posted a notice outside the Mansion House, sent a copy to

Lloyd's and took the original letter to the Stock Exchange where stocks immediately rose by 5 per cent. 'The joyful intelligence spread throughout this large city with the rapidity of lightning', reported the *Morning Chronicle*, but Mr Abraham Goldsmid[35] doubted the news, asked to see the letter and pronounced it a forgery. The seal was genuine but had been transferred from another document. At noon the Lord Mayor, who had written to thank Lord Hawkesbury for the good news, had a note from the Foreign Office saying that the letter was a forgery. 'Never was there seen such a scene of consternation and confusion'.[36] Stocks fell. The Stock Exchange was closed before 2 p.m. and a Committee of the Exchange decided that all bargains done on that day would be null and void. This was later rescinded for bargains for ready money.

Even foreigners were suspected of speculative dealing. Some years later it was reported that in May 1803:

> Talleyrand and his agents dispatched orders to three respectable houses in the City to buy up large sums in our Funds, upon the certainty that the then existing differences between Great Britain and France would be amicably adjusted. This purchase occasioned an immediate rise but four days later on other information there was a fall. Talleyrand and those in his confidence were consequently great losers by their speculations.[37]

In 1805 there were attempts to move the market with false reports of naval successes. In April 1805 Nelson was said to have won a great victory against a French and Spanish fleet, taking eight ships of the line and being in pursuit of the remainder. The report anticipated Trafalgar by six months.

In February 1814 a man dressed in an elaborate uniform and calling himself Colonel De Burgh appeared at Dover in the middle of the night at the Ship Inn seeking 'a speedy conveyance to London'. He said that he had just come from France with the news that Bonaparte had been killed in action. He wrote to the admiral at Deal asking him to forward the news by telegraph. On the same day in London there was a large volume of trading in the funds. After a Stock Exchange enquiry, the so-called Colonel was traced to a house in London inhabited by three men including Rear-Admiral Lord Cochrane, a popular naval hero and then MP for Westminster.[38] Very substantial sales of stock were shown to have been made on behalf of these people – stock which they had not owned for very long. Cochrane was subsequently convicted in a trial that is still controversial. Long after, he was pardoned and reinstated in the navy.

Charles Hales in *The Bank Mirror* was at pains to emphasize the creditworthiness of government funds and the liquidity of the market, but he also emphasized market-price risk:

> I would not, however, advise any timid person to place money in the Funds; for, instead of relieving themselves of anxiety, they increase it, on any depression of Stock, by false reports of designing men.
>
> Numbers of persons have sold out their property, upon bad news being circulated, at a considerable loss; while others, disregarding such reports, and placing a firm confidence in Government, have prudently bought in, and have been capital gainers.[39]

Possessors of capital are numerous in the novels. Male fortunes are often partly or wholly invested in land (see Chapter 3), but richer landowners would also have had money with their bankers and invested in securities. John Dashwood is one such man.

Women did not have their fortunes so attached to land. Sometimes women had an income derived from the family estate – such as the £2,000 annuity that the widowed Mrs Knight reserved to herself when she handed over the Godmersham estate to Jane Austen's brother Edward. Other women might have their capital invested as a mortgage on the family estate from which they would have received an income as interest. This might have been the position of Anne Elliot on marrying Wentworth because her father could give her 'but a small part of the share of ten thousand pounds'[40] to which she was entitled. Otherwise women often had their fortunes invested in 'the funds', or other financial assets.

The first place one might put money was on deposit with a

bank. They did not usually pay interest on customer's balances so this was not a means of getting an income. It is a measure of John Dashwood's wealth that he could buy East Kingham Farm because he 'happened to have the necessary sum in my banker's hands',[41] which was not earning interest.

Rightly or wrongly (as in Henry Austen's case), bankers were assumed to be rich. Lady Susan writes to Mrs Johnson about her brother-in-law Charles Vernon:

> Charles is very rich, I am sure; when a Man has once got his name in a Banking House, he rolls in money. But they do not know what to do with it, keep very little company, and never go to Town but upon business.[42]

We may doubt whether Charles was a successful banker because Lady Susan writes 'I really have a regard for him, he is so easily imposed on!'

There were many banks to choose from. The number of private banks increased from 119 in 1784 to over 600 in 1820. These were all unlimited liability partnerships with a maximum of six partners. Most were therefore quite small though most issued their own bank notes. Some did not last very long. The Original Security Bank was, briefly, prominent but closed in 1797 a year after its foundation and the partners were made bankrupts.[43]

The importance of these banks and their notes in the economy may be judged by the fact that in 1809 there were in circulation more notes issued by the country banks than by the Bank of England (£23.7 million vs £19.6 million). One of the important differences was that the country bank note denominations were generally much smaller – typically below £20 – and so most useful for commercial transactions. The fall in note issuance after the war was substantial so that in 1816 the country banks had in circulation £15.1 million compared to the Bank of England's £26.7 million.[44] It was this contraction in liquidity that helped Henry Austen's bank into insolvency.

Bank failures were not uncommon and there was no sort of depositor protection. In 1826 it was said that 300 banks had failed since 1800. There had been crises in 1797 and 1816. In the failure of Henry Austen's bank in 1815–16 his sister Jane lost £13, while her uncle, Leigh-Perrot, and brother, Edward Knight, lost very substantial sums. In the crisis of 1825 ninety-three banks failed. This was the catalyst for legislation in 1826 permitting the formation of joint stock banks which might be larger and therefore safer.

It was natural that investors in need of an income from their capital and seeking to avoid the credit risk of banks would move their capital elsewhere. As William Wordsworth wrote from Grasmere to his brother Richard in London, 'As to the disposal of the £1,500 I have no advice to give; it is plain I should think that there can be but one rule; viz that the money ought to be placed out on *solid* security, and next at as good a rate of interest as can be procured consistent with that end.'[45] The most popular investments for private individuals were government annuities – securities that paid a fixed semi-annual income and had no repayment date. They were variously referred to as funds or stocks. Some of them are still in existence. An estimated 250,000 people owned government stocks in 1815 and some 80 per cent of them received less than £50 a year in interest. This was not an investment confined to the very rich.

These issues of government annuities came into being during the eighteenth century and were added to regularly thereafter. The four most important were the 3 per cent Consols, so-called after the Consolidating Act of 1751, the 3 per cent reduced, which carried higher rates of interest before 1757, the 4 per cent consolidated annuities which dated from 1777 and the 5 per cents, which arose from a consolidation in 1784 of various navy, transport, victualling and ordnance debts. Jane Austen had £600 in the navy 5 per cent stock.

There were also other issues such as India bonds, India annuities and South-Sea annuities, issued not by the government but by the East India Company and the South-Sea Company.

In the period 1793 to 1815 the government issued at least one new loan each year, increasing the nominal value of the national debt by some £475 million. Typically new issues paid interest at 3 per cent and were sold at a discount to their face value. Payment for a new loan was usually staggered over a period of a year, which facilitated speculation. By the end of the Napoleonic Wars the accumulated British nominal national debt was £792 million. That was equivalent to more than 250 per cent of national income.[46] In 1811–15, government net borrowing averaged £25.3 million per year or 9 per cent of national income.

Because of the staggered payment for new loans, subscribers could control a larger amount of stock than they had money to buy outright. This allowed underwriters time to obtain subscribers for the stock they had underwritten as well as facilitating speculation. New money was raised by issuing parcels of different securities in a package known as an Omnium. City firms formed groups to bid for these loans and then, if successful, allocated loans to clients. By custom, however, certain officials including the directors and chief cashier of the Bank of England were entitled to allocations of new loans. One chief cashier, Abraham Newland, was said to have made a fortune of £200,000 in this way. Since the Bank of England advised the Treasury on its debt sales and attended the pricing meetings, there was a considerable potential conflict of interest. It was a case of buyer beware. Hales recommended 'at all events judge for yourself. Your Broker considers only his own interest – you are to consider yours.'

Louis Simond recorded in 1811 that, 'The profit of these whole-sale lenders to Government was formerly very considerable, (8 or 9 per cent) but the method devised by Mr Pitt of disposing of the loan to the lowest bidder, has reduced the ordinary profit to one or two per cent at most.'[47]

Women – spinsters and widows like the four Dashwoods – were important investors. Over a third of investors in 1810 were women which rose to almost half by 1840. Their holdings were typically smaller than men's. A study of women's wills granted probate in the Prerogative Court of Canterbury in 1830 shows that, of women who left more than £10 upon their deaths, over a quarter owned such investments.[48] They were not at the margins of property ownership.

Basic knowledge of this market was certainly available to women. The author of *A legacy of affection, advice, and instruction,*

from a retired governess, to the present pupils of an establishment for
female education (1827) had a section of her book entitled 'Nature of
Money and Property' which explained it clearly:

> The usual interest paid by government is 3l. per 100l., and the price
> of stocks merely means the sum which you are to pay some holder
> of an annuity of 3l. for that annual income from the government.
> Thus a traffic exists in annuities between those who hold them and
> those who have money to buy them. The price varies; it has been
> as low as 47 and as high as 97, and while I am writing is at the
> medium price of 78, which means that with 78l. you could buy an
> annuity of 3l. per annum, or with 780l. one of 30l.[49]

The Dashwood girls and their mother are to live on the income
from £10,000, which Fanny assumes will be £500 a year. This is a
widespread assumption – that incomes were typically 5 per cent
of capital – but it is a simplification. The capital of the Dashwood
ladies invested in the funds might well not have earned £500 a year
in reality.

Certainly there was a maximum interest rate of 5 per cent, set
by law, which might be charged on loans, though this could be circumvented by charging fees in addition to loan interest, and the
rule did not apply to government and other bonds. Loans, such as
mortgages, could be made at 5 per cent and many landed investors liked loans secured on land. Investors in government bonds
received whatever was the yield represented by the purchase price
they paid. As we will see this fluctuated substantially.

The price of an annuity is volatile when interest rates change.
The stocks which Jane Austen's contemporaries and her characters owned were roughly three times more volatile than the sort
of gilt that a modern reader might own. Those interested in bond
mathematics will note that the modified duration – a measure of
the sensitivity of price to changes in yield – of a ten-year gilt with a
coupon of 3 per cent would be roughly 8.5, while that of an undated
gilt with the same coupon would be 29.8. So investors faced considerable market risk, particularly in the 1790s, if they should ever
need to sell. This risk is the one referred to by John Dashwood

in *Sense and Sensibility* when talking about his purchase of East Kingham Farm: 'the stocks were at that time so low, that if I had not happened to have the necessary sum in my banker's hands, I must have sold out to very great loss.'[50]

Following the Treaty of Paris in 1783, the price of Consols rose to ninety-seven (one hundred being their nominal value) – yielding a little over 3 per cent, but after the start of the war with France in 1793 they fell over a number of years, trading as low as forty-seven and a quarter in 1798 – a yield of 6.35 per cent. The average price for the year 1798 was fifty and a half and the average yield was 5.94 per cent. While there were some large price changes in the early 1800s, in general the market became less volatile. The average yield on Consols during the first decade of the nineteenth century was 4.8 per cent; in the second decade the average fell to 4.57 per cent. So fortunes invested in government bonds alone probably would not have earned the 5 per cent widely assumed.

Those who we would today call retail investors seem to have taken market fluctuations in their stride. In June 1796 Matthew Flinders, the Lincolnshire apothecary, bought a nominal £100 of the 5 per cent stock for £95 12s. 6d. By August they had fallen below £89, he noted in his diary. But he was not discouraged from further investments. In November 1797 he bought £100 in the 3 per cent Consols for £49, including commission and went on to build up a holding of £900 in nominal terms on which he would have made good capital gains.[51]

In the early nineteenth century the market was less volatile so that Dr Thomas Trotter in the third, augmented edition of his *A View of the Nervous Temperament* (but not in the two earlier editions) considered that:

> the public funds of this country are one great cause of those torpid habits of living; where the security of property is so compleat, that any care about its safety is needless. A vast capital is by this means unproductive of anything to the public, but is a source of bad health to its owner. All enterprize is thus checked among a large part of the community, who become victims to diseased feelings, and to those kindred glooms which prey on still life.[52]

So while John Dashwood worried about the price of the funds in the 1790s, two decades later Mr Woodhouse's torpid life was untroubled.

Provided that one did not need to sell out of the funds and could live on the income, one could afford to be indifferent to the market manipulation and fluctuations. The credit of the government as to paying the interest was undoubted. However, if one needed to sell – as Willoughby might have done after his marriage to Miss Grey – the sum realized would have been uncertain.

In *Sanditon* Mr Heywood makes two journeys to London each year 'to receive his Dividends'.[53] The most likely months for those journeys are January and July when the 3 per cent Consols – by far the largest issue – paid their dividends. Hales describes the process that Mr Heywood would have followed on each visit to the Bank of England:

> The hours of payment, in most of the Funds, are from nine to eleven in the morning, and from one to three in the afternoon. In the Consols, [which form the most considerable part of the national debt] they are paid from nine in the morning till three in the afternoon. When you receive your Dividend, you must go under the first letter of your name. You must mention the principal sum, and your name. The clerk will then give you a warrant, which you sign, and he signs. You then take it into the Dividend office; and on presenting it, the money is instantly paid to you.[54]

Many people signed a power of attorney to authorize someone else to collect their dividends. Not doing so emphasizes Mr Heywood's cautious nature.

We have seen that transactions on the Stock Exchange were chiefly in the funds, that is Consols and other government bonds, and in Bank of England stock, South-Sea stock and so on, which were the issues of government-established monopolies such as the East India Company. There were alternative investments too. In 1811 prices of canal, dock, insurance, and waterworks shares were quoted for the first time. They did not in general offer great chances of profit.

An index of such shares[55] for the period 1811–18 shows a downward trend for most of 1811–13 with a modest recovery to May 1814, followed by post-1815 deflation and then a stronger recovery beginning in March 1817 lasting through 1818. Canal companies represented nearly half the paid-up capital of the equity sector on the London Stock Exchange in 1811. There was a rising trend in canal share prices until 1824 and then a rapid fall in the late 1830s.

English canal companies were mostly limited-liability companies established by Act of Parliament. In one of her letters in 1811, Jane Austen mentions the Weald of Kent Canal Bill that her brother Edward opposed and which, much delayed, eventually failed to find enough investors.[56] Inevitably there were great differences between canals. Construction costs, for example, might differ widely: £3,213 per mile on the Trent and Mersey, £3,374 on the Oxford and £16,666 on the Kennett and Avon.[57] Usually companies paid a fixed dividend – typically 5 per cent – during the long construction periods.

Despite the canal mania of the 1790s, canals often offered lower-risk, marketable capital securities which were attractive to a wide range of investors, until the railways came. The average dividend was 5.9 per cent[58] though some companies paid much higher dividends. In 1825 the ten most successful companies paid an average dividend of 27.6 per cent and the Sankey Brook Navigation in south Lancashire (carrying coal from St Helens to Liverpool) paid 33.3 per cent for eighty years from its opening in 1757. This was much above what railway companies paid later in the century. Some canal companies of course paid nothing (thirty-five of them in 1816).

Canals were not universally popular. Sir Frederic Morton Eden reported in *The State of the Poor* in 1797 that at Deddington in Oxfordshire:

> the general opinion, here, is that canals are a great injury to the poor, by enabling farmers to send their corn abroad: such erroneous ideas do not merit a refutation; but the farmers are very apprehensive that they will produce serious consequences. A boat laden with flower [sic] was lately seized by the populace, but was restored, on the miller's promising to sell it at a reduced price.[59]

On the other hand one contemporary writer who saw what later generations have seen was the Reverend Richard Warner who wrote in 1802:

> it has often struck me, that a great part of the natural beauties of our country might be seen to advantage by pursuing their banks; as the canals must necessarily follow the involutions of the vallies, the traveller would of course be led through all their romantic scenery, and be gratified with pictures, which a bird's-eye view from a hill must rob of half their effect, and which a turnpike-road will seldom afford him.[60]

Southey also wrote (in 1807) in praise of travel by canal.

> This was a new mode of travelling, and a delightful one it proved. The shape of the machine resembles the common representations of Noah's ark, except that the roof is flatter, so made for the convenience of passengers. Within this floating house are two apartments, seats in which are hired at different prices, the parlour and the kitchen. Two horses, harnessed one before the other, tow it along at the rate of a league an hour; the very pace which it is pleasant to keep up with when walking on the bank. The canal is just wide enough for two boats to pass; sometimes we sprung ashore, sometimes stood or sate upon the roof, — till to our surprise we were called down to dinner, and found that as good a meal had been prepared in the back part of the boat while we were going on, as would have been supplied at an inn. We joined in a wish that the same kind of travelling were extended everywhere: no time was lost; kitchen and cellars travelled with us; the motion was imperceptible; we could neither be overturned nor run away with, if we sunk there was not depth of water to drown us; we could read as conveniently as in a house, or sleep as quietly as in a bed.[61]

The popular speculative urge could be harnessed in other ways. William Pitt experimented with a type of investment plan called a tontine, whereby individuals would each invest a sum of money and would in return receive a life annuity. This life annuity would increase as the annuities of those who had died were put back into the pot to be redistributed among the surviving members. Matthew Flinders invested in the name of his daughter Elizabeth who died unfortunately aged twenty-four.[62] Tontines did not prove popular.[63]

Competence in financial matters is a quality valued in women in the novels. The late Lady Elliot restrained Sir Walter while she lived. Mrs Croft seems quite as business-like as the Admiral. Equally, lack of competence is deplored, for example, Mrs Dashwood plans to renovate Barton Cottage out of surplus income.

> In the meantime, till all these alterations could be made from the savings of an income of five hundred a-year by a woman who never saved in her life, they were wise enough to be contented with the house as it was.[64]

Knowing how volatile investments could be in an uncertain world, we understand even more why financial prudence was an important virtue.

One example of prudence is a story of the writer Mary Berry (1763–1852) who, with her sister Agnes, was so admired by Horace Walpole. Travelling in Italy they met a General Charles O'Hara with whom Mary fell in love. For six months in 1795–6 they were secretly engaged to be married. He was an incongruous fiancé for the sensitive and literary Mary. The general was a brave, if not always successful, soldier, with the unusual distinction of having surrendered in person to both George Washington and Napoleon Bonaparte. His financial affairs were troubled. His friends had helped him out of previous difficulties. It seems that his initial account of his circumstances was optimistic and he had had to admit as much to Mary. A practical woman with experience of managing her hopeless father, Mary then wrote to him setting out what they would need to live on together.

The letter, which probably dates from January 1796, gives us a good idea of what life in Society in London would have cost. The letter began 'the plan of life you at first proposed, my dear friend, ... would cost much more than you had any idea of, and much more even than the funds of which you then supposed yourself possessed.'[65] She proposed a small establishment in London. 'You will see I have cut off all *your* extravagances, your Saddle Horses, your separate carriage, and one of your Men-Servants',[66] but she was, she said, happy to travel with him anywhere because travelling would be cheaper than living in London. Her budget was as follows:

One pair of job horses inclusive of coachman's wages for 8 months of the year	£125
Annual repairs to Carriage about	£25
Two men servants at £20 apiece	£40
An upper man at the wages of	£55
Wages of 4 Women Servants: a Housekeeper, a Cook under her, a House maid and Lady's maid	£58
Liveries for the 3 Men Servants and the Coachman	£80
House rent and taxes	£200
Coals	£50
Candles	£25
Beer	£25
Wine	£100
Housekeeping at £40 a month	£480
	£1,263
To you	£800
To me	£200
Total	**£2,263**

The general doesn't seem to have found the prospect of such a life very attractive and after various manoeuvres the engagement came to an end in April 1796. He was by then Governor of Gibraltar where he lived for the rest of his life, consoled by two mistresses with each of whom he had several children. His soldiers nicknamed him 'the old cock of the rock'. One cannot help feeling that Mary's prudence saved her from an unhappy marriage.

Chapter 7

The Navy

MANY READERS IN JANE Austen's own time would have been familiar with the navy, whose exploits had for so long filled the newspapers. The novels, and even more her letters, show Jane Austen to have been well informed about a profession followed by two of her brothers. Twenty-seven naval ships are mentioned by name in her letters. The modern reader, however, may share the Musgrove family's 'very general ignorance of all naval matters'.

In *Persuasion* Lady Russell considered it a 'most uncertain profession'. Indeed it was. It is probable that the navy had about 100,000 fatal casualties in twenty years of war. But it was not dangerous for the reason one might think. Casualties in a major battle could be high: 1,098 were killed at the First of June (1794) and 1,690 at Trafalgar (1805). But the enemy were not the greatest danger. About half of all deaths in the navy were from disease (particularly yellow fever and typhus), about one-third by individual accident, 10 per cent by foundering, wreck, fire and explosion, and only 8 per cent by the enemy.[1] Promotion-hungry officers drinking to 'a bloody war or a sickly season' benefited more from the latter. The picture was the same with ships.[2] The navy lost only 10 ships through enemy action but about 100 from being wrecked. One of them was Charles Austen's ship *Phoenix*.

Just over a quarter of naval officers were from landed gentry families[3]; just under a quarter were the sons of naval officers; about one-eighth of officers were the sons of peers and baronets, and rather more than an eighth were the sons of clergymen and army officers. So roughly three-quarters of naval officers would generally have been considered to be born gentlemen, if not by Sir Walter Elliot. From the other quarter came Edward Pellew, probably 'the greatest sea officer of his time', who ended his life as Viscount Exmouth. Another, the son of a Lincolnshire apothecary, was Captain Matthew Flinders, the distinguished navigator and cartographer. He has a strong claim to be considered the person who named Australia, which he was the first to circumnavigate. It is said that in Australia there are more statues of Flinders (and some of Trim his cat) than of anyone save Queen Victoria.[4] This is just the sort of thing that Sir Walter Elliot so disliked about the navy.

If a commissioned officer was not born a gentleman, holding the king's commission gave a good claim to being considered a gentleman. Looking like a gentleman helped in cases of doubt. An experienced Scottish seaman called David Bartholomew was press-ganged in 1795. He did well, rose to master's mate and had passed his lieutenant's examination when the Revolutionary War ended and he was discharged. At the start of the Napoleonic War he so annoyed the First Lord of the Admiralty, St Vincent, with repeated applications for a commission that the First Lord summoned him and arranged for him to be press-ganged in the hall of the Admiralty. Uproar followed. A Select Committee of the House of Commons enquired into the matter. Because gentlemen were exempt from impressment, the matter turned on whether or not Bartholomew was close enough to being an officer to qualify for exemption as a gentleman. Five naval officers were consulted. The decision hinged on his appearance. Two thought he 'looked like a Boatswain' and thought that the impressment was justified, while three considered it a 'violation of the ways of the Navy'. The Committee had a look at Bartholomew themselves, decided that they could not 'concur in describing his appearance to be at all like that of a Boatswain, or any such inferior officer' and found in his favour.

In *Mansfield Park* Sir Thomas Bertram, we are told, assisted Mrs

Price 'liberally in the education and disposal of her sons as they became old enough for a determinate pursuit'. One boy was a clerk in a public office in London and another a midshipman on board an Indiaman. William Price was doing nothing unusual in going to sea at the age of eleven. The career of a would-be naval officer began young. In 1812 one mother was told that nineteen was at least six years too old to begin a sea life. Some of them were very young. Charles Boys, midshipman in the *Thetis* in 1793, was known for sucking his thumb.[5] Another, Hood Christian, aged eleven, was spanked by his father, a rear-admiral, in front of a boat's crew.[6]

Boys were sent to sea with any captain who would have them. Only in 1815 was Admiralty sanction required before a midshipman was entered in a ship's books. Known as 'young gentlemen', they hoped to become commissioned officers. Sometimes, if very young, they were entered on the books of a ship without having to go to sea. One consideration was that it cost less than going into the church as, in *Persuasion*, did Captain Wentworth's brother.

Connections of some sort were necessary for this first stage but they did not need to be very grand. The Lincolnshire apothecary, Matthew Flinders, had a niece, Henny, who was governess to the children of Commodore (later Admiral Sir) Thomas Pasley (1734–1808). Henny obtained places on Pasley's ships for her brother John and for Matthew Flinders, junior. Nelson's first connection of value was his uncle Maurice Suckling who was Comptroller of the Navy. The Reverend George Austen was not unworldly. He also understood how connections could be of use, writing to Warren Hastings in 1794 about Frank's career. Hastings himself enlisted the help of an Admiral Affleck, a member of the Admiralty Board.

In *Persuasion* we learn about the short career of Dick Musgrove (aka 'Poor Richard'):

> The Musgroves had had the ill fortune of a very troublesome, hopeless son; and the good fortune to lose him before he reached his twentieth year ... he had been sent to sea, because he was stupid and unmanageable on shore; ... he had at any time been very little cared for by his family, though quite as much as he deserved; seldom heard of, and scarcely at all regretted ... He had

been several years at sea, and had, in the course of those removals to which all midshipmen are liable, and especially such midshipmen as every captain wishes to get rid of, been six months on board Captain Frederick Wentworth's frigate, the *Laconia*; and from the *Laconia* he had, under the influence of his captain, written the only two letters which his father and mother had ever received from him during the whole of his absence; that is to say, the only two disinterested letters; all the rest had been mere applications for money.[7]

In poor Dick's defence his applications for money might have been entirely justified. We know from the Reverend George Austen's bank account with Hoare & Co. that he supported his naval sons early in their careers – midshipmen were not paid for their first two years – and the apothecary William Flinders helped his own son. In *Mansfield Park* Sir Thomas supports William Price. Lady Bertram gave William £10 at her husband's suggestion and when Fanny and William travel to Portsmouth, Sir Thomas pays for them to travel in a hired post chaise rather than on a public coach. When he is made a lieutenant Mrs Norris' characteristic comment is 'Now William would be able to keep himself, which would make a vast difference to his uncle, for it was unknown how much he had cost his uncle; and indeed it would make some difference to *her* presents too.'[8]

Poor Dick's comment on his captain was that he was 'a fine dashing felow, only two perticular about the school-master'. Dick's spelling is not surprising. Sea-going schoolmasters were not numerous. There was only one in the fleet that fought at Trafalgar. Nor were they well regarded. 'As late as 1793 the ship's teacher was rated for pay purposes with the cook's mate, the cooper and the trumpeter.'[9] Naval chaplains also played a part in the care and education of midshipmen. William Price 'met with great kindness from the chaplain of the *Antwerp*'.[10]

An Order in Council of March 1812 improved the pay and conditions of naval chaplains, the hope being that they might be induced to act as teachers. Chaplains had been very badly paid – about £12 plus 4d. per man in the ship's crew. Chaplains' pay was now raised to £150 per annum, with the right to a pension after eight years' service. They were to have their own cabins and to mess with a ship's lieutenants. If they acted as schoolmasters they would earn a further £20 plus £5 per pupil.

The Reverend Edward Mangin stood being a naval chaplain for just three and a half months in 1812 in the *Gloucester* (74) – the number in brackets being the number of guns, i.e. cannons, borne by the ship. 'With a gentleman's education but without sufficient income, my new undertaking had rather the air of desperation than of enterprise.'[11] He found that:

> nothing can possibly be more unsuitably or more awkwardly situated than a clergyman in a ship of war; every object around him is at variance with the sensibilities of a rational and enlightened mind; amidst preparations the most complex and ingenious for the purposes of plundering and murdering his fellow creatures, he must act and speak as becomes the promoter of 'peace and good-will towards men'.[12]

He complained that his instructions enjoined him 'not only to preach and pray, at stated times, but ... to do some things which are improper, and some which are impossible'. These included mediating between officers and seamen to divert punishment, and rebuking seamen for 'profane swearing and intemperate language'. Visiting the sick didn't go very well either. 'The entrance of the clergyman is, to a poor seaman, often a fatal sign.'[13]

His physical circumstances also repulsed him. His cabin 'in shape, precisely, and in size nearly the same as a grand-piano-forte' was on a deck which 'slept between five hundred and six hundred men; and the ports being necessarily closed from evening to morning, in this cavern of only six feet high, and so entirely filled with human bodies, (the smell) was overpowering'.[14]

Mangin thought the food was good but the water seemed to be 'the extract of the ditches around Sheerness'. Perhaps understandably the ward-room preferred bad wine: 'half a pint each day of the week and ... as much as we pleased on Sunday ... an average of a pint per day'. Mangin particularly disapproved of a Lieutenant Neill, 'the only independent man among us', who argued that 'a

pint of wine per day was the least that could be drank by gentlemen in the rank of King's officers.' The mess expenses were at a
rate of over £60 per annum each. It was all too much for the poor
man and he 'formed a resolution to leave the service, by the earliest
fair opportunity'.[15]

Not everyone found the role so unpleasant. The Reverend James
Stanier Clarke, the Prince Regent's librarian, who suggested that
Jane Austen might send a clerical character to sea, had been a naval
chaplain and published a book, *Sermons preached in the Western
Squadron during its services off Brest, on board H.M. ship Impetueux*, in
1798. His suggestions were quoted – they hardly needed parody –
by Jane Austen in 1816 in the unpublished *Plan of a Novel, according
to Hints from Various Quarters*.

One might add that since the crews were drawn from many
countries, a Church of England chaplain was unlikely to have an
entirely willing congregation. Southey, writing to Coleridge in
December 1807, said that his main reason for opposing Catholic
emancipation was that its consequence 'would be to introduce an
Irish priest into every ship in the navy'.

Most naval schoolmasters were not accomplished and, given
their small number, there seem to be rather too many stories to
their general discredit. On the *Pegasus* (28) in 1786 the schoolmaster Mears tried twice to murder Prince William (later William IV)
with a knife. Several were spectacular alcoholics. The education
of a midshipman was therefore mostly practical. William IV was
supposed to have said that 'there was no place superior to the quarterdeck of a British man of war for the education of a gentleman.'[16]

In *Mansfield Park* William Price is a midshipman of a very different sort to poor Dick Musgrove. For one thing he is acknowledged
as an excellent correspondent. 'Young as he was, William had
already seen a great deal. He had been in the Mediterranean – in
the West Indies – in the Mediterranean again – had often been
taken on shore by the favour of his Captain, and in the course of
seven years had known every variety of danger, which sea and war
together could offer.'[17]

Even Henry Crawford is impressed: 'he felt the highest respect
for a lad who, before he was twenty, had gone through such bodily

hardships, and given such proofs of mind. The glory of heroism, of usefulness, of exertion, of endurance, made his own habits of selfish indulgence appear in shameful contrast.'

Although the education of young gentlemen at sea was haphazard, there was a prejudice against the shore-based alternative, the Royal Naval College at Portsmouth. It was seen as a threat to the patronage exercised by captains. Nevertheless, it provided a methodical education according to a plan of learning with an emphasis on mathematics. While the sons of naval officers received free board and tuition, the sons of clergymen did not. Mr Austen had to pay annual fees of £25 as well as the cost of maintaining Frank – about £50.[18]

Compared to the unreformed public schools of the day it offered a good education. Francis Austen went to the College in April 1786, and spent almost three years there before joining HMS *Perseverance* in the rank of 'college volunteer'. His brother Charles was there from July 1791 to September 1794 before joining HMS *Daedalus*.[19] But it was noted that of the famous frigate captains of the day, only Philip Broke of the *Shannon* and Thomas Byam Martin went to the College. In all it probably provided 2.5 per cent or less of officers.[20]

Some distinguished officers came by other routes. William Hotham was put on a ship's books at seven but went to Westminster School until he was thirteen. Then, after a few months at sea, he went to the Royal Naval Academy for a while, finally joined his ship and was a lieutenant four years later. Frank Austen was also made a lieutenant four years after leaving the Academy.

We see in William Price, visiting Fanny after seven years at sea, 'a young man of an open, pleasant countenance, and frank, unstudied, but feeling and respectful manners'. Sir Thomas is pleased to see in his protégé 'the proof of good principles, professional knowledge, energy, courage and cheerfulness'. And William has the grace to call himself a 'poor, scrubby midshipman'. He tells Fanny that he might not get a partner at the Portsmouth Assembly because 'The Portsmouth girls turn up their noses at anybody who has not a commission. One might as well be nothing as a midshipman. One is nothing indeed.'[21]

Before considering how one became 'something', it is helpful to understand how officers were paid and rewarded. Naval pay was not particularly high, even with allowances. A rear-admiral, such as Admiral Croft, might be paid £823 a year. A captain's pay and allowances varied with the number of men and guns on his ship. Commanding a first-rate ship might bring with it an income of £800 while commanding a sixth-rate paid £285. In 1805 Henry Austen wrote to congratulate his brother Frank on his new command: 'We all heartily wish you joy of the Canopus, which I see is an 80 Guns Ship, & which I calculate will nett you £500 per Ann.'[22] Henry was always an optimist. A captain, obliged to entertain his officers and others, might find himself short of money since he was not paid until the ship's books of account had been approved.

A commander's pay did not range so widely as that of a captain, being typically in the region of £250 or so. A lieutenant was paid about £112.

But these are all full-pay figures. When not at sea officers were on half-pay. So in *Persuasion*, beside whatever income from capital they had, Admiral Croft's half-pay as a rear-admiral would have been £547 a year, Captains Wentworth and Harvill would have had about £192 and Benwick about £155. Midshipmen received no half-pay at all.

In 1806 Wentworth was a newly promoted commander on half-pay of about £118 a year with no fortune. 'He had been lucky in his profession, but spending freely, what had come freely, had realized nothing.'[23] We can only speculate on how he might have spent his money. Sailors were not known for orderly conduct when spending prize money. Dr Trotter, who had much naval experience, commented, 'I have observed something like temporary insanity, in several officers, who had at once been elevated from extreme poverty to a fortune, by prize-money.'[24]

In April 1794 Pellew in the *Arethusa* captured two French frigates. The frigates of the Western Squadron shared ample prize money and celebrated famously. In Plymouth five sailors hired a coach, filled it with women, drink, a fiddler and an organ-grinder. 'They careered in triumph around the town for days until the money ran out.'[25]

An officer might have been less obvious but the general

direction of his probable enjoyments may be inferred. Captain Augustus Hervey in the previous century, for six months had on board his ship in the Mediterranean a Mademoiselle Sarrazin from Marseilles. Hervey wrote in his journal:

> I was extremely sorry to part with her, tho' she was ever sick at sea, too, poor thing; she was the best tempered creature that ever breathed, always in a good humour, cheerful and ready to oblige; she made time pass away very agreeably.[26]

She must have been most obliging, for Captain Hervey gave her £360 when she left his ship. This relaxed tradition survived, despite the efforts of evangelical admirals. George Watson, a seaman in the *Fame* (74), under Captain R.H.A. Bennett in 1809, recorded of his captain that:

> He loved the society of women, as most men do, and nearly all the time he was with us, had one in the ship with him, and at the period I am speaking of, there was a Miss Jennings on board as his mistress and had left England with him. She was a lovely looking woman, and modest in a great degree, compared with the majority of her sex who plough the seas on the same footing, and while she was much respected by the captain, she was also held in estimation both by the officers and men.[27]

Unfortunately, Miss Jennings became pregnant and was sent home. She was replaced by a beautiful Spanish girl 'of a genteel and handsome figure, and had large black and brilliant eyes; she dressed gaily and lightly, and appeared always at ease, and full of pleasure and cheerfulness'.[28] At Mahon the Captain took divine service every Sunday as ordered by Lord Collingwood, there being no chaplain on board. George Watson remembered that:

> often instead of directing my thoughts to Heaven, they were chiefly fixed, with my eyes accompanyihg them, on Miss L, our commander's mistress, who generally sat looking at us from the windows under the poop.[29]

Commander Wentworth, 'full of life and ardour', might so easily
have behaved in a similar way. Such was the navy's reputation it
was said that when Lord Howe's battered fleet returned to port
after the Glorious First of June in 1794 thirty thousand women
came aboard to comfort the heroes.

However he spent his money, Commander Wentworth had 'no
hopes of attaining affluence, but in the chances of a most uncertain
profession, and no connexions to secure even his farther rise in that
profession'.[30]

We have seen the dangers of the profession, the need for interest to further a career and above all the importance of luck. Jane
Austen knew about this last from her brother Frank's career. He
was in command of the *Canopus* in Nelson's fleet before Trafalgar
but missed the battle, and all the honours and rewards that followed, by being away from the fleet getting fresh food and water.

Although Wentworth is 'brilliant' and 'headstrong', one can
see why Lady Russell deprecated the connection, 'little taste for
wit' as she had. For the daughter of a baronet, a commander's half-
pay was not enough of an income on which to marry. Jane Austen
knew that some girls would take the risk of marrying a naval
officer in the hope of future prosperity. Eliza de Feuillide wrote to
Philadelphia Walter in October 1792 about the Captain Williams
who was to marry Dr Cooper's daughter Jane: 'His present fortune
is small, but he has expectations of future preferment.'[31] Jane
judged well. He ended his life as Admiral Sir Thomas Williams
and became Charles Austen's mentor, but Jane died in 1798 in
a carriage accident. Frank Austen's fiancée waited two years to
marry him.

In the novels there is the moving account of Captain Benwick's
engagement to Fanny Harville which lasted a year or two waiting
for fortune and promotion. 'Fortune came, his prize money as a
lieutenant being great; promotion, too, came at last, but Fanny
Harville did not live to know it.'[32]

Generally, the life of a naval officer's wife was an anxious one
with long years of separation. News of absent husbands was infre-
quent and often incorrect. When the mail reached Newcastle with
news of Trafalgar, the coachman announced that Nelson and all the

admirals had been killed. Collingwood's wife, Sarah, out shopping, fainted in the street.[33] Uncertainty might continue after a naval officer's death. Some widows only discovered that their husbands were bigamists on applying for a widow's naval pension and learning of a rival claim.

When Anne meets him again seven years later Wentworth is a different proposition:

> All his sanguine expectations, all his confidence had been justified. His genius and ardour had seemed to foresee and to command his prosperous path. He had, very soon after their engagement ceased, got employ; and all that he had told her would follow, had taken place. He had distinguished himself, and early gained the other step in rank ...[34]

At this stage in his life, Wentworth must now be rich. On a captain's half-pay of at least 10s 6d a day (from 1814) and an income of 5 per cent on £25,000, he would have had an annual income of about £1,440 a year.

The thing that made all the difference to the fortunes of a naval officer was prize money. The army sometimes earned prize money, too, but it was rare and not particularly large. After the Walcheren expedition, for example, booty taken on the island was divided amongst the army. General officers had about £562, field officers – the army equivalent of naval captains – about £211, so it was not life-changing in the way that naval prize money could be. The rank and file got less than a pound each, so the unequal distribution was fairly similar to that with naval prize money.[35]

Jane Austen is careful to establish Wentworth's gallantry first before describing his prize-taking. We learn that Wentworth made his name when in the *Asp* – an old and not very seaworthy sloop – he captured a French frigate and brought her in to Plymouth. This was an exceptional feat. The frigate would have had much heavier guns than the *Asp*. Such things did happen, although rarely, in real life. In May 1801 Commander Thomas Cochrane in the *Speedy*, a sloop which he described as 'little more than a burlesque on a vessel of war ... about the size of an average coasting brig', with

14 4-pounder guns (a broadside of 28 lb) and a crew of 54, fought, boarded and captured the Spanish frigate *El Gamo*, with 32 guns (a broadside of 190 lb) and a crew of 319. At the height of the action all of the *Speedy*'s crew boarded the enemy ship, leaving only the doctor, Mr Guthrie, at the helm. Cochrane, with a surviving crew of 42 fit men, brought the *El Gamo* and 263 unhurt prisoners into Port Mahon.[36]

We are to understand that Wentworth is a very capable and brave officer indeed. One might add that his passivity and inactivity after Louisa Musgrave's fall on the Cobb at Lyme are rather out of character. Capturing an enemy warship was glorious and often led to promotion (unlike the capture of a merchantman) and it was more profitable on average, if much more dangerous, than capturing merchantmen. Strongly built warships were usually acquired by the navy, often despite battle damage. Besides the value of the hull, there was the value of the stores, armaments and rigging, and head money (see p.146). French frigates were more heavily manned than English ships so head money could be significant. The most valuable frigate captured (*Le Niemen* in 1809) yielded a net £28,480 in prize money but a more typical figure was £13,000–£14,000 so that the captain's share would have been, say, £3,000–£3,500.

Capturing privateers, as Wentworth does, was more frequent but much less profitable – privateers were often lightly built for speed and not heavily manned. Average net prize proceeds were not much over £1,000 (captain's share c.£250) – which is why Wentworth comments about 'privateers enough to be entertaining'.[37]

Jane Austen's letters mention the prospect or absence of prizes in the careers of her brothers. When Charles' ship *Endymion* took a prize Jane wrote to her sister Cassandra:

He has received 30£ for his share of the privateer & expects 10£ more – but of what avail is it to take prizes if he lays out the produce in presents to his Sisters. He has been buying Gold chains and Topaze Crosses for us – he must be well scolded.'[38]

(Le Faye. D. (ed.), *Jane Austen's Letters*, 4th edition (OUP, 2011). Reproduced by permission of Oxford University Press.)

In *Mansfield Park*, William Price brings Fanny an amber cross from Sicily, though the purchase of a gold chain is beyond his means.

One of the difficulties was the possibility for long delay in the payment of prize money. Charles Austen's experience in *Endymion* is a good example. The *Endymion*, commanded by Sir Thomas Williams, took a number of prizes in the spring of 1800 but had to wait to report them when she returned to Spithead in May. It was only on 20 October 1800 that the *Portsmouth Telegraph* could report that the crew of *Endymion* would be paid for capturing two ships, *La Scipio* and *La Paix*, and the money was not paid out until May 1801. It was only then that Charles could buy the famous crosses and chains for his sisters.[39]

Later in his life Charles Austen was not a financially successful captain. Between 1805 and 1808 he took thirteen prizes on the North American Station when in command of the sloop *Indian* (18). His prizes included French, Spanish, Swedish and American vessels. The capture of a French privateer *La Jeune Estelle* earned him something over £570. But one capture spent five years going through the prize courts and the costs consumed much of the prize money. In another case, after proceedings lasting two years, another capture was ruled on appeal not to be a lawful prize, leaving Charles and another captain liable for the costs of the case.[40]

In 1811 when he returned after a seven-year absence with a new Bermudan wife and two pretty daughters, Cassandra Austen wrote to Philadelphia Walter, now Mrs George Whitaker, 'There must be always something to wish for, and for Charles we have to wish for rather more money. So expensive as every thing in England is now, even the necessaries of life, I am afraid they will find themselves very, very poor.'[41] She was right and Charles Austen had to have his family on board his ship as Cassandra recorded in March 1812:

Charles and his Fanny came to us for a few days previous to their taking possession of their aquatic abode, he is Captn. of the *Namur* at Sheerness and she and his children are actually living with him on board. We had doubted whether such a scheme would prove practicable during the winter, but they have found their residence very tolerably comfortable and it is so much the cheapest home she could have that they are very right to put up with little inconveniences.[42]

Fanny's enthusiasm for ship-board life waned gradually. Sheerness was not the most salubrious anchorage. Her children spent quite a lot of time ashore staying with relatives. Eventually she died in childbirth. She was twenty-four.[43]

Prize money arose when a ship and its cargo captured by the navy were found to be lawful prizes by the High Court of Admiralty and 'condemned'. Naval ships claimed the right in wartime to stop and search other ships. Some might be enemy ships which would fight – and resistance was sufficient evidence to justify confiscation as a prize. The status of merchant ships could be very uncertain. Ships of neutral countries sailing between neutral ports were generally safe. But there were many possible combinations of nationality – of ship, of cargo, of origin or of destination – and papers were often forged. A ship running a blockade or taking part in some trade which would be banned in peace-time could be a lawful prize. Though potentially very rewarding, prize-taking could be a hazardous business. A captain was personally liable for all the costs if his ship took as a prize a ship and/or cargo that was subsequently judged not to be a lawful prize.

Admiral Sir Thomas Byam Martin recorded a case in Jamaica:

One of our ships detained a ship under American colours on suspicion of her being French property. The case was carried before the Court of Admiralty at that place, and while the investigation was in progress, and at the moment when the captain of the vessel (an American) was swearing through thick and thin as to the neutral character of the property, and supporting his false swearing by exhibiting false papers, there was brought into court a bundle of papers which had been taken out of the maw of a shark, and on unfolding them it was found that they were the actual bona-fides papers of this very ship which had been thrown out of the cabin window as the ship was entering Port Royal harbour. The American was so astonished and confounded that he was ready to sink into the floor.[44]

If single-ship capture was not difficult enough, prizes might be captured not singly but in numbers and not by one warship but by several. The complexities and arguments arising could drag out the settlement for years.

The law relating to prizes was based on the Convoy and Cruizers Act of 1708 and the Prize Act of 1793 (replaced by the 1805 Prize Act) – appropriately sub-titled An Act for the Encouragement of Seamen. Being a form of international law, cases were heard by the High Court of Admiralty. The court in London was better run than some of its satellite courts – the one in Malta being particularly unsatisfactory. Marine law cases were of sufficient interest to naval officers for law reports to form a regular part of the *Naval Chronicle*.

This may seem like a form of licensed piracy but the court could be robust in standing up for neutral interests. On 7 March 1801 the Admiralty Court in London heard a case which the *Naval Chronicle* summarized as follows:

The *Jonge Vrow Wilhelmina*, a neutral vessel, Capt. Jacobus, commander, belonging to Pappenburgh, and engaged in a course of trade on the coast of Holland, perfectly consonant to the Laws of Nations, was stopped and boarded by the *Ajax*, a Guernsey privateer. The Captain of the privateer, through the medium of an interpreter, intimated to Captain Jacobus, that he had good reason to think he was engaged in a contraband commerce, which the inspection of his ship's papers would expose; but that if he would give him a certain sum of money, he would release his ship. The Captain of the *Wilhelmina*, alarmed at the circumstance of having his ship boarded, and apprehensive of his voyage being delayed, readily consented to the demand, in order to get off, and paid the Captain of the *Ajax* what he thought proper to extort. No sooner had this transaction been concluded, than the *Ajax* made prize of the neutral ship, and carried her in to Guernsey, where the Prize Commissioners condemned her. The ground of the condemnation was, that the pretence by which the Captain of the *Ajax* obtained a sum of money to release the ship, was an innocent stratagem to make the captain of the neutral ship confess the truth, and that the payment of it by the latter was an absolute admission of his carrying on an illicit commerce.[45]

The judge in London, Sir William Scott, would have none of it.

> He expressed himself in unqualified terms of indignation at the conduct, not only of the Captain of the Guernsey privateer, but of the Commissioners who had sanctioned it ... he could no otherwise describe it, than as oppressive, unjust, and fraudulent; an infraction of the Rights of Neutral nations; a disgrace to the justice of our own, and a violation of its positive laws ... all the satisfaction he could make to the injured Neutral Owners, they should receive at his hands; and to that effect he decreed, that the *Wilhelmina* should be restored to them, and all the loss, damages, expenses, and costs occasioned by her detention, fully paid by the Captain of the privateer, or by his owners.[46]

Prize money was divided on a formal scale. The net sum after court, lawyers' and agents' costs was typically a little over 80 per cent of the value of the prize.[47] It was divided into eighths. The captain of the capturing ship received three-eighths unless operating under the command of a flag officer, which was generally the case, who took one of the eighths (the 'flag eighth'). A captain would usually expect therefore one quarter of the net prize money and the same proportion of head or salvage money. There was surprisingly little resentment at this system though there was a popular wish that the enemy's shot should be distributed in the same proportion as prize money. In June 1808 a new distribution was introduced which reduced the share of flag officers and captains, left the shares of other officers broadly unchanged and increased the crew's share, with a sliding scale recognizing seniority. After 1808 a captain's share became two-eighths less a possible flag share of one-third of that figure, so that a net captain's share fell from 25 per cent to 16.7 per cent. Lord Mulgrave, the first lord who made this change, was not popular with captains.

The greatest opportunities for profit were enjoyed by frigate captains and admirals. In *Persuasion* Wentworth remembers, 'Ah, those were pleasant days when I had the *Laconia*! How fast I made money in her. A friend of mine and I had such a lovely cruise together off the Western Isles.' The next summer he had the same luck in the Mediterranean.[48] A frigate captain on service detached from a fleet, and preferably acting on direct Admiralty orders, would have the chance of taking prizes with very little sharing. Admirals, entitled to a share of any prizes captured by any of the ships under their command, tended to interpret 'command' pretty broadly and it would be a brave captain who argued too strenuously against his admiral.

Some admirals made great fortunes: Keith, Pellew, Rainier, and Hyde Parker were thought each to have made between £200,000 and £300,000 during their careers, hence the reference to the possibility of a rich admiral being found to be a tenant of Kellynch Hall in *Persuasion*.

Admiral Croft – a rear-admiral of the white – having acquired a very handsome fortune wants to settle in Somersetshire from which he comes. He was at Trafalgar and then for several years in the East Indies. Mr Shepherd, Sir Walter's agent, describes the Admiral as 'quite the gentleman in all his notions and behaviour'. His wife, 'a very well-spoken, genteel, shrewd lady', is the sister of the former curate of Monkford and, of course, of Frederick Wentworth. Eventually Sir Walter is comforted to think that Admiral Croft might be an acceptable tenant: 'an admiral speaks his own consequence, and at the same time, can never make a baronet look small.'[49] He turns out to be the best-looking sailor Sir Walter has ever met, which allayed his other great dislike of the navy.

Sir Walter was right that life in the navy could age a man prematurely. Gilbert Blane, Physician to the Fleet, wrote of seamen that:

> in consequence of what they undergo, they are in general short lived, and have their constitutions worn out ten years before the rest of the laborious part of mankind. A seaman at the age of forty-five, if shewn to a person not accustomed to be among them, would be taken by his looks to be fifty-five, or even on the borders of sixty.[50]

We may speculate whether 'in the summer of 1814' Admiral Croft might have been among those officers promoted on 4 June 1814 to the rank of rear-admiral of the white or whether he was one of the twenty-four rear-admirals of the white made before that date, many of whom advanced to rear-admiral of the red on 4 June 1814. Anne's knowledge of his rank might be attributed to having read of that summer's promotions. It was perhaps Jane Austen's tact that put him below the real-life Admiral Sir Thomas Williams who was made vice-admiral of the red in June 1814.

Admiral Croft when walking with Anne in Bath sees across the street an Admiral Brand and his brother, 'shabby fellows, both of them ... they played me a pitiful trick once'.[51] Flag officers frequently quarrelled amongst themselves. One quarrel about prize money, between Nelson and St Vincent, came to court. Of course it was not publicly described as a quarrel about money. When the matter came to be heard at the Court of King's Bench at the Guildhall in front of the Lord Chief Justice on 4 March 1801, the *Naval Chronicle* described the matter thus: 'the persons interested were all of the highest reputation ... they were also friends to one another; and this controversy was by no means of a pecuniary nature, but arose out of the different opinions that had been entertained on the subject, as to the custom of the service.'[52]

While most prizes were quite modest individually, some could be enormous. One splendid example was the capture in October 1799 of two Spanish ships – *El Thetis* and *Santa Brigida* – by four English frigates – *Naiad, Ethalion, Triton* and *Alcmene*. The two ships had a cargo of treasure which was sold to the Bank of England for £661,206 13s. 9d. The distribution of this prize money included £40,731 to each captain, £5,091 to each lieutenant and £182 to each seaman.[53] The distribution was very unequal but a seaman's share was still equivalent to about nine or ten years' pay for an able seaman.[54]

Besides prize money there was a bounty, known as 'head money' payable at a rate of £5 per member of the enemy crew in a captured or destroyed warship. This was distributed in the same manner as prize money but from a government fund. After a bloody and destructive action it was not always easy to establish the original number of the enemy's crew. When the 130-gun

Imperial was driven ashore at the battle of Santo Domingo in 1806, the testimony of a single, illiterate survivor was sufficient.[55]

Freight money was received only by admirals and captains – a payment for carrying non-naval cargoes of treasure. It was based upon ancient usage rather than law. In 1801 freight money for public treasure was stopped, an order partly repealed in 1807. William Dillon, then a frigate captain, made £2,000 carrying £200,000 of East India Company treasure from Portsmouth to India in 1815. An admiral's share could be considerable too. In the two years 1803–4, Lord Keith's agents calculated that as Commander-in-Chief in the Mediterranean he had received a little over £47,500 in freight money alone.[56] But he was also spending £8,000 a year on entertainment as commander-in-chief – about four times his pay.[57]

Captain Wentworth admits he was lucky. Indeed it was possible for an able and active officer to make very little money. One such was Captain George Duff. Born in 1764, he had been in thirteen engagements before he was sixteen. He was appointed captain and commander of the *Martin*, a sloop, in 1790 and soon after married Sophia Dirom, a childhood friend. The *Naval Chronicle* noted that 'Captain Duff had no opportunity in the course of the last war … of materially improving his fortune'.[58] The young William Dillon served in the *Glenmore* under Duff and remembered, 'We were invited to dine in rotation with our Captain, at whose table the strictest frugality prevailed … the instant the quantity allowed was expended we rose, and the party broke up. It had more the bearing of a ceremonial meeting than a sociable one.'[59] None of Duff's subsequent service led him to capture prizes and he was killed at Trafalgar on the quarterdeck of his ship the *Mars* (74) where a cannon ball took off his head. He left his wife with three surviving children. His letters to his wife show how worried he had been about his small capital.

Naval officers seem to have invested their prize money quite conventionally. Lord Collingwood, Nelson's second in command at Trafalgar, left about £163,743 of which almost £100,000 (market value) was in Consols, bought gradually over many years. We know that when the price of Consols fell he thought of buying an estate as well so that 'our property might rest on more points than one'.[60]

Having looked at money, or the lack of it, in the navy, we can turn to the system of promotion. Jane Austen knew well the importance of connections and influence – 'interest' – to obtain promotion in the navy. Her brothers Francis and Charles, who lived to be admirals, both had family connections who helped them. James Austen had married Anne Mathew, the daughter of a General Mathew (and grand-daughter of a duke). A Mathew girl married 'Dismal Jimmy' Gambier, the evangelical naval officer, who was a patron to Francis Austen. Charles Austen, for his part, depended on Admiral Sir Thomas Williams who had married Jane Cooper, an Austen first cousin.[61]

Even Nelson, who had first gone to sea with his maternal uncle, saw nothing wrong in the system. He wrote to Sir Peter Parker, Admiral of the Fleet, about his grandson.

> I have kept him as Lieutenant of the Victory, and shall not part with him until I can make him a Post Captain, which you may be assured I shall lose no time in doing … I owe all my Honours to you, and am proud to acknowledge it to all the world.'[62]

There was a family-like quality to the navy – for good or bad. Philemon Pownoll, one of the captors of the *Hermione* in 1762, taught Edward Pellew and John Borlase Warren, subsequently famously successful officers. Pellew named his eldest son Pownoll. Unfortunately Pownoll Pellew's career is a not-very-edifying example of patronage exerted on a subject of modest abilities. By his father's influence he was made a lieutenant without the usual years of experience; a commander at seventeen, he was promoted to post rank at twenty. He was given by his father particular opportunities to take prizes in the East Indies. Subsequently Pownoll became an MP and succeeded his father as the second Viscount Exmouth.

In *Mansfield Park* Fanny is sure that their uncle will do everything in his power to get William made a lieutenant. A midshipman had to have served at least six years and, in theory, be twenty years old (nineteen after 1806) before he could take the examination for lieutenant – the only formal examination in a naval officer's career. The minimum age requirement was sometimes circumvented. It

was said that the porter at the navy office could produce birth cer-
tificates for a crown.

The ordeal might be lessened by friends and connections among
the examiners. James Gardner was examined by 'an intimate friend
of my father's' and a particular friend of Admiral Parry, his great-
uncle, in 1795. He was passed despite giving a wrong answer to the
only serious question he was asked! It is perhaps to the credit of the
navy that he remained a lieutenant for thirty-five years.[63]

But passing the examination was not enough. A lieutenant's
commission was to a specific ship, and midshipmen who had
passed for lieutenant could linger unappointed. In the period after
the Peace of Amiens in 1803 more than 1,200 unemployed lieutenants applied to the Admiralty for posts. In 1813 the list of such men
was nearly 2,000 long. But it was a problem for all naval officers.
Even when the navy was at its largest in 1814 with 713 ships in commission, only half of the 4,920 naval officers on the active list were
employed. By 1816 after the peace there were only 278 ships in commission while the number of officers had grown to 5,937, so that
only 17 per cent of them were employed. The increase in officers
was largely a result of the midshipmen being given commissions as
lieutenants at the end of the war so that they would be entitled to
half-pay for life.[64]

It is clear that William Price is in this position. It is Henry
Crawford's introduction of William to his uncle the Admiral – he
takes him to dinner with the Admiral in Hill Street – which leads
to William's commission as second-lieutenant of HM Sloop *Thrush*.
The Admiral used his influence with a friend, named only as
Sir Charles, who approached the First Lord of the Admiralty on
William's behalf. Mary Crawford is anxious to emphasize to Fanny
the kindness her brother has shown to William: 'I know he must
have exerted himself very much, for I know the parties he had to
move. The Admiral hates trouble, and scorns asking favours; and
there are so many young men's claims to be attended to.'[65]

On his appointment, William Price, exercising his own small
interest, takes his 11-year-old brother Sam to sea for the first time
in the *Thrush*.

When made a lieutenant, William Price is full of:

schemes for an action with some superior force, which (supposing the first lieutenant out of the way – and William was not very
merciful to the first lieutenant) was to give himself the next step, or
speculations upon prize money, which was to be generously distributed at home, with only the reservation of enough to make the
little cottage comfortable, in which he and Fanny were to pass all
their middle and later life together.[66]

Once made a lieutenant, the next step was to be made a commander. One might stay a lieutenant for a long time. One such was
John Richards Lapenotiere, who passed for lieutenant in 1793 and,
aged thirty-five, was still a lieutenant in command of the *Pickle* (6),
a 73-foot schooner of 127 tons, in 1805 at Trafalgar, where she was
the smallest British ship. The *Pickle* took Collingwood's dispatches
the 1,000 miles to Falmouth, and Lapenotiere then travelled by
road the 266 miles to London as fast as he could. He did it in under
thirty-seven hours, at an average speed of just over seven miles an
hour. He was promoted to commander and awarded a Patriotic
Fund sword valued at 100 guineas. Others were not so lucky. The
Navy List of February 1814 includes one Jacob Adams, a lieutenant
made on 26 September 1777.

Once a commander there came the most important step, to be
raised to the rank of post-captain. The quickest way to promotion
was to distinguish oneself in action. In March 1800 Francis Austen,
when in command of the sloop *Peterel* (16), a part of Nelson's
Mediterranean fleet, was in an engagement with three French
vessels. Two were driven onto the rocks and the third captured.
This was achieved with a short-handed crew and led to his promotion from commander to captain.

Unlike the army, promotion could not be bought in the navy.
Owing to their nature, attempts at direct bribery may be hard to
uncover. We know of one lieutenant who in 1810 offered the First
Lord £2,000 to make him a commander. He quickly realized his
mistake. He apologized, sensing disaster, was sent back to his ship
and remained a lieutenant for twenty-nine years.[67] Naval promotion was largely on merit, not merely on social status. Among
Nelson's 'band of brothers' was Captain George Blagdon Westcott

(1753–98). Westcott was the son of a baker from Honiton in Devon. He was killed at the Battle of the Nile in 1798, by a musket ball to the throat, when in command of *Majestic* (74). 'A good officer and a worthy man', wrote Collingwood to Nelson after the battle.[68] Had he survived the battle, his seniority of appointment would have obtained him an Admiral's flag. Nelson later wrote to Lady Hamilton 'At Honiton, I visited Captain Westcott's mother – poor thing, except from the bounty of Government and Lloyd's, in very low circumstances. The brother is a tailor, but had they been chimney sweepers it was my duty to shew them respect.'[69] Over lunch Nelson asked whether she had received her son's Nile medal. When she said she had not, he unpinned his own medal from his coat and gave it to her, saying he hoped she would not value it less because Nelson had worn it.[70]

There was competition for commands. When Captain Wentworth comments on the poor condition of his first command, the *Asp*, Admiral Croft interjects, 'Phoo! phoo! ... what stuff these young fellows talk ... Lucky fellow to get her! – He knows there must have been twenty better men than himself applying for her at the same time. Lucky fellow to get anything so soon, with no more interest than his.'[71]

A small blemish on a record could reduce one's chance of a sea-going command. After the loss of his ship the *Phoenix* (36) in 1816 Charles Austen waited ten years for another, having to serve in a post as a coastguard. But the means of his getting his next ship are a tribute to naval initiative. Living near Portsmouth, he noticed one day the flag of the *Aurora* (44) being lowered to half-mast. He took a boat, confirmed that the captain had died, posted to London to the Admiralty to tell them the news and asked for the command himself. He was given it. In *Aurora* Charles sailed for Jamaica within four days of her former captain's death and was away for four years.[72]

Once a captain, while ability might affect appointment to a sea-going command, time would ensure an automatic rise up the Navy List almost irrespective of merit. Nelson was one of nine post-captains of 1779 made rear-admiral of the blue on the same day. This is why Anne Elliot can think of Captain Wentworth as being 'as high in his profession as merit and activity could place him'.[73] In *Mansfield Park*, Miss Crawford is dismissive: 'Post-captains may be very good sort of men in their way, but they do not belong to *us.'* Her opinion of the navy is that the profession 'is well enough under two circumstances; if it makes the fortune, and there be discretion in spending it.'[74]

The picture of the navy in the novels has blemishes. In *Mansfield Park* we are told that 'Admiral Crawford was a man of vicious habits' who after his wife's death chose 'to bring his mistress under his own roof'. This prejudices Miss Crawford against all admirals.

> Of various admirals I could tell you a great deal: of them and their flags, and the gradation of their pay, and their bickerings and jealousies. But in general, I can assure you that they are all passed over, and very ill used. Certainly, my home at my uncle's brought me acquainted with a circle of admirals. Of rears and vices, I saw enough. Now, do not be suspecting me of a pun, I entreat.[75]

This is the speech that Edmund Bertram thought 'very wrong, very indecorous'.

Some admirals lived to be very old. Francis Austen lived to be ninety-one and died an Admiral of the Fleet. The most splendid example was Provo Wallis. Born in 1791, he was entered on a ship's books at the age of four, under the illegal practice of false muster, but did not actually go to sea until he was nine. In 1813 he was second-lieutenant of the *Shannon* when it fought and captured the American frigate *Chesapeake*. Captain Broke was seriously wounded and the first-lieutenant was killed. Young Wallis, in temporary command, brought the prize in to Halifax for which he was made commander. Further promotion followed in time. In 1870 a system of retirement from the navy was introduced but with a provision that any veteran officer who had commanded a ship in the French Wars should not have to retire. Wallis qualified by virtue of his few days' command of the *Shannon*. In 1877 he became Admiral of the Fleet and died in February 1892 aged 100. He had been in the navy for ninety-six years.

Chapter 8

The Church

WE FIND IN THE novels a critical view of the Church that is remarkable from the daughter and sister of clergymen. It is not the criticism of an unbeliever – far from it – but that of a well-informed observer.

There are numerous clergymen in Jane Austen's novels as there were in her life. Besides her own family, Austens, Leighs, Cookes and Coopers, other families who were close friends and had clergymen among them included the Lefroys, Terrys, Digweeds, Chutes, Powletts, Portals and Fowles. The number of clergymen mentioned in her letters is large – more than one hundred.

So the Church is a subject with which she was familiar. She knew how it worked, the rules, the getting of preferment and the characters of many clergymen. Quite apart from their spiritual role, the clergy made up a significant portion of the *intelligentsia* and exercised influence over public opinion. They were important in local government as justices of the peace and Poor Law guardians.

However, the Church's reputation did not stand high. The clerical office was not 'equal in the point of dignity with the highest rank in the kingdom' as Mr Collins asserted, nor thought smart enough by Edward Ferrars' family. A layman, John Byng, wrote at the close of a tour in the Midlands in 1789:

about religion I have made some enquiry, (having been in so many churches) and find it to be lodged in the hands of the Methodists; as the greater clergy do not attend to their duty, and the lesser neglect it; that where the old psalm singing is abolished, none is established in its place; as the organ is inconvenient and not understood; at most places the curates never attend regularly, or to any effect, or comfort, so no wonder that the people are gone over to Methodism.[1]

The inadequacies of the Church of England created something of a vacuum which was filled by numerous other churches. Anglicans showed some curiosity about these 'others'. Mary Hardy in Norfolk who heard regularly two sermons each Sunday, went also to Quaker meetings, to Methodist and to Dissenting chapels. Her husband went to a synagogue during a visit to London.

Southey recorded a story told of the Mayor of Tiverton in Devon who was reluctant to allow Methodists to hold services in his town:

'What, sir,' said he, 'Why, what reason can there be for any new religion in Tiverton? Another way of going to Heaven when there are so many already? Why, sir, there's the Old Church and the New Church, that's one religion; there's Parson Kiddell's at the Pitt Meeting, that's two; Parson Westcott's in Peter Street, that's three; and old Parson Terry's in Newport Street, is four. – Four ways of going to Heaven already ! – and if they won't go to Heaven by one or other of these ways, by – they shan't go to Heaven at all from Tiverton, while I am mayor of the town.'[2]

Louis Simond visiting Westminster Abbey admired the music very much but:

Whatever sentiments of elevation and piety the music might have produced, were soon unfortunately brought down to the ordinary worldly level by the sermon it was our fortune to hear. The preacher was a purple-faced short-necked man, forcing his hollow, vulgar, insincere voice through a fat narrow passage. He told us, or

154

rather read out of a paper in his hand, that it was wrong to wish to die, yet not right to be afraid neither; and that St Paul taught us to keep a happy medium.[3]

There were excellent preachers in London, as elsewhere. Some became well-known figures. Elizabeth Grant of Rothiemurchus remembered hearing the much-admired Reverend Edward Irving at the Caledonian Church in Hatton Garden and noted waspishly 'the little chapel he served was crammed with all the titles in London; and such a crush on entering as to cause screaming and fainting, torn dresses, etc.'[4]

Looking back at the eighteenth century the Reverend Sydney Smith wrote in his *Edinburgh Review* article on Church parties that:

> the thermometer of the Church of England sank to its lowest point in the first thirty years of George III. Unbelieving bishops, and a slothful clergy, had succeeded in driving from the Church the faith and zeal of Methodism which Wesley had organised within her pale. The spirit was expelled and the dregs remained. That was the age when jobbery and corruption, long supreme in the State, had triumphed over the virtue of the Church; when the money changers not only entered the temple, but drove out the worshippers; when ecclesiastical revenues were monopolised by wealthy pluralists; when the name of curate lost its legal meaning, and, instead of denoting the incumbent of a living, came to signify the deputy of an absentee.[5]

Certainly there is no shortage of anecdotes to support the view of a neglected Church, both in its function and its fabric. In 1783 the canons of Hereford Cathedral decided that 'the fines in future for all Leases that shall be granted by the Chapter shall be paid immediately and the Money instantly divided amongst the members of the Chapter.'[6] The canons, while sharing money between themselves, neglected both their estates and their cathedral. On Easter Monday 1786 the whole of the cathedral's west tower collapsed. The neglect of church buildings was not confined to cathedrals. In 1803 Reverend William Jones, Vicar of Broxbourne, wrote in his diary, 'My church has not been repaired, not even white-washed, for 50 or 60 years, not within the memory of the oldest man in the parish.'[7] Jane Austen's own parish church at Chawton was also in disrepair.

A further complication inside churches related to pews. Southey, impersonating a Catholic Spaniard, wrote 'They have an abominable custom of partitioning their churches into divisions which they call pews, and which are private property; so that the wealthy sit at their ease, or kneel upon cushions, while the poor stand during the whole service in the aisle.'[8]

The consequence of this spiritual and physical decay was evident both to clerics and to laymen. Sydney Smith wrote, 'The English clergy, though upon the whole a very learned, pious, moral, and decent body of men, are not very remarkable for professional activity', and he wrote of Mrs Fry, the prison reformer, 'Mrs Fry is very unpopular with the clergy: examples of living, active virtue disturb our repose, and give birth to distressing comparisons: we long to burn her alive.'[9]

The condition of the Church was evident to visitors like Louis Simond.

Returning from Scotland, where the clergy are particularly grave and decorous, we are the more struck with the smart appearance of the English clergy. I observed a few days ago, at the house of one of these reverend persons, a pair of sparring-gloves; and the sight put me in mind of Dr Moore's anecdote about the young man who thought he had a vocation for the church, 'because he liked field-sports so much.' You meet in the best society a number of young clergymen, brought up in the expectancy of some good living, of which their families or friends have the presentation. Those young men have received an education which sets any talents they may have off to the best advantage, — they are idle enough to be *aimable*, and welcome everywhere, like our Abbes formerly. A well brushed suit of black forms the essential of their establishment; nobody inquires where they lodge nor at what ordinary they eat their meal. We have in the upper part of the house where we lodge one of these young expectants of the good things of the church. From his garret he went the other day to Carleton-house to be presented, – he dines out every day, – is of all the parties, – and comes home at two o'clock in the morning.[10]

Given all this it is perhaps not surprising that some of the clergy-men in the novels are pretty unimpressive: Mr Collins and Mr Elton are two such. Dr Grant, the epicurean Vicar of Mansfield, suc-ceeds to a stall in Westminster and to a larger income and once in London, 'brought on apoplexy and death, by three great institution-ary dinners in one week'.[11] Not all are bad clergymen. Dr Shirley in *Persuasion* has been a diligent parson for more than forty years. We are told that Edward Ferrars readily discharged his duties in every particular at Delaford. Edmund Bertram was no doubt serious and diligent but he was also a pluralist – it seems that he held the ben-efices of Thornton Lacey and Mansfield together.

At the head of the Church were the bishops. Miss Steele says of Edward, 'as soon as he can light upon a Bishop, he will be ordained'.[12] Allowing for all Miss Steele's failings, there is a sense here of the generally casual approach to ordination. When the mid-dle-aged Henry Austen went to be ordained by Brownlow North, Bishop of Winchester in December 1816 he had taken trouble to study the New Testament in Greek. The Bishop 'after asking him such questions as he thought desirable, put his hand on a book ... a Greek Testament, and said "As for this book, Mr Austen, I dare say it is some years since either you or I looked into it."'[13]

The other reference to a bishop is in *Persuasion* when Charles Musgrove defends that other eldest son Charles Hayter: 'It would not be a *great* match for Henrietta, but Charles has a very fair chance, through the Spicers, of getting something from the Bishop in the course of a year or two.'[14] This short sentence encapsulates how church appointments were made – by personal recommenda-tion, whether or not on grounds that we would consider adequate. The Spicers are not otherwise mentioned so we are not told how they have influence with the bishop.

As we see in the novels, bishops were not the only sources of preferment in the Church. The Church was not monolithic; Lady Catherine de Bourgh, Sir Thomas Bertram and Colonel Brandon are examples of lay patrons. Almost 62 per cent of the rights to present to rectories and vicarages lay in private hands. Bishops controlled just 12 per cent. The Crown, deans and chapters and the universities also controlled significant numbers.[15]

What they all controlled was the right to present to a living – the advowson – which was in law a piece of property that could be bought and sold. John Dashwood, typically, remarks on the value of the presentation to the living of Delaford – seven times the annual income. Though Jane Austen's father and her brothers James and Henry benefited from this practice, she must have disliked the commercial aspect of the system. She would surely have felt that the ownership of an advowson should be seen as a trust and not as a financial asset.

We see Sir Thomas Bertram's blushing at the expedient he is driven to in disposing of the next presentation of the living at Mansfield so as to recover some of the money spent by his extravagant elder son Tom. But a yet stronger feeling is at the injury to Edmund. 'You have robbed Edmund for ten, twenty, thirty years, perhaps for life, of more than half the income which ought to be his … which he is now obliged to forego through the urgency of your debts.'[16]

Dr Grant was 'a hearty man of forty-five' when he came to Mansfield so could have remained for a long time but, as Tom Bertram said, 'he was a short-necked, apoplectic sort of fellow, and, plied well with good things, would soon pop off.'[17]

What was the character of the bishops in Jane Austen's time? Sydney Smith commented:

> It is in vain to talk of the good character of bishops. Bishops are men; not always the wisest of men; not always preferred for eminent virtues and talents, or for any good reason whatever, known to the public. They are almost always devoid of striking and indecorous vices; but a man may be very shallow, very arrogant, and very vindictive, though a bishop.[18]

Of course it is also true that some of the bishops were good and diligent men. Spencer Madan was Bishop of Peterborough from

1794 to 1813. He was described as 'a man of austere and simple piety'. In 1813 at the age of eighty-four and starting on his last round of confirmations and visitation he said that 'he preferred to die in the discharge of his duty rather than live a little longer by neglect of it.'[19]

In general, though, bishops were not thought to be much different from other men of their class. A.J.C. Hare recounted a tale, probably apocryphal, told to him by Dean Alford. Archbishop Harcourt of York was not sure if it was proper for him to hunt. He consulted friends: 'Of course I should never join the meet, but you know I might fall in with the hounds by accident.' His friends concluded that the archbishop might hunt if he did not shout.[20]

Looking at the list of the higher clergy it is noticeable how many different offices, both secular and ecclesiastical, many of them held, sometimes including several benefices. The rather scurrilous *Extraordinary Black Book* claimed to have found one bishop with eleven benefices. Many bishops were well-connected and had obtained their preferment on that account.

The higher clergy were rich. Contemporary estimates seem, if anything, to have underestimated their wealth. Colquhoun[21] estimated that in 1812 the forty-eight spiritual lords or bishops had an average income of £5,010 and a total of £240,480. There was no correlation between the value of an episcopal appointment and the work involved. There were over 1,000 benefices in the diocese of Lincoln but only 150 in Durham,[22] which was more than twice as well paid.

We can see what contemporaries thought were the incomes of the higher clergy and we can see from tax returns that some had much greater incomes. The *Court Companion* in 1804 published a list of leading clergymen with the supposed value of their bishoprics.

The list gives us a striking picture of the highest ranks of the Church. First come the two English archbishops: Dr John Moore, Archbishop of Canterbury, Primate of all England, President of the Corporation of Sons of the Clergy, and of the Society for Propagating of the Gospel, a trustee of the British Museum, and a governor of the Charterhouse, with an income of £8,000; and Dr

William Markham, Archbishop of York, primate of England, and Lord High Almoner to the King, with an income of £7,000.

Among the bishops we might select just five examples with the value of their bishoprics: Dr Beilby Porteus, Bishop of London, Dean of the Chapel Royal, a governor of the Charterhouse, a trustee of the British Museum, and a Vice-president of the Asylum – £6,200; The Hon. Dr Shute Barrington, Bishop of Durham, Custos Rotulorum of the principality of Durham,[23] uncle to Viscount Barrington – £8,700; The Hon. Dr Brownlow North, Bishop of Winchester, uncle to the Earl of Guilford, prelate of the Order of the Garter, – £7,400; The Hon. Dr James Yorke, Bishop of Ely, uncle to the Earl of Hardwicke – £4,000; and Dr George Pretyman, Bishop of Lincoln, Dean of St Paul's – £3,200.

Most had other sources of income as well so that their actual total incomes were higher than those publicly estimated. The Archbishop of Canterbury, John Moore, paid tax on a taxable income of £15,200 in 1799/1800.[24] That would imply a gross income of over £20,000 of which about £11,000 on average came from his archbishopric. The Archbishop of York paid tax on £14,300, twice as much as the £7,000 attributed to him – and the Bishop of London on £8,000 (not £6,200) in the same year.

We have seen that the patronage of bishops was quite limited. In exercising what patronage they had there is evidence that some bishops thought of their own relatives first. One, quite extreme, example is that of George Pretyman (later Tomline), shown above as Bishop of Lincoln, who came from a family of Suffolk gentry. He had been tutor to William Pitt and was well rewarded, eventually becoming Bishop of Winchester. He was said to be worth £200,000 when he died in 1827. His son Richard was 'one of the most notorious pluralists in England',[25] holding some of his livings for forty years. George Pretyman's other son George and his nephew John also held multiple benefices. The next generation's benefices were numerous.[26]

Richard Pretyman, son of the bishop, was Precentor and Canon Residentiary of Lincoln, Rector of Middleton-Stoney, Rector of Walgrave, Vicar of Hannington, and Rector of Wroughton. George Pretyman, son of the bishop, was Chancellor and Canon

Residentiary of Lincoln, Prebendary of Winchester, Rector of St Giles, Chalfont, Rector of Wheathampstead, and Rector of Harpenden. John Pretyman, nephew of the bishop, was Prebendary of Lincoln, Rector of Sherrington, and Rector of Winwick.

If we turn from the episcopate to patronage, we find in the novels several examples of lay patrons exercising their powers. One of the clearest expressions of why the exercise of patronage was thought normal in the Church comes from Fanny Price in *Mansfield Park*:

'It is the same sort of thing', said Fanny, after a short pause, 'as for the son of an admiral to go into the navy, or the son of a general to be in the army, and nobody sees anything wrong in that. Nobody wonders that they should prefer the line where their friends can serve them best, or suspects them to be less in earnest in it than they appear.'[27]

Equating the Church with the armed services might strike the modern reader as incongruous or inappropriate but both were career choices open to gentlemen who needed to work. In a slightly later period the great Duke of Wellington tried to obtain a bishopric for his brother the Reverend Gerald Wellesley. He failed in that but eventually secured him other preferments so substantial that the Reverend Gerald was said to be the second richest parson in England, with an income of £5,000 a year.

Patronage, it has been argued, stabilized the class system. As Clive Dewey has written, 'access to undemanding jobs reduced the speed with which the untalented fell out of their caste and, on the other hand, the pursuit of patrons turned ambitious arrivistes into assiduous sycophants'.[28] One might think of Edward Ferrars, in *Sense and Sensibility*, on one hand and, in *Pride and Prejudice*, Mr Collins on the other.

However, some of the examples of patronage in action in the novels carry implied or explicit criticism. We find Sir Thomas Bertram having to sell the right to the next presentation to Mansfield, which goes to the indolent Dr Grant. Lady Catherine de Bourgh's presentation to the living of Huntsford, on no more basis than a chance acquaintance, of the recently graduated and very foolish Mr Collins does much to bring the practice into disrepute. The ordination and presentation of Wickham, as planned by Mr Darcy's father, might well have been a much greater error.

Mistakes in patronage did not happen just in novels. There are various versions of the history of Dr Claudius Crigan, Bishop of Sodor and Man, who was presented to his see by the Dowager Duchess of Athol in 1784 – a unique power. An Irishman, Dr Crigan was of modest origins but managed to get to Trinity College in Dublin and was ordained. A handsome man, he was said to have insinuated himself into the good graces of a lady close to the Dowager Duchess, who wanted to appoint a man who would not live too long so that one of her sons could have the appointment in turn. Crigan knew this, and for the crucial interview had himself made up to look much older and feigned asthma. He was approved and subsequently consecrated. The Duchess was not pleased when she found out, nor much mollified to be told, 'Ah, your Grace can hardly imagine what a good thing a bishopric is to cure an asthma.'[29] Dr Crigan enjoyed his good fortune for nearly thirty years, dying in office in 1813.

Colonel Brandon's presentation of the untried, and as yet unordained, Edward Ferrars to care for the parish of Delaford seems at first more benevolent than wise but Edward turns out to be a good and diligent clergyman. On balance it would be hard to argue that Jane Austen was a critic of the system of private patronage though she was certainly critical of its abuses.

Jane Austen would have known her brother James' jokes about the consequences of such a system of patronage. A young man hoping for clerical preferment needed to make himself agreeable. James Austen joked in *The Loiterer*:

> I must suppose they have, during their stay at Oxford, taken care to make themselves tolerable masters of Whist, have obtained a competent knowledge of Cribbage, and are not entirely ignorant of Piquet and Backgammon. Of the former of which games to be ignorant, would be inexcusable, and an acquaintance with the latter will be found extremely convenient when they spend a Tête-à-Tête

evening with the Squire of the Parish; whose good opinion it ought to be their first endeavour to cultivate; as much of the happiness or misery of their lives must, after all depend on his conduct. Nor can this be found a difficult task, if to the above-mentioned qualifications, they add also an extensive and accurate knowledge in all sporting matters.[30]

In *Pride and Prejudice* we find an acknowledgement of the importance of patrons when Mr Bennet writes cynically to Mr Collins: 'I must trouble you once more for congratulations. Elizabeth will soon be the wife of Mr Darcy. Console Lady Catherine as well as you can. But, if I were you, I would stand by the nephew: he has more to give.'[31]

Government patronage was no better. Sydney Smith, a Whig, particularly disapproved of Dr Robert Nares (1753–1829), a Tory, who was chaplain to the Duke of York and held numerous benefices, including the Archdeaconry of Stafford. Nares founded *The British Critic* in 1793 and ran it for twenty years. Smith wrote to Francis Jeffrey:

That Nares is in point of talents a very stupid and a very contemptible fellow no one pretends to deny. He has been hangman for these ten years to all the poor authors in England, is generally considered to be hired by the Government, and has talked about Social Order till he has talked himself into 6 or £700 per annum. That there can be a fairer object for critical severity I cannot conceive.[32]

(from *The Letters of Sydney Smith*, edited by Nowell C. Smith (OUP, 1953). Reproduced by permission of Oxford University Press.)

But then in his turn Sydney Smith became a beneficiary of government patronage. He was presented to the living of Foston-le-Clay in Yorkshire in 1806. Smith called on Lord Erskine, the Lord Chancellor, to thank him. According to Rodgers, Smith was told, 'Oh, don't thank *me*, Mr Smith. I gave you the living because Lady Holland insisted on my doing so; and if she had desired me to give it to the devil, *he* must have had it.'[33]

Another route to advancement was to make a good marriage. Southey joked:

> The customs of England do not exclude the clergyman from any species of amusement; the popular preacher is to be seen at the theatre, and at the horse race, bearing his part at the concert and the ball, making his court to old ladies at the card-table, and to young ones at the harpsichord: and in this way, if he does but steer clear of any flagrant crime or irregularity (which is not always the case; for this order, in the heretical hierarchy, has had more than one Lucifer), he generally succeeds in finding some widow, or waning spinster, with weightier charms than youth and beauty.[34]

Southey also wrote that:

> It was formerly a doubt whether the red coat or the black one, the soldier or the priest, had the best chance with the ladies; if on the one side there was valour, there was learning on the other; but since volunteering has made scarlet so common, black carries the day.[35]

One of the great grievances in the Church was absenteeism – clergymen not living in their parishes. The proportion of parishes with resident incumbents was less than half in the early nineteenth century, though it rose to 88 per cent by 1879. In 1810 the figure was 43.1 per cent, which by 1814 had fallen to 35.8 per cent.

Jane Austen disapproved of this, as a passage in *Mansfield Park* makes clear. Sir Thomas Bertram would have been deeply mortified if Edmund had not chosen to live at Thornton Lacey:

> a parish has wants and claims which can be known only by a clergyman constantly resident, and which no proxy can be capable of satisfying to the same extent. Edmund might, in the common phrase, do the duty of Thornton, that is, he might read prayers and preach, without giving up Mansfield Park; he might ride over every Sunday, to a house nominally inhabited, and go through divine service; he might be the clergyman of Thornton Lacey every

seventh day, for three or four hours, if that would content him. But it will not. He knows that human nature needs more lessons than a weekly sermon can convey; and that if he does not live among his parishioners and prove himself by constant attention their well-wisher and friend, he does very little either for their good or his own.[36]

When Edmund Bertram, Fanny Price and Mary Crawford talk about the Church, in the wilderness at Sotherton, the less-than devout Mary Crawford speaks about absentee clergy:

One does not see much of this influence and importance in society, and how can it be acquired where they are so seldom seen themselves? How can two sermons a week, even supposing them to be worth hearing ... do all that you speak of? Govern the conduct and fashion the manners of a large congregation for the rest of the week? One scarcely sees a clergyman out of his pulpit.[37]

From the mouth of the most irreligious character comes the argument for clergymen being resident in their parishes. Perhaps we can see Mary Crawford's irreligious habits of mind as one result of the church's failings. It is certainly the example of Dr Grant that informs her well-known outburst about the motivation of a clergyman:

Oh! no doubt he is very sincere in preferring an income ready made, to the trouble of working for one; and has the best intentions of doing nothing all the rest of his days but eat, drink, and grow fat. It is indolence, Mr Bertram, indeed. Indolence and love of ease – a want of all laudable ambition, of taste for good company, or of inclination to take the trouble of being agreeable, which make men clergymen. A clergyman has nothing to do but to be slovenly and selfish – read the newspaper, watch the weather, and quarrel with his wife. His curate does all the work, and the business of his own life is to dine.[38]

Jane Austen continues the theme of reform. Edmund argues that:

We do not look in great cities for our best morality. It is not there that respectable people of any denomination can do most good; and it is certainly not there that the influence of the clergy can be most felt. A fine preacher is followed and admired; but it is not in fine preaching only that a good clergyman will be useful in his parish and his neighbourhood, where the parish and neighbourhood are of a size capable of knowing his private character, and observing his general conduct.[39]

In Sydney Smith's experience country parishes were not a great deal better than urban ones. In 1801 he commented:

In London, I dare say, there are full seven-tenths of the whole population who hardly ever enter a place of worship from one end of the year to the other. At the fashionable end of the town the congregations are almost wholly made up of ladies, and there is an appearance of listlessness, indifference, and impatience, very little congenial to our theoretical ideas of a place of worship. In the country villages half of the parishioners do not go to church at all and, almost all, with the exception of the sick and the old, are in a state of wretched ignorance and indifference with regard to all religious opinions whatever.[40]

Smith went on to say that in a district of the diocese of Lincoln where the population was 15,042, of whom 11,282 were adults, it was found that the average congregation was 4,933 and the average number of communicants was 1,808. Not one in three attended service and not one in six adults received the sacrament.

In his guise as a Catholic Spaniard visiting England Southey joked:

The Church festivals, however, are not entirely unobserved; though the English will not pray, they will eat; and, accordingly, they have particular dainties for all the great holydays. On Shrove Tuesday they eat what they call pancakes, which are a sort of wafer fried, or made smaller and thicker with currants or apples, in which case they are called fritters. For Mid Lent Sunday they have huge plum-cakes, crusted with sugar like snow; for Good Friday, hot buns marked with a cross for breakfast; the only relic of religion remaining among all their customs.[41]

But at the start of the nineteenth century there were the first stirrings of reform. In *Mansfield Park* Edmund Bertram refers to 'a spirit of improvement abroad' in the Church. He is speaking of reading in church but it is clear that the idea has a wider application:

> among those who were ordained twenty, thirty, forty years ago, the large number, to judge by their performance, must have thought reading was reading, and preaching was preaching. It is different now. The subject is more justly considered. It is felt that distinctness and energy may have weight in recommending the most solid truths; and, besides, there is more general observation and taste, a more critical knowledge diffused than formerly; in every congregation, there is a larger proportion who know a little of the matter, and who can judge and criticize.[42]

Jane Austen's awareness that the Church should be judged and criticized is in contrast to the attitudes of many of her contemporaries.

The key to a career in the Church was a particular education which in itself may have been a cause of some of the ills. Having a degree from Oxford or Cambridge was an almost essential qualification for ordination in the Church of England, a good grounding in pagan literature being thought a suitable education for a clergyman as well as a gentleman. It was noted in consequence that some sermons had more classical than biblical references.

Jane Austen was slightly in awe of this classical learning, protesting to the Reverend James Stanier Clark, the Prince Regent's librarian, that she was 'the most unlearned & uninformed Female who ever dared to be an authoress'. She felt that:

> A Classical Education, or at any rate, a very extensive acquaintance with English Literature, Ancient & Modern, appears to me

quite Indispensable for the person who wd. do any justice to your Clergyman.[43]

(Le Faye. D. (ed.), *Jane Austen's Letters*, 4th edition (OUP, 2011). Reproduced by permission of Oxford University Press.)

Elizabeth Grant of Rothiemurchus had an uncle who was Master of University College, Oxford, with whom she stayed for some time in 1810: 'Two facts struck me, young as I was, during our residence at Oxford; the ultra-Tory politics and the stupidity and frivolity of the society ... there was little talent and less polish and no sort of knowledge of the world.' She went on: 'the Christian pastor, humble and gentle, and considerate and self-sacrificing ... had no representative, as far as I could see, among these dealers in old wines, rich dinners, fine china and massive plate.'[44]

One did not have to be very clever to get into the universities; just male and able to afford the life of an undergraduate. Two of Jane Austen's brothers had scholarships to St John's College, Oxford, as 'founder's kin'. James Austen wrote in *The Loiterer* a letter signed H. Homely, ostensibly from an elderly clergyman remembering his rather moderate education:

> I was the only child of honest, though not wealthy parents, who discovering in me early symptoms of very extraordinary abilities (a discovery which parents frequently make) could not prevail upon themselves to deprive the literary world of so promising a genius; and therefore; instead of breeding me up to assist my father in his shop, they were determined to make a scholar of me. To this end, at the age of nine I was sent to the free school of the town in which we resided, where, in the nine succeeding years, I completed my classical education, that is, I could construe Latin pretty well with an *Ordo verborum*, and generally knew Greek when I saw it. At this juncture I had the good fortune of being recommended by the Master of our School to the Head of — College, in Oxford, and soon after had the inexpressible pleasure of being elected to a scholarship worth at least 15l. *per annum*.[45]

Once at Oxford, life was not demanding. Even if we discount John

Thorpe's account of his guests drinking five pints of wine each, undoubtedly then, as now, much was drunk. James Austen's fictitious correspondent, H. Homely, in the letter quoted previously, wrote:

> on looking about me I concluded, from several reasons, that I was the happiest man alive. In the first place I was totally my own master, and might do what I pleased; that is, I might do nothing at all. Secondly, I was convinced that I had money enough to last for ever. And thirdly, I had already made several friends, who were willing to lay down their lives to oblige me. This latter opinion, indeed, I had very reasonably drawn from seeing with what ardour they proposed to me, and with what eagerness they joined in every species of pleasure, merely to amuse me. To be sure, it often came to my lot to be general paymaster, but this might be the effect rather of their thoughtlessness, than any intention to defraud, or any inability to disburse; and flushed, as I then was, with the enjoyment of present, and the schemes of future pleasure, I thought (if I thought at all) that the continuance of such friends was cheaply purchased by defraying some of their extravagancies.[46]

Southey mocked:

> It is of little consequence whether they shoot water-fowl, attend horse-races, frequent the brothel, and encourage the wine trade in one place or another; but as a few years of this kind of life usually satisfy a man for the rest of it, it is convenient that there should be a place appointed where one of this description can pass through this course of studies out of sight of his relations, and without injuring his character; and from whence he can come with the advantage of having been at the University, and a qualification which enables him to undertake the cure of souls.[47]

He was writing about Cambridge.

For young men making their way in the world the universities were an opportunity to make friends and contacts who could be helpful in later life. It is held against Mr Collins that he had not formed 'any useful acquaintance' at university. James Austen's account of a fictitious undergraduate's life continued:

> To convince you, Mr. Loiterer, that my daily employment left not much time for study or reflection. I shall, without sending you a journal, briefly inform you, that the morning was dissipated in doing nothing, and the evening in doing what was worse; the first part wasted in idleness, the latter drowned in intemperance. As it would be tedious to relate in what various scenes I played the fool and the rake, or to describe the many different expedients, which I adopted to lessen my knowledge, my fortune, and my health: suffice it to say, that in about six years I had so far succeeded as to have very little left of any, and when I took my degree, I was as ignorant as emaciated, and as much in debt as the first peer of the realm. I had lost everything which I ought to have preserved; I had acquired nothing but habits of expense, which long outlived the means of gratifying them, and a relish for indolence at a time when I had my bread to earn.[48]

It was perhaps as well that the oral examination for an ordinary degree after three years was not burdensome.

Of those 172 men matriculating at Cambridge in 1810[49] almost two-thirds became clergymen. Just over a tenth became lawyers, and just under a tenth followed their fathers as landed gentlemen. Smaller numbers became doctors, members of parliament or officers in the armed forces.

Before ordination some undemanding study of a few theological texts was usual. Armed with a testimonial of suitability from one's college, the next step was to apply to a bishop to be ordained. Some bishops thought that the testimonial was enough and that the candidate's familiarity with scripture, the liturgy and the thirty-nine articles could be assumed. We see Edmund Bertram going through this easy process in *Mansfield Park*.

Once ordained one might choose to aim for a fellowship at a college to prolong one's academic life, as did George Austen and his sons James and Henry. Fellowships were worth about £100 per annum and had to be given up on marriage. Fellows were supposed to study for a degree in theology but many did not. The elderly Dr Shirley in *Persuasion*, Dr Grant in *Mansfield Park* and, in *Sense and Sensibility*, Nancy Steele's beau Dr Davies, are the only clergymen in the novels so qualified.

After ordination what were the career prospects of clergymen? In *Pride and Prejudice* Mr Collins graduated at Easter and seems to have been appointed Rector of Hunsford very soon afterwards. This was far from typical. The profession was crowded and the competition was intense to obtain even the most meagre of benefices or preferment. James Austen's fictitious advertisement for 'a Curacy in a good sporting country, near a pack of fox-hounds, and in a sociable neighbourhood ... must have a good house and stables'[50] was far from reality. Mary Crawford's doubts about a career in the Church were well founded.

Looking at the same group of Cambridge graduates mentioned previously,[51] of those who joined the clergy, about a tenth became fellows, only a quarter were beneficed within five years and nearly a third were never beneficed at all.

Even for the fortunate, the sudden change from Oxford to a country living might not be agreeable. James Austen wrote in mock-solemn manner in *The Loiterer*:

> Young men in the bloom of life, and in the Heyday of their blood, cut off from all that renders life agreeable, removed from the Scene of their Triumphs, and the Witnesses of their Glory, and condemned to pass many years in solitary obscurity and insipid quiet. To be obliged to wear black to those who have been usually dressed in brown or blue; to be under the necessity of going twice in a week to Church, to those, who for some time, have never gone at all, are very serious mortifications.[52]

The irreligious Mary Crawford thought it was 'madness' to seek ordination without having a living in prospect but the first step for most clergymen, unless fortunate like Henry Tilney or Edmund Bertram, or extraordinarily lucky, like Mr Collins, was to obtain employment as a curate.

In *Persuasion* the Elliot family did not much regard curates. Sir

Walter considered the curate of Monkford – Captain Wentworth's brother – to have been a nobody and certainly not a gentleman. His daughter, Mary Musgrove, thought little of Charles Hayter. He was 'nothing but a country curate. A most improper match for Miss Musgrove, of Uppercross.'[53] This was not just another example of the Elliot pride; they had good economic reasons for doubting the wisdom of marrying a curate. It is hoped by Henrietta Musgrove that Dr Shirley could be persuaded to retire to Lyme, only seventeen miles away, and to appoint Charles Hayter as his curate. Jane Austen's contemporaries would have known this to be a very moderate preferment, lasting at best only for Dr Shirley's lifetime.

There were four sorts of curacy.[54] A stipendiary curate was employed by a non-resident incumbent. A temporary curate was employed to cover the absence of an incumbent for such short-term reasons as illness. An assistant curate worked under a resident incumbent. A perpetual curate ranked as a vicar but usually without the right to tithes or glebe which were enjoyed by an impropriator. The impropriator paid the curate a stipend but could not sack him. The first three sorts of curacy were more or less impermanent and particularly so on the death of the incumbent.

In 1810 there were 1,587 resident curates (assistant and stipendiary) in England and Wales. This number increased to 2,537 by 1831.[55] Sydney Smith described a curate as 'the poor working-man of God – a learned man in a hovel, good and patient – a comforter and a teacher – the first and poorest pauper of the hamlet; yet showing that, in the midst of worldly misery, he has the heart of a gentlemen, the spirit of a Christian, and the kindness of a pastor'.[56]

Perhaps unsurprisingly some fell below this standard. Dr Thomas Somerville, Minister of Jedburgh and a noted historian, went to a funeral at Fairfield near Buxton in 1793. He recorded that 'the ceremony of the burial was performed with indecent hurry by an intoxicated curate in a dirty surplice'.[57]

Sydney Smith's first parish was a miserable experience. His daughter wrote that:

> the village consisted but of a few scattered cottages and farms, in
> the midst of Salisbury Plain. Once a week a butcher's cart came

over from Salisbury; it was only then that he could obtain any meat, and he often dined, he said, on a mess of potatoes, sprinkled with a little ketchup. Too poor to command books, his only resource was the Squire, during the few months he resided there; and his only relaxation, not being able to keep a horse, long walks over those interminable plains.[58]

Curates were notoriously poorly paid. In 1802, 'it was reported that even according to the incomplete returns made to the board of Queen Anne's Bounty and to the exchequer there were 5,597 livings of under £50 per annum.'[59] Irene Collins concluded that, because of the competition for curacies, 'curates in the 1790s were lucky to receive more than £35. Henry Austen's stipend at Chawton in 1818 was still only £54 12s 0d.'[60]

A survey of curacies in the diocese of Oxford in 1799 found one paying £20 a year, nineteen paying £20–£29, sixteen paying £50–£59 and one paying £75.[61] In the diocese of Worcester Bishop Hurd found at the end of the eighteenth century that while 40 curates were paid £50 or more, 113 had only £30–£50.[62] However, some curates might do duty in more than one parish, hold a college chaplaincy or earn money as a schoolmaster in addition. So altogether most curates probably earned between £60 and £70 a year at the end of the eighteenth century.

As one contemporary wrote about curates:

> ... placed in a situation where they are expected to sustain the rank of a gentleman, they have scarcely the means of procuring even the common necessaries of life, much less of obtaining those superfluities which are considered as essential appendages to that rank.[63]

William Jones, curate at Broxbourne, wrote sadly in his journal on Easter Day 1784, 'Providence seems now to frown on me, & to blast all my schemes – An increasing family and a decreasing income ... on casting up my accounts I found that the expenses of the last quarter exceeded £36, which sum is almost double my income for the same quarter.'[64]

Later in life he remembered:

> we, literally and frequently, had not enough of the plainest, com-
> monest provisions. I can truly say that I often pretended to have
> had enough, in contradiction to the cravings of my under-stomach
> … we had very little meat, & I grew so thin by my short allowance,
> that the alteration was actually noticed to me by some of my neigh-
> bours, but none of them had the kind sagacity to guess at the cause,
> & contribute to redress it![65]

His lack of money continued for years. His wife must have had a
hard time. He recorded on 30 March 1797: 'my wife, tho' wanting in
mildness and gentleness to me, is in every other respect an excellent wife, frugal and attentive to all her domestic concerns'. He
noted that according to her estimate they would be quite unable
to support their family of nine children. But in the end, and to his
great joy, he was presented to be vicar by the Bishop of London on
4 June 1801. 'Blessed be Heaven! I now enjoy what my soul has long
wished for', he wrote.[66] Jones had run a school – 'teaching is a life
of drudgery and difficulty' – and after twenty years as a curate,
which he called his 'servitude', he became the Vicar of Broxbourne
for a further twenty years.

Jones would have disagreed utterly with Sydney Smith who
wrote in the *Edinburgh Review* in 1808:

> The poverty of curates has long been a favourite theme with novel-
> ists, sentimental tourists, and elegiac poets. But, notwith-standing
> the known accuracy of this class of philosophers, we cannot help
> suspecting that there is a good deal of misconception in the
> popular estimate of the amount of the evil. A very great propor-
> tion of all the curacies in England are filled with men to whom the
> emolument is a matter of subordinate importance. They are filled
> by young gentlemen who have recently left college, who of course
> are able to subsist as they have subsisted for seven years before,
> and who are glad to have an opportunity, on any terms, of acquir-
> ing a practical familiarity with the duties of their profession. They
> move away from them to higher situations as vacancies occur.[67]

Many curates were not by birth young gentlemen and, as we have seen, higher situations might not come their way for many years, if at all. Curates could augment their incomes in various ways. Woodforde noted how he grew vegetables when he was curate of Babcary in Somerset. Wilberforce told the Commons in 1806 of a curate who was also a weaver.[68] Another played the fiddle in a village pub on weekday evenings.[69] These steps were necessary because curates, most already poor, were left behind by the inflation of the 1790s in a way that clergymen who benefited from tithes were not.

If, on the other hand, the curate had private means, he might be able to be more active in social life. Some of the clergymen Jane Austen knew went hunting, including her brother James, who had written jokingly at Oxford that hunting and shooting might bring preferment. Edmund Bertram hunts and might well have continued after ordination. In *Persuasion* Charles Musgrove regrets that though Charles Hayter's curacy will be 'in the centre of some of the best preserves in the kingdom' Charles will not value it as he ought as 'Charles is too cool about sporting. That's the worst of him.' This tells us something of the scholarly Hayter as well as the sport-mad Musgrove.

In James Austen's *Loiterer* writings the young curate is imagined travelling to his new curacy with 'Dr. Trusler's Sermons, a Fishing Rod, and a Gun ... two or three Pointers and Spaniels, a Hunter, and a Poney' and James Austen's final injunction is that the young curate, when playing whist, should not let 'the Squire name the Trump; not even if he is the Patron of the Living, unless they have a positive promise of the next Presentation, and the Incumbent is at least four-score'.[70]

The Reverend William Jones wrote scathingly about young men who obtained preferment in the Church but then haggled 'with poor curates, 'til they can find those who will starve with fewest symptoms of discontent'. According to Jones, they were 'far more anxious to attain the fame of being "excellent shots", giving the "view halloo", well-mounted in the field, & being "in at the death" – than raising their voices in the desk or pulpit, or feeding the flock, whom they are eager to fleece.'[71]

Jones was not inventing such vicars. A graduate of Jesus College,

Cambridge, Benjamin Newton, Rector of Wath near Ripon, was a diligent cleric, a magistrate and a founder of the Bedale Savings Bank, but he also shot, hunted foxes, coursed hares, went racing, dined with the local gentry and went to balls at Ripon. His diary has many entries such as this for 2 November 1816: 'Went hunting, found a fox at Norton and killed at the Plaister Pits. Found another at Melmerby, ran very hard and lost at Littlethorpe.'[72]

Newton was fortunate in having as a patron Lord Ailesbury, to whom he had once been tutor. The living was a good one. In December 1816 he took £676 to his banker in Ripon after his tithe day and had arrears of only £59. He enjoyed his good fortune. In January 1817 he paid for a pipe of wine which cost £105 10s. 6d. Half was sold on to two fellow clergymen.[73]

The reality for many curates seeking preferment was pretty bleak. We have seen the difficulties of Reverend William Jones. Another, James Palmer, curate of Headington, wrote to a Balliol friend in 1806, 'If I had been the 19th cousin of a lord I might have attained hopes of a living; but I have not one drop of Duke's blood in me that I know of, and have none to patronize or assist me, so that probably I shall continue a curate all my life.'[74] Palmer was also unlucky in other respects. He was killed by a fall from his horse two years later.

Many were reduced to applying for any and every possibility of preferment and watching closely the health of elderly incumbents. William Bagshaw Stevens, Headmaster of Repton, applied for more than twenty livings in 1792–1800. He wrote to his friend Thomas Coutts in March 1795, 'For some time to come I shall be a very Death-Watch among the Ancient Incumbents'. The ancient incumbents withstood the winters better than he hoped. Of one he noted, 'Old Edward was here the other evening as blithe as a bird and as tight as a drum'.[75]

But there were so many poor livings that pluralists were not necessarily rich. The Reverend James Hakewell held four Oxfordshire livings together from 1767 to 1799 (Fritwell, North Aston, Weston-on-the-Green and Tusmore). The richest was worth £40 and the four together produced £117 in 1786.[76]

What was the work of a parish clergyman? Sydney Smith

described his role in his parish at Foston near York as 'village parson, village doctor, village comforter, village magistrate'. Once presented to a living, a clergyman became in effect a temporary landed gentleman. He had to decide how to conduct himself. Sydney Smith made a resolution never to shoot:

> first, because I found, on trying at Lord Grey's, that the birds seemed to consider the muzzle of my gun as their safest position; secondly; because I never could help shutting my eyes when I fired my gun, so was not likely to improve; and thirdly, because, if you do shoot, the squire and the poacher both consider you as their natural enemy, and I thought it more clerical to be at peace with both.[77]

A clergyman was very hard to remove from his living if he proved unsuitable. Proceedings in ecclesiastical courts were slow and expensive. Consequently it was very hard to get rid of a clergyman, however dreadful, once he had been appointed. So in *Sense and Sensibility* Colonel Brandon was placing great faith in an untried young man, Edward Ferrars.

One, admittedly extreme, example was Dr Edward Drax Free, a fellow of St John's College, Oxford, where James and Henry Austen might have known him, and Rector of Sutton in Bedfordshire.[78] Parson Woodforde in his diary described his own election by the fellows of New College to the living of Weston Longville. A certain amount of canvassing before and drinking afterwards was normal. The fellows of St John's also elected Dr Edward Drax Free to a college living but may have needed little persuasion.

Almost all the land in the village of Sutton – an agricultural community of some 300 people – was owned by the Burgoyne family. It was an estate similar, one might imagine, to Delaford. In the middle of the eighteenth century the Burgoynes had sold the advowson to St John's, who, in 1808, presented Dr Free to the living which was worth about £250 a year, similar to Delaford.

Dr Free's first daughter was born in 1811. Unfortunately he was not married to the child's mother, nor did he marry any of the four other women by whom he had children in the following twelve years. He was a truly awful man. Red-faced, coarse, rude and quarrelsome, he was a grasping collector of tithes and was variously accused of drunkenness, lechery, poaching, shoplifting and swindling. He sold the lead from the church roof, kept horses and cattle in the churchyard and pigeons in the organ loft. And yet he was not finally deprived of his living until 1830 after six years of litigation in the Church courts and two petitions to parliament.

It is not true that private patronage was all bad. We have seen that one of the worst men was appointed by an Oxford College but Sydney Smith, appointed by noble patronage, was in fact an excellent clergyman, diligently looking after the physical and spiritual needs of his parishioners.

We now turn to the incomes of parish clergy. There are four benefices in the novels whose value we know:

	£
The living of Thornton Lacey (Edmund Bertram)	700
The living of Mansfield (Mr Norris, Dr Grant and Edmund Bertram)	650
James Morland's living	400
The living of Delaford (Edward Ferrars)	200

How would Jane Austen's contemporaries have seen these incomes?

One contemporary source of information was Patrick Colquhoun's *A Treatise on the Wealth, Power, and Resources of the British Empire* (second edition, 1815). Colquhoun summarized the incomes of those in the Church. Below the bishops he estimated 1,500 eminent clergymen with an average income of £720 and 17,500 lesser clergymen with an average income of £200.[79] As we have seen there were among the lesser clergymen many poor curates who had a great deal less than £200 a year.

Both Mansfield and Thornton Lacey would have been considered very good livings. Holding the two together, as Edmund Bertram does eventually, made him a most fortunate clergyman.

Edward Ferrars and Elinor Dashwood are not so much in love as to think that £350 a year is enough. James Morland's living was similarly on the cusp of what would have been considered an adequate income. Jane Austen's contemporaries might well have agreed with Colonel Brandon that £200 a year would make Edward Ferrars comfortable as a bachelor without enabling him, as a gentleman, to marry, even if the living could be improved to £250 'at the utmost'.[80]

One of the reasons why clergymen were not well paid was that a great many parishes were small. Steventon had thirty families when George Austen arrived in 1764. The neighbouring Ashe and Deane were smaller still. Chawton was bigger, with a population of 347 people at the 1811 census.[81]

The temptation, even sometimes the necessity, to hold two livings simultaneously is clear. It seems at the end of *Mansfield Park*, after Dr Grant's death, that Edmund holds both Thornton Lacey and Mansfield, giving him an income of about £1,350. About two-thirds of clergymen held one living and only 6 per cent held more than two, among whom was James Austen.[82] Indeed Jane Austen's attitude to James' income was robustly of the eighteenth century. She wrote to Cassandra in December 1808:

> We have now pretty well ascertained James's Income to be Eleven Hundred Pounds, curate paid, which makes us very happy – the ascertainment as well as the Income.[83]

> (Le Faye. D. (ed.), *Jane Austen's Letters*, 4th edition (OUP, 2011). Reproduced by permission of Oxford University Press.)

How were these incomes obtained? A parish priest had two main sources of income – tithe and glebe. Tithe was the right to one-tenth of the product of all cultivated land in the parish. 'In 1814 72% of the annual value of English agricultural land was tithable and just over 8% of the income from the ownership of land accrued to titholders.'[84] Tithes might be paid in kind or, increasingly, in money based on an estimate of the yield. These compositions might need to be renegotiated as areas or yields changed. Characteristically, negotiating tithes came first in Mr Collins' list of a rector's duties. When we understand how unpopular tithes were, we can appreciate more fully the foolishness of his comment.

Jane Austen was familiar with tithes as a matter of great importance to all clergymen if she was not herself particularly interested
in the subject. In an early work, she wrote of the trouble tithes
could cause:

> The living of Chetwynde was now in the possession of a Mr
> Dudley, whose family unlike the Wynnes were productive only
> of vexation and trouble to Mrs Percival and her niece. Mr Dudley,
> who was the younger son of a very noble family, of a family more
> famed for their pride than their opulence, tenacious of his dignity,
> and jealous of his rights, was forever quarrelling, if not with Mrs
> Percival herself, with her steward and tenants concerning tithes.[85]

There were in fact two sorts of tithe: the greater tithes levied on
cereal crops, hay and wood and the small or lesser tithe, levied on
produce such as lamb, chickens, and fruit.[86] A landowner might
'impropriate' the great tithes – as was the case in nearly half the
parishes in England – which might amount to three-quarters of
the whole tithes. Whoever held the great tithes was technically
the rector. So in *Sense and Sensibility* when Colonel Brandon tells
Edward that Delaford is a rectory he is telling him that as incumbent he will receive all of the tithes. It is also to this division of
tithes that Mr Collins is alluding when he says that a rector's agree-
ment for tithes should be 'not offensive to his patron'.

A contemporary, Sir Frederic Morton Eden, wrote, 'grateful
as I am, along with the great mass of my fellow subjects, for
the blessings of the Reformation, the transfer of tithes to lay-
impropriators is not that part of it which I contemplate with the
most satisfaction.'[87] Jane Austen joked about it in her unpublished
parody *Plan of a Novel, according to Hints from Various Quarters*
in which a clerical character 'expires in a fine burst of Literary
Enthusiasm, intermingled with Invectives against holders of
Tithes'.

The subject of tithes is complicated. At Bromfield in Cumberland
it was possible for five different tithing men to have, each of them,
a legal claim to tithe in one field.[88] Events as far back as the twelfth

century could still have a bearing on what tithes could be collected. Similarly, what constituted great or small tithes could vary. Wood might be a small tithe if the vicar had collected it by custom, and a parish's most productive crop might be a greater tithe whatever it was. Where a thing was grown might matter, too. Hop tithes were held to be small tithes if grown in gardens or small allotments, but being valuable, were greater tithes elsewhere.[89] The extent to which tithes were paid in kind rather than in cash varied greatly from county to county. Tithing in kind required labour, horses and tithe barns so composition for a cash payment was much simpler.

Tithes were generally unpopular. Tithe was a tax on gross produce, not on profit, and might often be equivalent to as much as a quarter of the rent paid by a tenant farmer. William Jones wrote:

> I am confident that I am defrauded by many of my parishioners of various vicarial dues and rights, to which the laws of Heaven and earth entitle me ... and mine is by no means a singular case: for the very word 'tithe' has ever been as unpleasing and odious, to farmers especially, as 'cuckoo' to the married ear. Those who pay them pay them very partially.[90]

Three years later he was still 'at a loss for words to express the meanness and grudging illiberality with which many of my parishioners pay me a trifle in lieu of my tithes, etc.; & the scandalous injustice of many others, who refuse to pay me at all.'[91]

Parson Woodforde at Weston Longville in Norfolk, as many other parsons, gave a 'frolick' to those who paid him tithes where they were given a good dinner and plenty to drink. He was not a grasping man – being unmarried may have had a bearing on that – and in 1803 his successor doubled the tithe composition.[92]

Some tithes rose sharply during Jane Austen's life. The agricultural boom of the war years benefited some clergymen who saw their tithes double, but others had a much smaller share in the increase in agricultural prosperity. After the war agricultural incomes and thus tithes fell. The total of tithe income, both lay and clerical, in England was £1,857,720 in 1806, rising to £2,385,141 in 1812. This was an increase of 28.4 per cent but if we look at the experience of different counties we see that tithes in Rutland rose by 101.2 per cent while those in Worcestershire fell by 18.4 per cent. In Hampshire, Jane Austen's county, tithes rose by 31.9 per cent.[93]

Tithe income was also taxable, and was related to the land tax, property tax, income tax (from 1799) and poor rates. In some cases where a clergyman had increased his tithe revenue, his parishioners retaliated by increasing the amount of poor rate levied on him.[94] Tithes were eventually commuted by the Act of 1834.

The other principal source of income, glebe, was an area of land owned by the church for the benefit of the incumbent. It was often added to by enclosure – sometimes doubling or more. So the clergy had a vested interest in enclosure from which they often benefited. Indeed clergymen were often favoured on enclosure by being granted land close to their houses or to other land. This glebe land turned parsons into farmers.

By both renegotiating tithes and better farming of glebe land a benefice could be improved. When Colonel Brandon says that the Delaford living is 'certainly capable of improvement' that is what he is referring to. There could, therefore, be some uncertainty as to the value of a living. In 1796 the value of the living of Chawton was variously assessed as £300 or £400 per annum – the house was 'exceedingly bad' which may have accounted for a part of the difference of opinion.[95]

Some clergymen made the most incongruous farmers. The Clergy Residence Act passed in 1803 but only slowly compelled clergymen to reside in their parishes. Sydney Smith wrote, 'A diner out, a wit, and a popular preacher, I was suddenly caught up by the Archbishop of York and transported to my living in Yorkshire, where there had not been a resident clergyman for 150 years. Fresh from London, not knowing a turnip from a carrot, I was compelled to farm three hundred acres.'[96]

Edward Ferrars might have had a similar experience. Three months' absence was allowed each year. Smith came to be happy in the country. 'I give myself quietly up to horticulture, and the annual augmentation of my family'.[97] There was a contemporary debate as to whether farming on any scale was a suitable occupation for a clergyman.

The parson's house was sometimes very poor. Henry Crawford describes a typical parsonage as being 'a scrambling collection of low single rooms, with as many roofs as windows'.[98] Rich men might refurbish or rebuild them. Jane Austen's cousin, the Reverend Thomas Leigh, remodelled the parsonage and its surroundings at Adlestrop from 1763 onwards.[99] There is in *Mansfield Park* an idyllic description of Thornton Lacey which is to be Edmund Bertram's parish:

> a retired little village between gently rising hills; a small stream before me to be forded, a church standing on a sort of knoll to my right – which church was strikingly large and handsome for the place, and not a gentleman or half a gentleman's house to be seen excepting one – to be presumed the Parsonage – within a stone's throw of the said knoll and church.[100]

Henry Crawford has great ideas for changing the place: the farmyard is to be removed, the house turned to face the east instead of the north, a new garden made, and something done with the stream. He is particularly eloquent on how the house might be given a higher character: 'from being the mere gentleman's residence, it becomes by judicious improvement, the residence of a man of education, taste, modern manners, good connexions'. He hopes that 'its owner [will] be set down as the great landholder of the parish by every creature travelling the road; especially as there is no real squire's house to dispute the point'.[101] So in Crawford's plan the parsonage is to be a pretence in both senses, by being artificial and making a claim. Contrast this with Catherine Morland's delight in the thought of 'the unpretending comfort of a well-connected parsonage' at Woodston.[102] In his plan, Crawford expresses the difference in money, too. He wants the house to look 'above a mere parsonage house – above the expenditure of a few hundreds a year', to be instead like the house of an old country family 'spending from two to three thousand a year'.[103] Jane Austen's disapproval is clearly indicated.

Edmund agrees only about the farmyard and insists that the house may be made comfortable 'without any very heavy expense, and that must suffice me; and, I hope, may suffice all who care about me'.[104] It will be in fact a house better suited to Fanny Price than to Mary Crawford.

Henry Tilney's parsonage at Woodston is a 'new built substantial stone house, with its semicircular sweep and green gates'. General Tilney thinks that there are 'few country parsonages in England half so good'.[105] Catherine Morland would not have disagreed with him.

In 1812 Sydney Smith approached Peter Atkinson the younger who carried on Carr's architectural practice in York to design a new rectory at Foston. Perhaps reflecting the increased wealth and social aspirations of many clergy, Atkinson produced plans which would have cost £3,000 to build. Smith exclaimed, 'You build for glory, Sir: I for use' and sent back the plans with a payment of £25.[106]

Jane Austen herself knew what a rich parsonage was like. Visiting her cousins at Adlestrop parsonage she would have found a butler, two livery servants, a gardener, his helper and five women servants. The Reverend Thomas Leigh had a substantial private income (£513 in interest income in 1805) as well as his benefice, worth (like Thornton Lacey) about £700.[107]

For all clergymen (or their widows) there might be an obligation to pay 'dilapidations' on leaving a parsonage. Mrs Norris' poor view of her successors, the Grants, 'had begun in dilapidations'.[108]

Having looked at income, it is interesting to see how clergymen spent their incomes. We know how the Reverend James Plumptre, Vicar of Hinxton in Cambridgeshire, spent his money (about £205) in 1802.[109] Just over one-third went on housekeeping, over a fifth on books (including books to give away) and more than 10 per cent in charity.

In 1799 Parson Woodforde, at Weston Longville in Norfolk, spent more – about £250 and possibly as much as £300 – his records are incomplete. Gregarious and fond of food as he was, though unmarried, his housekeeping expenses were more than 58 per cent of his total. Mrs Norris suspects that Dr Grant's household was similarly expensive. Proportionately compared to Plumptre, Woodforde gave half as much in charity and spent much more on physic – his health was failing.

When James Austen was first married he spent over £200 on furniture and furnishings for his new home. He had an income of about £300 and it is not surprising that it was inadequate to pay for his wife's carriage and his hunting.

On the death of a clergyman his family might suffer a great, perhaps catastrophic, diminution in income. This was Jane Austen's own experience when her father died. In *Emma*, the predicament of Mrs Bates would have been a familiar one to contemporaries. Beneficed clergymen were, after all, only temporary gentlemen.

So, in summary, we see in the novels not an attack on the organization of the Church but a consistent, critical view of how it worked in practice. Venal or foolish patrons and rude or lazy clergymen, who together bring the Church into disrepute, are not spared.

Chapter 9

Shopping

IN THE NOVELS NUMEROUS shops are mentioned, including milliners, gunsmiths, jewellers, chandlers, print shops, book sellers, music sellers, stationers, bakers and, that prototype of a department store, Ford's in *Emma*, which is part woollen draper, part linen draper and part haberdasher's. In Jane Austen's own letters, too, there are many references to shopping in Hampshire, in Bath and in London.

In *Sense and Sensibility* Marianne finds it tedious to go shopping in Bond Street in London with the foolish Mrs Palmer 'whose eye was caught by everything pretty, expensive or new: who was wild to buy all, could determine on none, and dawdled away her time in rapture and indecision'. Above all, Mrs Palmer lacks *taste*, a crucial Austen quality.

Mrs Palmer's rapture and indecision were perhaps an understandable reaction to the splendour of London's shops which so entranced foreign as well as domestic visitors. One of these, a young French noblewoman, Sophie von La Roche, visited in 1786. She wrote that, 'Behind great glass windows absolutely everything one can think of is neatly, attractively displayed, and in such abundance of choice as almost to make one greedy.'[1]

Sophie described Oxford Street thus:

We strolled up and down lovely Oxford Street this evening, for some goods look more attractive by artificial light. Just imagine, dear children, a street taking half an hour to cover from end to end, with double rows of brightly shining lamps, in the middle of which stands an equally long row of beautifully lacquered carriages, and on either side of these there is room for two coaches to pass one another; and the pavement, inlaid with flagstones, can stand six people deep and allows one to gaze at the splendidly lit shop fronts in comfort. First one passes a watchmaker's, then a silk or fan store, now a silversmith's, a china or glass shop. The spirit booths are particularly tempting, for the English are in any case fond of strong drink. Here crystal flasks of every shape and form are exhibited: each one has a light behind it which makes all the different coloured spirits sparkle. Just as alluring are the confectioners and fruiterers, where, behind the handsome glass windows, pyramids of pineapples, figs, grapes, oranges and all manner of fruits are on show. We inquired the price of a fine pineapple, and did not think it too dear at 6s.[2]

Sophie was particularly impressed by a pastry-cook's shop and by a pet shop.

A pastry-cook's attracted our attention for some time, as it is surrounded, like a large spacious room, by glass cases, in which all kinds of preserved fruits and jellies are exhibited in handsome glass jars; in the middle of the shop however, there stood a big table with a white cover containing pyramids of small pastries and tartlets and some larger pastries and sweetmeats; wine glasses of all sizes, with lids to them and full of liqueurs of every conceivable brand, colour and taste were attractively set out in between, as might be expected at a large and very elegant table. What we women liked best of all though, was a large but delightful covering made of gauze, which hid nothing from view and at the same time kept the flies off.[3]

Sophie recalled:

We also passed shops where animals were for sale, which goods were both novel to us and comical. Peacocks were placed on pretty perches, bright cages with songsters hanging in between; there were cases of monkeys, large bird cages containing turtle-doves, others with fine domestic fowls; lap-dogs of every type followed in nicely padded kennels; pointers lay at the bottom on leads, and by their side baskets of all kinds of game – all grouped so artistically that the whole made a charming picture.[4]

Southey's Don Manuel Espriella remembered 'The oddest things which I saw in the whole walk were a pair of shoes in one window floating in a vessel of water, to show that they were water-proof; and a well-dressed leg in another, betokening that legs were made there to the life.'[5]

Having read such accounts, one might have more sympathy with Mrs Palmer.

Not all shopkeepers needed elaborate external show. Elizabeth Grant remembered the premises of Rundell & Bridge, the silver-smiths and jewellers on Ludgate Hill in London which she visited during the winter of 1809–10, 'so dirty and shabby without, such a fairy palace within, where on asking a man who was filling a scoop with small brown-looking stones what he was doing, he told me he was shovelling rubies'.[6] Some years later Richard Rush, in effect the American ambassador, remarked:

Outside it is plain; you might pass by without noticing it; but on entering, the articles of silver were piled in heaps, even on the floor. Going further into the building the masses increased. In a room upstairs, there was part of a dinner-service in the course of man-ufacture. The cost of an entire service varied from thirty to fifty thousand pounds sterling, according to the number of pieces and workmanship; sometimes it was much higher. A candelabra for the middle of a table, had just been finished for a customer, at fourteen hundred pounds. A dress sword for another customer was shown; the cost was four thousand guineas.[7]

The development of shopping spread from London to the

provinces. The growth of shops, not just in London, but in cities such as Norwich, Bristol and Manchester around the turn of the century was striking.[8] As prosperity increased there was a proportionate reduction in the importance of shops selling wearing apparel and an increase in shops selling consumable household goods, household furnishings, books, jewellery and silver. In 'wearing apparel' the shares of drapers and haberdashers declined while that of milliners and straw hat-makers grew.

Provincial towns could be impressive. Sophie von La Roche found Colchester 'large, old and beautiful'. She 'enjoyed the fine shops, which jut out at both sides of the front doors like big, broad oriels, having fine large windowpanes, behind which wares are displayed, so that these shops look far more elegant than Paris.'[9] In towns, the main shopping streets were shaped by this growth – wider pavements, street lighting, covered walkways, arcades.[10] Shops tended to cluster in a few streets. Civic authorities had reason to attract the wealthy to their towns – in the manner of *Sanditon*, if on a larger scale. Social facilities such as assembly rooms, theatres, coffee houses, and subscription libraries entertained the wealthy. A virtuous circle was created in which a growing polite society supported more and more sophisticated services and shops which, in turn, drew more consumers.

Going to Bath, Catherine Morland's 'entrée into life could not take place till after three or four days had been spent learning what was mostly worn' just as Jane Austen used to report to Cassandra in her letters from Bath. Catherine found, too, that in the country shops were more numerous, remarking on 'all the little chandlers' shops' during her visit to Woodston, the 'large and populous village'[11] which was Henry Tilney's parish.

In *Emma* the trend has reached Highbury – also described as 'a large and populous village' but 'almost amounting to a town'. Shopping has become a social activity. Ford's shop is 'the principal woollen-draper, linen-draper and haberdasher's shop united; the first shop in size and fashion in the place.' Frank Churchill exclaims at seeing Ford's shop: 'Ha! This must be the very shop that everybody attends every day of their lives, as my father informs me. He comes to Highbury himself, he says, six days out of seven, and has always business at Ford's.'[12]

He and Emma go in and look at gloves. There are several other mentions of the shop in the novel. It was there that, by chance, Harriet Smith met Robert Martin and his sister Elizabeth, who were pleasant to her. A 'charming collection of new ribbons from town' at Ford's is remarked on. Emma is content to watch the passing street scene from the door of Ford's while waiting for Harriet.

Jane Austen laughs gently at the spread of fashionable shops in *Sanditon*:

> 'Civilization, civilization indeed!' cried Mr Parker, delighted. 'Look, my dear Mary, look at William Heeley's windows. Blue shoes, and nankin boots! Who would have expected such a sight at a shoemaker's in old Sanditon! This is new within the month. There was no blue shoe when we passed this way a month ago. Glorious indeed! Well, I think I *have* done something in my day.'[13]

Shopping had not always been such a social activity. Before the development of shops much distribution of goods was by pedlars, hawkers, travelling packmen or at fairs and markets. Many of these outlets were suspected of distributing smuggled goods and suffered from government legislation. Pedlars became chiefly sellers to the urban poor. Hawkers were licensed and so we can trace their decline. Pitt, in introducing a tax on shops, promised to abolish hawkers but in the end taxed them and restricted the places in which they could sell.[14] In 1782–3 there were 221 licensed hawkers in London, 242 in Staffordshire, but 85 in Devon, 43 in Somerset and only 1 in Dorset.[15] Travelling packmen were replaced by printed circulars, pattern cards and travelling commercial salesmen.

In one of her earlier letters Jane Austen, writing from Steventon, recorded a visit from the 'lace man'[16] – probably an itinerant seller – but there are no further mentions of such visits, suggesting that perhaps it was an old-fashioned way of buying and was declining.

While markets were frequent – typically weekly – and contin- ued to be large distributors of food products, fairs do not seem to have become less numerous although their business declined. A survey of fairs in six counties in the north Midlands showed both the number of places holding fairs and the number of fairs increasing between 1799 and 1824.[17] However, this increase in numbers of fairs seems not to have matched the growth in population. At Chester, in the north-west of England, the two fairs every year each lasted two weeks. They were held in purpose-built halls and were active well into the nineteenth century although linen hall rents – a proxy for trade – declined gradually from 1787 and sharply after 1810.[18] This reflected a gradual falling-off in business done at fairs in general. Their role as places of entertainment, particularly for the poor, remained.

The main trade was in livestock, pedlar's wares and textiles. James Austen bought a horse at Winchester Fair in 1800. The importance of agriculture influenced the dates of fairs, with peaks in May and, to a lesser extent, in October. Fairs were often places where, by custom, accounts were settled, or rents collected. William Howitt wrote, 'There are cheese, cattle, horses, poultry, geese, and a hundred other things to be sold: and multitudes of household articles, clothing and trinkets to be bought; and besides all this, a vast [amount] of seeing and being seen to be done.'[19] At a large fair, like Nottingham's October Goose Fair, there would be travelling menageries, circuses, bands and 'all kinds of strollers, beggars, gipsies, singers, dancers, players on harps, Indian jugglers, Punch & Judy exhibitors, and similar wandering artists'.

In 1815 Jane Austen wrote apologetically to Anna Lefroy that Charles' daughter, Cassy, when given the choice, had preferred going to the Alton fair to dining with the Lefroys.[20] It seems that Jane Austen enjoyed a good fair herself, writing to Caroline Austen, 'Our fair at Alton is next Saturday, which is also Mary Jane's birthday, & you would be thought an addition on such a great day.'[21] According to *Owen's Book of Fairs*, the Alton fair happened on the Saturday before 1 May, with an emphasis on sheep and lambs, and on 29 September when cattle and toys were prominent. Presumably the latter was what attracted Cassandra. At Godmersham Jane Austen declined an invitation to the Goodnestone fair. Fanny seemed to like them more. In 1813 Jane Austen wrote of:

Fanny being gone to Godnestone [*sic*] for a day or two to attend the famous Fair which makes its yearly distribution of gold paper and coloured Persian through all the family connections.[22]

(Le Faye. D. (ed.), *Jane Austen's Letters*, 4th edition (OUP, 2011). Reproduced by permission of Oxford University Press.)

Shops became more numerous so that periodic fairs were at a disadvantage. Transport became more regular and with it new means of distribution were adopted. As people became more fastidious, the disorderly reputation of fairs in town-centre locations was used in attempts to move, restrict or close them.

The number and variety of shops grew in the eighteenth century. These shops might be fine premises on a high street, or small backstreet shops. The development of shop-keeping as separate from the business of a merchant was slow: some shop-keepers thought it beneath them to seek customers actively or to display prices. Some didn't like the process at all: sellers of wines and spirits insisted on keeping the name of merchant – which they still enjoy. In an early work – *A Collection of Letters* – Jane Austen has a Lady Greville ask the heroine, "'Pray Miss Maria in what way of business was your Grandfather? for Miss Mason and I cannot agree whether he was a Grocer or a Bookbinder." I saw that she wanted to mortify me, and was resolved if I possibly could to Prevent her seeing that her scheme succeeded. "Neither Madam; he was a Wine Merchant."'[23]

Shop-keeping became more competitive. Advertising, mail-order selling and competition on price were frequent. Commercial information spread more widely. Provincial sellers of tea were much interested in news of the China Fleet, and their customers could read newspaper reports of the tea auctions in London and then argue about prices.

In parallel with the development of shops and shopping there was a revolution in consumer spending. No longer content with buying only necessities and decencies, shoppers of many classes sought luxuries. Foreigners exclaimed at the English appetite for luxury. It may be that this was a necessary adjunct to the Industrial Revolution. Southey wrote:

luxury here fills every head with caprice, from the servant-maid to the peeress, and shops are become exhibitions of fashion. In the spring, when all persons of distinction are in Town, the usual morning employment of the ladies is to go a-shopping, as it is called; that is, to see these curious exhibitions. This they do without actually wanting to purchase anything, and they spend their money or not, according to the temptations which are held out to gratify and amuse.[24]

This development of shopping as a social activity was seen in the country, also. In *Emma* everyone goes to Ford's. In *The Watsons* there is a gentle joke made of the old mare pulling Miss Watson's small open carriage 'making only one blunder, in proposing to stop at the milliner's before she drew up at Mr Edwards' door.'

Jane Austen's aunt by marriage, Mrs Leigh Perrot, may have found the temptations too much for her. While she was acquitted of shop-lifting in Bath, after ten character witnesses, including a peer, two MPs and two clergymen, had spoken on her behalf, there is some evidence that she was a kleptomaniac. *The Lady's Magazine* in April 1800 devoted six pages to an account of the seven-hour trial, with a portrait of the lady. It was a very public matter. Despite this shaming incident, her later mean-spirited behaviour to the Austen family makes one inclined to think ill of her. Her own counsel, Joseph Jekyll, MP, thought that she was a kleptomaniac and guilty'.[25]

The rich in the eighteenth century built magnificent new houses with splendid furniture, porcelain and silver. Novelty became a craze. The middling classes spent, too, emulating their neighbours and betters.

The conservative reaction to all this consumption was to try to suppress 'bare-faced luxury'. The argument went back to Mandeville's *Fable of the Bees*, subtitled 'Private Vices, Public Benefits'. Prosperity stemming from self-indulgence was controversial. Cobbett, for example, was appalled at the competition in show and luxury.

England was a multi-layered society in which there was much movement. The newly prosperous encouraged optimism. Servants imitating their masters was one way in which ideas and tastes were transmitted through society. So prevalent was this that it was remarked that often servants were indistinguishable in appearance from their masters. Southey's Espriella noted that 'the finest gentlemen to be seen in the streets of London are the men who serve at the linen-drapers' and mercers'.[26]

The scale of the resulting 'consumer revolution' was very large. Seddon & Sons, Furniture makers of Aldersgate Street, in 1796 had over 400 employees – gilders, mirror-workers, locksmiths, carvers, seamstresses, sawyers and joiners. The growth in the consumption of 'luxuries' outpaced the growth in population. In the last fifteen years of the eighteenth century the population increased by about 14 per cent. Tea consumption rose by almost 98 per cent and that of printed fabrics by almost 142 per cent.[27]

Jane Austen was familiar with shopping in London and often enjoyed it. In 1814 she wrote, probably to Anna Lefroy:

> I was particularly amused with your picture of Grafton House; it is just so. – How much I should like finding you there one day, seated on your high stool, with 15 rolls of persian before you.[28]
>
> (Le Faye. D. (ed.), *Jane Austen's Letters*, 4th edition (OUP, 2011). Reproduced by permission of Oxford University Press.)

Jane Austen had been to Grafton House, which Deirdre Le Faye identifies as the premises of the drapers Wilding & Kent on the corner of Grafton Street and 164 New Bond Street, in 1811, where, after having had to wait half an hour before being attended to, she bought bugle trimming and silk stockings. She visited again with Fanny Knight in 1813 when Edward waited with 'wonderful patience for three quarters of an hour'. She learnt to go to Grafton House early in the morning to avoid having to wait. Even so, she did not enjoy shopping among crowds, writing in 1815 of 'the miseries of Grafton House'.[29]

On the 1811 shopping expedition she wrote to Cassandra:

I am sorry to tell you I am getting very extravagant & spending all my Money; & what is worse for you, I have been spending yours too: for in the Linen draper's shop to which I went for check'd Muslin, & for which I was obliged to give seven shillings a yard, I was tempted by a pretty coloured muslin, & bought 10 yds of it, on the chance of your liking it.[30]

(Le Faye. D. (ed.), *Jane Austen's Letters*, 4th edition (OUP, 2011). Reproduced by permission of Oxford University Press.)

Jane Austen visited one of the most sophisticated shops in London, that of Josiah Wedgwood, with her brother Edward and his wife Fanny. They chose a dinner service; 'the pattern is a small Lozenge in purple between Lines of narrow Gold – & is to have the Crest.'[31] The order was entered in the Wedgwood 'Crest Order Book 1813–17' on 18 September 1813. The complete service appears to have been of 167 pieces. Its cost is not known. Besides numerous different sizes of serving dishes, there were six dozen table plates (presumably the most used and therefore more likely to become worn or to be broken), two dozen soup plates and two dozen small flat plates.[32] Much of the service still survives.

It was not an accident that brought Jane Austen to Wedgwood's smart shop off Piccadilly.[33] The European china fever of the mid-eighteenth century had shown Wedgwood the importance of royal or noble patronage. His achievement was to help channel this demand from porcelain to pottery and from the aristocracy to the wider population. A mixture of growing wealth, changing habits – the consumption of tea, coffee and chocolate – developments in technology and transport, and Wedgwood's own discoveries, contributed to his success. But none of these was a unique or long-lasting advantage.

Wedgwood never competed on price, generally selling well above his competitors. He relied on quality and fashionable appeal. His success lay in capturing the world of fashion. He worked hard to win the patronage of the royal family and then publicized it constantly. He was prepared to accept commissions of great difficulty from Queen Charlotte and the Empress Catherine of Russia. New designs were shown first to certain aristocratic patrons. They in turn alerted him to anticipated changes in fashion. Gilding on vases, for example, was stopped at the suggestion of Sir William Hamilton.

Wedgwood wrote 'few ladies, you know, dare venture at anything out of the common stile 'till authorised by their betters – by the Ladies of superior spirit who set the *ton*'.[34] Care was taken to make his London showrooms attractive to ladies and to keep out 'common people'. Careful thought was given as to how the wares could best be displayed. He advertised assiduously. There was a succession of exhibitions and famous commissions were often shown to the public before being shipped to the purchaser.

Visitors were dazzled by the sophisticated display. Sophie von La Roche recorded, 'At Wedgwood's to-day I saw a thousand lovely forms and images; vases, tea-things, statuettes, medallions, seals, table-ware and a service on which pictures of the finest villas and gardens of the last three reigns were painted; were I a traveller of means this would have accompanied me home to Germany.'[35]

The people of the middling sort thus attracted were more prudish than their aristocratic contemporaries. When 'the ardour of the Greek gods was too readily apparent, Wedgwood was quick to cloak their pagan immodesty – gowns for the girls and fig leaves for the gods were usually sufficient'[36] but some classical originals were completely redraped.

Jane Austen did not write as a puritan, disapproving of all luxury and pleasure. But nor did she run after every fashion – not least because the expense would have been beyond her. She was aware of fashion certainly, for example writing to Cassandra in October 1808, 'We must turn our black pelisses into new, for Velvet is to be very much worn this winter', though she was cautious generally in what she spent on clothes. In the same letter she mentioned an experiment in dyeing old dresses, which was not satisfactory.

Fashion had certainly begun to be pursued more widely. The fashion doll and the fashion plates in women's magazines spread the ideas. William Hazlitt commented most aptly, 'Fashion is gentility running away from vulgarity, and afraid of being overtaken by it. It is a sign the two things are not very far asunder.'[37]

Fashion has often been expressed in hats. The women's hats in the three Stubbs' paintings of *The Haymakers* reflect accurately the fashions of the years in which they were painted: 1783 had a sharp forward tilt, 1785 the immensely high, soft crown worn over the mob cap and in 1795 there was the enormous picture hat swept up at one side.[38]

In *Pride and Prejudice* Kitty and Lydia visit a milliner and then order a lunch they cannot pay for. Lydia says to Elizabeth:

'Look here, I have bought this bonnet. I do not think it is very pretty; but I thought I might as well buy it as not. I shall pull it to pieces as soon as I get home, and see if I can make it up any better.' And when her sisters abused it as ugly, she added, with perfect unconcern, 'Oh! But there were two or three much uglier in the shop.'[39]

Hats became a symbol of excess and indeed were excessive themselves. Hannah More, writing from Bungay in Norfolk in 1777, noted:

the other night we had a great deal of company – eleven damsels to say nothing of men. I protest I hardly do them justice when I pronounce that they had, amongst them, on their heads, an acre and a half of shrubbery, besides slopes, grass-plats, tulip beds, clumps of peonies, kitchen-gardens, and green-houses. Mrs. Cotton and I had an infinite deal of entertainment out of them, though, to our shame be it spoken, some of them were cousins; but I have no doubt that they held in great contempt our roseless heads and leafless necks.[40]

Jane Austen, writing in 1799 to Cassandra from Bath, noted:

Flowers are very much worn, and fruit is still more the thing. Eliz: has a bunch of Strawberries, & I have seen Grapes, Cherries, Plums, and Apricots. There are likewise Almonds and raisins, french plums, & Tamarinds at the Grocers, but I have never seen any of them in hats.[41]

(Le Faye. D. (ed.), *Jane Austen's Letters*, 4th edition (OUP, 2011). Reproduced by permission of Oxford University Press.)

There is a tone of detached amusement. The tone is quite different in *Pride and Prejudice* after Lydia's elopement with Wickham
and the moral point is clearly made. Lydia's shopping habits were
of a piece with her ungoverned wildness. Elizabeth says: 'she has
been given up to nothing but amusement and vanity. She has
been allowed to dispose of her time in the most idle and frivolous
manner, and to adopt any opinions that came her way.'[42]

But not all shopping is foolish or evidence of moral failings.
When, in *Mansfield Park*, Fanny returns to her family in Portsmouth,
she finds her two sisters squabbling over a silver knife left to Susan
by Mary, a third sister who died. Fanny buys a silver knife for
Betsey. It is done thoughtfully and hesitantly:

> she was so wholly unused to confer favours, except on the very
> poor, so unpractised in removing evils, or bestowing kindnesses
> among her equals, and so fearful of appearing to elevate herself as
> a great lady at home, that it took some time to determine that it
> would not be unbecoming in her to make such a present.[43]

The purchase is a success. 'The deed thoroughly answered; a
source of domestic altercation was entirely done away, and it was
the means of opening Susan's heart to her, and giving her something more to love and be interested in.'

Fanny has had no money to command and it is a liberating
moment when she can spend her own money as she likes. She has
£10 given to her by Sir Thomas. To her this is wealth:

> wealth is luxurious and daring – and some of hers found its way
> to a circulating library. She became a subscriber – amazed at being
> anything *in propria persona*, amazed at her own doings in every way;
> to be a renter, a chooser of books! And to having any one's improve-
> ment in view in her choice! But so it was. Susan had read nothing,
> and Fanny longed to give her a share in her own first pleasures.[44]

There are thoughtful presents such as these, and the large
new shawl that Mrs Dixon sends to Mrs Bates. There are also
thoughtless presents: Willoughby's present of a horse to Marianne,

which she can't afford, and the expensive and very elegant-looking Broadwood pianoforte which Frank Churchill buys secretly for Jane Fairfax and which must seem out of place in the Bates' impoverished household.

The contrast is clear between affordable material comforts preferred by the right-thinking and the extravagant display of the foolish, selfish and wrong-headed.[45] Robert Ferrars' exemplifies all of the latter. He is willing to make the Dashwood ladies wait, looking at them unashamedly as he does so. Besides his manners, his claims to taste are made fun of in references to the correctness of his eye, the delicacy of his taste and the inventiveness of his fancy. He is buying a toothpick-case. Elinor remembers 'a person and face of strong, natural sterling insignificance, though adorned in the first style of fashion.'[46]

Edward Ferrars imagines what shopping the Dashwood girls would do if Margaret's wish for 'a large fortune apiece' came true. 'What magnificent orders would travel from this family to London,' said Edward, 'in such an event! What a happy day for booksellers, music-sellers, and print-shops!'[47] This is shopping with intelligence and taste, though Edward goes on to tease them about their enthusiasms.

There is also a social dimension to the matter of consumption. The barouche-landau owned by Mrs Elton's brother Mr Suckling is one such example. At a time when 'new money' was everywhere, what did gentlepeople, or those claiming gentility, do to distinguish themselves? Clearly anybody with some money, however foolish or vulgar, could buy things in imitation of the fashionable. Nancy Steele's curiosity about Marianne's clothes and her minute observation is one such example. It has been argued that, for the 'unlanded gentry', a great deal of shopping was not so much aspirational but to do with acquiring the things that confirmed your status in that group. Mrs Elton's pearls would have been one such attempt.

As Penelope Byrde has pointed out, the fashion for pale and particularly for white muslin was a mark of gentility, however well they washed.[48]

One reaction was the way in which male fashion changed under Brummel's influence to an emphasis on sophistication of cut rather than materials, a fastidious path the vulgar might not easily follow. The hardest thing of all to copy was the great country house.

The country house has been described as 'an embodiment of social and cultural capital'. Consumption in such houses was not just fashion-driven but involved 'more "dynastic" forms of consumption which emphasised traditional concerns of the elite: patronage, display and heritance'. This consumption drew on 'value systems and status markers not available to the middling sorts'.[49]

The eighteenth-century household accounts of the Leighs of Stoneleigh Abbey – Jane Austen's cousins – have been analysed. About 60 per cent of their purchases were made in London, with 30 per cent in two local towns – Coventry and Warwick. Luxuries generally came from London while less important things were bought in local places: silk came from London, but servants' liveries were bought locally.

Among the purchases by the Leighs during the eighteenth century (1710–89)[50] silver, furniture and books were large items, together accounting for almost half their purchases. All of these might be means whereby the family could show its taste.

Jane Austen makes fun of Lady Catherine de Bourgh's pretensions to taste: 'There are few people in England, I suppose, who have more true enjoyment of music than myself, or a better natural taste. If I had ever learnt, I should have been a great proficient.'[51]

There are two other characters who do not understand taste. Mr Collins misunderstands the matter when he talks about the cost of the chimney-piece at Rosings. General Tilney, too, is inclined to talk about the cost of gilding. Theirs is a failure of taste that condemns them.

One might also claim sophisticated knowledge with a well-stocked library, elaborately bound, and the possession of instruments such as globes. Mr Darcy could not 'comprehend the neglect of a family library in such days as these'.[52] Mr Bingley, by contrast, is not bookish and has inherited no family library since his family's money was made in trade. Some aristocrats certainly did not neglect their family libraries. The Duke of Devonshire paid almost £10,000 for the entire library of Thomas Dampier, the Bishop of Ely, who died in 1812.

Large-scale dinner parties were one way in which a country-house family might distinguish itself from the lives of the middling sort. An American called Willis wrote an account of staying at Castle Gordon. He asked a page 'how many sit down to dinner?' and was answered 'Above ninety, sir, besides the Duke and Duchess.'[53] Such parties would typically involve footmen in livery and silver engraved with crest or arms. Such style was imitated by lesser landowners. We have seen Jane Austen helping her brother Edward Knight to choose armorial china from Wedgwood.

A Frenchman, François de la Rochefoucauld, described staying with the Duke of Grafton at Euston and contrasted the informality of the day with the formality of dinner: 'The standard of politeness is uncomfortably high – strangers go first into the dining room and sit near the hostess and are served in seniority in accordance with a rigid etiquette. In fact for the first few days I was tempted to think that it was done for a joke.'[54]

The Frenchman also noted that 'the English seize every opportunity to use things which are expensive in themselves. At all events their tables are made of the most beautiful wood and always have a brilliant polish like that of the finest glass.'[55]

François was alarmed at the amount drunk after dinner and appalled by the conversation. 'Sometimes conversation becomes extremely free upon highly indecent topics – complete licence is allowed and I have come to the conclusion that the English do not associate the same ideas with certain words that we do.'[56] Lord John Russell recalled that often men would have to be carried home drunk from dinner parties.

> Some curious incidents arose when some of the valets were not themselves too sober, and substitutes had to take their places, and some of the masters were put into the wrong coaches, and carried to the wrong houses about midnight or later, much to the astonishment … of the wives and other members of the households.[57]

So Elizabeth Bennet's 'stuffy uncle Phillips, breathing port wine' was not untypical.

However, all of these things could occasionally be imitated, if at great cost. The bill-broker Benjamin Goldsmid had a house at Roehampton where he received King George III. His biographer wrote, admiringly if not very fastidiously, that:

> Everything is here on a scale of magnificence and beauty equal to any Nobleman's country seat. Drawing, Music and Dancing Rooms, furnished with the highest taste and latest fashions, with a profusion of ornamental as well as useful articles ... Drawings and Paintings of the most eminent Artists, as well as family Portraits were to be seen in every part of the house.
>
> Books were not the only furniture of this study, he had also there the most useful philosophical apparatus of every kind, to put in practice whenever it was required the theories contained in the curious volumes that were ranged around.
>
> Here amidst the works of the greatest geniuses foreign and domestic, he invited his friends to retire and partake of the luxuries of mind, the feast of reason and the flow of the soul. Here the Bookish man or the practical Philosopher might retire, and enjoy himself according to his taste or fancy with these silent friends without interruption.[58]

Not quite everybody followed the fashion for expensive china. Sydney Smith, comfortable in his parish of Combe Florey in Somerset, spoke of his dinner plates:

> ... every one a different pattern.... It is true, Mrs Sydney, who is a great herald, is shocked because some of them have the arms of a royal duke or a knight of the garter on them, but that does not signify to me. My plan is to go into a china-shop and bid them show me every plate they have which does not cost more than half-a-crown; you see the result.[59]

Turning to gender, historians have identified certain differences between men and women in what they bought and how they thought about what they owned. Women in their wills describe their possessions and bequeath them carefully to friends as well as family. Women left more specific bequests of linen, jewellery, silver and clothing than men.[60] It seems that tea things were particularly precious to middle-class women and carefully bequeathed. The tea ceremony was one in which women were central.[61] Perhaps we see something of the importance of such items to women in one of Jane Austen's letters.

In 1811 Jane Austen was in London staying with her brother Henry and correcting the proofs of *Sense and Sensibility*. She also had shopping commissions to perform, including a visit to Wedgwood's shop. The result of that visit was recorded in a letter later in the year.

> On Monday I had the pleasure of receiving, unpacking and approving our Wedgwood ware. It all came very safely, & upon the whole is a good match, tho' I think they might have allowed us rather larger leaves, especially in such a Year of fine foliage as this. One is apt to suppose that the Woods about Birmingham must be blighted. – There was no Bill with the Goods – but that shall not screen them from being paid. I mean to ask Martha to settle the account. It will be quite in her way, for she is just now sending my mother a Breakfast set from the same place. I hope it will come by the Wagon tomorrow; it is certainly what we want, & I long to know what it is like.[62]

(Le Faye. D. (ed.), *Jane Austen's Letters*, 4th edition (OUP, 2011). Reproduced by permission of Oxford University Press.)

As Linda Slothouber has pointed out, tableware was an important marker of social status.[63] Mrs John Dashwood is jealous of the breakfast china that the Dashwood ladies take to Devon – 'a great deal too handsome, in my opinion, for any place that *they* can ever afford to live in'.

In *Northanger Abbey* Henry Tilney challenges the male stereotype of a man interested only in buying furniture and silver, guns and horses. He understands muslins, always buys his own cravats and buys for his sister – obtaining prodigious bargains. He claims such knowledge of muslin that he teases Catherine that her dress will not wash well.

Lest this be thought an improbable invention, John Sparrow, warden of All Souls, wrote an essay[64] in which he suggested that the Reverend Sydney Smith might have been an influence in the creation of Henry Tilney. Smith also was 'about four or five and twenty, was rather tall, had a pleasing countenance, a very intelligent and lively eye, and, if not quite handsome, was very near it.' Smith, too, was in Bath in late 1797, buying materials for Mrs Hicks Beach, the wife of his patron, and writing to her in detail about the quality and prices of various stuffs. There is no evidence that they ever met but it remains an interesting speculation.

Chapter 10

Carriages

A MODERN NOVELIST CAN illuminate a character by specifying the type of car they drive. So, too, with carriages. William Howitt wrote, 'How the man who drives his close carriage looks down upon him who only drives his barouche or phaeton; how both contemn the poor occupier of a gig.'[1] Jane Austen was careful to specify what sort of vehicle many of her characters drove. This chapter tries to put these in context.

The Reverend George Austen had a carriage for a while,[2] but the Austen ladies at Chawton Cottage had only a donkey carriage drawn by a single donkey. It was open to the weather. One day in July 1816, Jane Austen wrote:

> Mary Jane and I have been wet through once already today, we set off in the Donkey Carriage for Farringdon as I wanted to see the improvements Mr Woolls is making, but we were obliged to turn back before we got there, but not soon enough to avoid a Pelter all the way home.[3]
>
> (Le Faye. D. (ed.), *Jane Austen's Letters*, 4th edition (OUP, 2011). Reproduced by permission of Oxford University Press.)

Later the same year she remarked that December was not a season for donkey carriages so she had declined an invitation to dinner.

She joked to Alethea Bigg:

> our Donkeys are necessarily having so long a run of luxurious idle-
> ness that I suppose we shall find they have forgotten much of their
> Education when we use them again.[4]
>
> (Le Faye. D. (ed.), *Jane Austen's Letters*, 4th edition (OUP, 2011). Reproduced by
> permission of Oxford University Press.)

Unprotected though it was, a donkey carriage at least offered the
prospect of independent travel, if only on quite short journeys. For
much of her life Jane Austen, like most gentlewomen, depended on
others to convey her and had to comply with their plans.

Jane Austen wrote in her letters with relish about carriages.
Writing to Cassandra from Bath in May 1801 she expressed a great
desire to go out in a phaeton with a Mr Evelyn and then recorded
her enjoyment of the event:

> I am just returned from my Airing in the very bewitching Phaeton
> and four, for which I was prepared by a note from Mr. E soon
> after breakfast. We went to the top of Kingsdown and had a very
> pleasant drive.[5]
>
> (Le Faye. D. (ed.), *Jane Austen's Letters*, 4th edition (OUP, 2011). Reproduced by
> permission of Oxford University Press.)

In May 1813 she described her pleasure in being driven by her
brother Henry in his curricle from Chawton to London. 'I never
saw the Country from the Hogsback so advantageously.'[6] In
London that month, looking unsuccessfully for paintings that
might resemble Mrs Darcy, she wrote:

> I had great amusement among the Pictures; & the Driving about,
> the carriage been open, [sic] was very pleasant. I liked my solitary
> elegance very much, and was ready to laugh all the time, at being
> where I was. – I could not but feel that I had naturally small right to
> be parading about London in a Barouche.[7]
>
> (Le Faye. D. (ed.), *Jane Austen's Letters*, 4th edition (OUP, 2011). Reproduced by
> permission of Oxford University Press.)

Carriages represented a luxury and freedom to which she was not much accustomed.

From an early age Jane Austen naturally was familiar with carriages and was amused at the way in which people indulged themselves. In *The Memoirs of Mr. Clifford: an Unfinished Tale*, dedicated to her brother Charles, when she was between twelve and fifteen, we find:

> Mr. Clifford lived at Bath; & having never seen London, set off one monday morning determined to feast his eyes with a sight of that great Metropolis. He travelled in his Coach & Four, for he was a very rich young Man & kept a great many Carriages of which I do not recollect half. I can only remember that he had a Coach, a Chariot, a Chaise, a Landeau, a Landeaulet, a Phaeton, a Gig, a Whisky, an italian Chair, a Buggy, a Curricle & a wheelbarrow. He had likewise an amazing fine stud of Horses. To my knowledge he had six Greys, 4 Bays, eight Blacks & a poney.[8]

Let us begin with two-wheeled carriages, which were taxed at an annual rate of between £3 and £4. So-called 'taxed carts', however, were subject to a lower annual charge of 10 (later 12) shillings. Taxed carts had less than four wheels, were drawn by one horse and were built only of wood and iron without any lining or springs and were to be used chiefly 'in the affairs of husbandry, or for the purpose of carrying goods in the way of trade' but occasionally they conveyed people. They had to be worth less than £12.[9] That was an annual tax equal to at least 5 per cent of the value. Taxed carts were not very large or comfortable. Jane Austen wrote to Cassandra:

> In consequence of a civil note that morning from Mrs Clement, I went with her and her husband in their tax-cart – civility on both sides; I would rather have walked, and no doubt they must have wished I had.[10]

> (Le Faye. D. (ed.), *Jane Austen's Letters*, 4th edition (OUP, 2011). Reproduced by permission of Oxford University Press.)

Now we turn to gigs. These were small two-wheeled carriages

drawn by a single horse – the runabouts of their day. In *Persuasion* Admiral Croft has lately bought a gig. He and his wife take long drives and have frequent accidents. 'My dear Admiral, that post! – we shall certainly take that post.'[11] Mr Collins also has a gig. Edward Ferrars, remembering his distaste for a career at the bar, comments on 'young men, who had chambers in the Temple, made a very good appearance in the first circles, and drove about town in very knowing gigs'.[12] The Duke of Wellington later complained about seeing in London too many young men in gigs with no visible means of support.

Another young enthusiast is the tiresome John Thorpe. Mr Thorpe is so proud of his gig which is 'town built', that is to say in London. 'Curricle hung you see, seat, trunk, sword case, splashing-board, lamps, silver moulding, all you see complete, the iron work as good as new, or better. He asked fifty guineas; I closed with him directly.'[13]

But buying a gig was only the first expense. John Thorpe's cost him 50 guineas. Jane Austen's contemporaries would have known that he would have had to spend roughly the same each year to run it,[14] including the cost of the servant – presumably an occasional groom – who travels with him. Duty and repairs etc. would have been about £12 a year and the cost of keeping the horse and its groom would have been about £42.[15]

Thorpe thinks James Morland 'a fool for not keeping a horse and gig of his own'[16] but Catherine is sure he could not afford it. Mr Thorpe's loud, incoherent response suggests that he thinks himself less rich than Morland and so is presumably even less able to afford his gig.

A gig was not very smart. In *Sanditon* Sir Edward Denham and his sister have only a simple gig. Miss Denham was one who 'felt her consequence with Pride and her Poverty with Discontent, and who was immediately gnawed by the want of a handsomer Equipage'.[17]

The smart thing to drive was a curricle – 'the Porsche of its time'.[18] In *Persuasion* Mr Elliot drives 'a gentleman's carriage – a curricle'. So do many other young gentlemen in the novels: Mr Darcy, Mr William Goulding (of Hyde Park, whose family dine with the Bennets), Mr Rushworth, Charles Musgrove, Henry Tilney, Willoughby and Mr Musgrave in *The Watsons*. Only Willoughby, with an income of about £700 a year, cannot afford both his curricle and his hunters. Men must have talked about curricles as they do about cars today. Colonel Brandon found fault with the hanging (the suspension as we now call it) of Willoughby's curricle.

Catherine Morland, once in Henry Tilney's curricle, was 'as happy a being as ever existed' and was easily persuaded of a curricle's merits.

> A very short trial convinced her that a curricle was the prettiest equipage in the world; the chaise and four wheeled off with some grandeur, to be sure, but it was a heavy and troublesome business, and she could not easily forget its having stopped two hours at Petty France. Half the time would have been enough for the curricle, and so nimbly were the light horses disposed to move, that, had not the general chosen to have his own carriage lead the way, they could have passed it with ease in half a minute. But the merit of the curricle did not all belong to the horses: Henry drove so well, so quietly.[19]

A curricle drawn by two horses would have cost more than £100 to buy new (excluding harness) and probably £100 a year to run, including depreciation of the carriage. If we were to adjust for the increase in prices this amount would be about £7,000 today. If we put this expense in a social context the annual cost of a curricle would be about £105,000 today.

There is further evidence of expense implied in Catherine's artless remarking on how 'nimbly were the light horses disposed to move'.[20] Unlike, for example, Mr Bennet whose horses both work on the farm and pull his carriage, Henry Tilney is driving thoroughbred horses. In December 1804 *The Morning Post* had a piece entitled 'The leaders in fashionable carriages' which asked 'who it was that first introduced blood horses into our modern coaches: a species of refinement unknown to our ancestors, who were satisfied with the cart breed'.[21] *The Morning Post*'s answer to the second question was an Irish rake.

The late Lord Barrymore was the first who sported blood horses in carriages. In the spring of the year 1792, in Rotten Row, he made his grand *entre* in the ride where everyone was running chariot and coach horses; and immediately upon his entrance he overturned Sir John Lade in his curricle, which gave the worthy Baronet so great a disgust for that kind of conveyance, that he for several years discontinued their use.[22]

As one might imagine, the variety of carriages was enormous. There were, too, regional variations and oddities. Mrs Lybbe Powys in 1781 remarked:

> the most droll thing in Yarmouth are their little carts, alias hackney-coaches, in which everybody goes about, as their rows or what in London we should call alleys, are too narrow for any other carriages to pass ... the riding ... is truly comic; and their uncommon jolting hardly to be borne, and those not used to driving them would immediately overturn them, as the wheels are underneath and no farther out than their shafts.[23]

The construction of coaches – sometimes a matter of high fashion – was both complicated and evolving. We need not go into the intricacies of futchells, nunters and territts, but a general comparison of costs will help us understand the references as Jane Austen's contemporaries would have known them.

One way of bringing order to this confusing world is to rank carriages by their initial purchase cost excluding harness and horses. As we have seen there were substantial running costs to be paid in addition. The prices below are from William Felton in 1796.[24]

Type of carriage	New price (£/s./d.)	Owners in Jane Austen's novels
Travelling coach	201–1–6	General Tilney, Sir Thomas Bertram, Mr Bennet, Mr Musgrove
Town chariot	192–13–0	Mrs Jennings, Mrs Rushworth
Travelling post chaise	177–10–6	Mrs Jennings, Mr Bingley, Lady Catherine de Bourgh
Landaulette	156–10–3	Mrs Wentworth, Mrs Darcy

Post chaise	115–3–6	Lady Bertram, Mrs Rushworth, Mr Suckling
Fixed curricle	103–5–0	Mr Darcy, Mr Goulding, Mr Elliot, Charles Musgrove, Mr Rushworth, Mr Willoughby, Henry Tilney, Tom Musgrave
Small phaeton	67–0–0	Miss de Bourgh and possibly Elizabeth Darcy
Curricle gig	58–9–3	Admiral Croft, John Tilney, Mr Collins
Whisky	24–10–0	The Watson family

Being luxury items, coaches could be very expensive, running to £250 or more. In his retirement Philip Godsal, who had been one of the leading coach-makers in London, bought in 1818 a new chariot with many extras from his old firm, now called Baxter & Macklew, for just over £356.

Felton suggested that over four years one could spend almost half the cost of a carriage again in repairs, new wheels and repainting. At the end of four years a carriage would be worth about one-third of its new cost. So very roughly the annual capital cost of a carriage might be about 30 per cent of its new cost in its first years.[25] However, many people must have kept their carriages much longer, like the Heywoods in *Sanditon* whose coach 'had been new when they married and fresh-lined on their eldest Son's coming of age ten years ago'.[26]

Buying a coach was only a first expensive step. Carriages and carts were taxed. Four-wheeled carriages were taxed annually at £8 16s. for a first carriage and £9 18s. for a second. If one had three or more carriages the tax on the second and each subsequent vehicle was £11. This encouraged people to have two rather than three carriages.

Carriages were not particularly big by our standards. Felton wrote:

Open bodies have this advantage, that three can sit with tolerable ease on the same length of seat as would only accommodate two in a confined one. A full-sized seat for a close body to contain three, is from four feet to one or two inches more; that of an open body, from three feet four, to three feet five or six inches. This size is sufficient for two in the close, and from two feet seven inches, to two feet eight or ten inches, in the open bodies.[27]

So we may have a little more sympathy with Mary Musgrove when she had to suffer sharing a carriage with her parents-in-law: 'They are both so very large, and take up so much room! And Mr. Musgrove always sits forward. So there I was crowded into the back seat with Henrietta and Louisa. And I think it very likely that my illness to-day may be owing to it.'[28]

John Thorpe refers to his gig as 'town built' – rather grandiose for a gig but a reference to the centre of the carriage-making trade. The centre of the industry in London was in Long Acre, Covent Garden, where there were twenty-one coach-makers in 1790. The three leading makers were Hatchett, Wright & Lukin, and Godsal. They employed a wide range of very skilled craftsmen and artists. Several distinguished painters and sculptors decorated carriages. So high was the reputation of English carriage-makers that in September 1817, not long after the defeat of France, *The Morning Chronicle* reported 'we understand that the French Government has offered a contract for 900 mail coaches to some of the London coach builders, at £150 each, to be built in France.'[29] The last phrase bears witness to an interesting early example of attempted technology transfer.

Sophie von La Roche visited Hatchett's premises in 1786. He employed several hundred workmen in his service in three floors of spacious rooms.

> At home we have no conception of such a saddler, with premises for cartwrights, smiths, harness-makers, sculptors, painters, upholsterers, gilders, girdlers – all kinds of workmen necessary for coach- and harness-making and other accessories, working under his supervision and producing the loveliest masterpieces of their kind … The painters and lacquer workers were on the third floor. All the main flights of stairs are broad, and so arranged that the banisters may be taken down and the finished vehicle allowed to slide down on ropes.[30]

It is outside the scope of this book but nonetheless interesting to note the links between carriage-building and the other decorative arts not just in London but in the country. Henry Hill (*d.* 1778) of Marlborough, for example, had a wide-ranging business; 'he was a coachmaker as well as a comprehensive furnisher and decorator; also an estate agent and auctioneer, and a local agent for the Sun Insurance Company, and he even found time to sell fish (trout and crayfish) to at least one client'.[31] He worked for Lord Bruce (later Marquis of Aylesbury) in 1776 repairing a cabriolet, providing a Wilton carpet for a landau, making curtains, repairing and recovering chairs and refurbishing a table as well as other decorative services.

Carriages were important as items of public display. English carriages were popular abroad. Sophie von La Roche saw a drawing of the coach made for the Nabob of Arcot which she was told had cost 15,000 guineas. Hatchett sold one to Catherine the Great of Russia and Godsal made one for Napoleon's mother.

Godsal was also commissioned to make the Irish State Coach. At once the patriotic Mayor of Dublin commissioned a mayoral coach from a Dublin maker. When Godsal's coach reached Dublin it was so superior that the Mayor's coach had to go back to be redesigned. Unfortunately on its first outing in Dublin the Irish State Coach met a low arch and was badly damaged.

We find new carriages being bought to mark special events, particularly weddings. In *Sense and Sensibility* it is reported that a new carriage is being built for the wedding of Willoughby and Miss Grey. In *Mansfield Park*, the chaise at Sotherton is a year old when it is used to convey the newly married couple from the church to the house. This is the only thing that the neighbourhood objected to when the wedding was discussed. In a juvenile fragment *The Three Sisters*, the capricious 'heroine' Mary Stanhope has an offer of marriage from a Mr Watts, 'an old Man, about two and thirty, very plain ... he has a large fortune.' She writes to a friend, 'he promised to have a new Carriage on the occasion, but we almost quarrelled about the colour, for I insisted upon its being blue spotted with silver, & he declared it should be a plain chocolate; & to provoke me more said it should be just as low as his old one. I won't have him I declare.'[32]

The idea of a carriage being blue spotted with silver would have seemed less ridiculous to Jane Austen's contemporaries than it may do to the modern reader. Carriages were of many colours and a matter of high fashion. William Felton in his *Treatise on Carriages* wrote that a carriage 'has now, in the higher circles of life, become a distinguishing mark of the rank and taste of the proprietor'.[33]

In December 1804 *The Morning Post* noted that 'It has been often asked to whom is the town indebted for the present taste in the building of carriages' and commented that it was the Prince of Wales who:

> introduced the patent yellow picked out very fully with black, with linings of drab cloth, and black and yellow lace, finished with red morocco reclining cushions. This style was so admired, that in less than six months from its commencement, not a fashionable carriage was to be seen of any other colour, and it still continues as prevailing as ever.[34]

The Prince's carriage must have looked rather gaudy. We know, too, that his dominance of fashion was exaggerated. It was fashionable to have a new carriage built for royal birthday parades. Lists of newly built birthday carriages in the *Morning Post* of January 1804, included many in yellow (The Prince of Wales, two royal dukes, Sir Henry Dashwood, T.R. Beaumont, William Pitt, the Dowager Lady Boyd, Admiral Sir Robert Kingsmill, and others).[35] But the fashion was not absolute. In the same newspaper were noted carriages in deep claret (the Marquis of Thomond), dark corbeau (the Earl of Peterborough), japan black (Colonel Vaughan), dark green (Lord Broke), olive green (George Canning), and a fine pearl (Sir Thomas Gooch, Bt). Women, too, had their own carriages built: for example, Miss Callender had a landaulette in dark blue and Madame de Bonneuil a chariot in light blue.

Setting up one's coach was, as a public display of wealth, a form of particularly conspicuous consumption. In *Sense and Sensibility* Miss Steele says of her friends the Richardsons: 'very genteel people. He makes a monstrous deal of money, and they keep their own coach'. In *Emma* Mrs Elton's brother-in-law, Mr Suckling, keeps two.

There is in *Emma* an account of a joke which, for its effect, depends on knowing the cost of buying and keeping a coach and the earnings of apothecaries. Frank Churchill asks Mrs Weston 'what became of Mr Perry's plan of setting up his carriage?' This is information he had from one of Jane Fairfax's secret letters. He covers his mistake by saying that he must have had a dream. Mr Weston doubts Perry can afford it and says the news is at least premature.

In *Emma* we hear quite a lot about Mr Woodhouse's apothecary and 'great friend' Mr Perry, 'an intelligent, gentlemanlike man' who indulges Mr Woodhouse's hypochondria. 'As Perry says, where health is at stake, nothing else should be considered.' Contemporary readers would have appreciated that Jane Fairfax had told the story as a joke on how much money Perry was supposed to be making from his hypochondriac patient Mr Woodhouse. They would have known the circumstances of apothecaries from their own lives.

To understand Mr Perry we must make a digression into the medical world. The medical profession – physicians, surgeons and apothecaries – was not particularly well-regarded in the early-nineteenth century. It was said that physicians looked down on surgeons while surgeons looked down on apothecaries. One medical man, Thomas Trotter (1760–1832) a Scottish naval physician, at least had the grace to admit to his failings: 'I was frequently mortified with seeing my patients get worse under my treatment.'[36]

At this time doctors trained at one of the medical schools and became members of the Royal College of Physicians. Much of what they were taught was nonsense. Apothecaries, on the other hand, undertook practical apprenticeships and tended to know more about what actually worked.[37]

The poet Keats trained as a surgeon at Guy's Hospital in London. In 1816 he worked as a dresser – in effect an assistant surgeon – under William Lucas, junior.

Dogged by ill-health, including premature deafness, 'Billy' Lucas had never been strong enough to study anatomy in the unhealthy dissecting-room of his day; but the influence of a successful father proved stronger than this handicap, and in 1799 he duly succeeded to the parental position as surgeon in the hospital. Here he began a career of butchery which even his generous colleague, Astley Cooper, was to recall with critical horror: 'he was neat handed but rash in the extreme, cutting amongst most important parts as though they were only skin, and making us all shudder from the apprehension of his opening arteries or committing some other error.[38]

Perhaps because of this unedifying example, Keats gave up medicine.

Good apothecaries kept abreast of medical developments and often corresponded with the leading scientists of the day. One such man was Matthew Flinders (1751–1802), a surgeon, apothecary and man-midwife of Donington in Lincolnshire. Matthew lived in a two-storey brick-built house in the middle of the town with his shop attached to the house. He had some land and kept a horse and a cow. He had two servants – a maid and a boy. He fathered thirteen children by two wives. He served his apprenticeship in London under Richard Grindall, FRS, one of the surgeons extraordinary to the Prince of Wales and warden of the Surgeons Company in 1788.

Flinders inherited a practice from his father which was among rather poorer people than we might imagine Mr Perry's practice around Highbury to have been, and Flinders may not have been quite so 'gentlemanlike'. He was able to save money, typically between £150 and £200 each year, during the latter part of his career, and, inheriting property, left a fortune of about £6,000. So he was doing much better than the average medical man. He kept a horse, usually costing £10–£15 to buy, and very occasionally hired a chaise. Sometimes he and his wife would ride double on his poor horse, but in thirty years of successful professional life he never owned a carriage. So Perry's carriage would have been unlikely.

Moving up to four wheels, the costs rose considerably. A coach or carriage with four wheels would have cost about £40 a year in duty, repairs and other incidental expenses. Carriages needed new

wheels quite regularly and the value of the old set was by tradition a perquisite of the coachman. If we assume at least £130 for
four horses, then the retrenching Sir Walter Elliot in *Persuasion* was
saving himself a significant sum – perhaps £170 a year – in giving
up his carriage and four horses. 'The last office of the four carriage
horses was to draw Sir Walter, Miss Elliot, and Mrs Clay to Bath.'

Some coaches were not intended for rough travel. Sydney Smith
recorded a visit to his Yorkshire parsonage by Lord and Lady
Carlisle from Castle Howard:

> a cry was raised, that a coach and four, with outriders, was plung-
> ing about in the midst of a ploughed field near the house, and
> showing signals of distress. Ploughmen and ploughwomen were
> immediately sent off to the rescue, and at last the gold coach, as
> Lady Carlisle used to call it, which had mistaken the road, was
> guided safely up to the house, and the kind old Lord and Lady, not
> a little shaken, and a little cross at so rough a reception, entered the
> parsonage.[39]

Amongst four-wheeled carriages a barouche was particularly fine.
Lady Catherine de Bourgh has one. Of Mrs Ferrars it is said that
'it would have quieted her ambition to see him [Edward] driving a
barouche'.[40] Miss Elliot enjoys making it known that she is being
called for at a shop in Milsom Street, Bath, by Lady Dalrymple's
barouche. And then there is Mr Suckling's barouche-landau which
is so often mentioned by Mrs Elton.

In *Mansfield Park* Henry Crawford has a barouche with two men
to look after it. He is a young man of fortune, with an income of
£4,000 a year, and a good estate, Everingham, in Norfolk. Henry
collects his sister's harp from Northampton and also takes the
party to Sotherton in it. The barouche holds four people easily with
another on the box next to Henry, who drives it.

The barouche-landau – to which Mrs Elton refers – was a relatively new and originally fashionable type of carriage. The first
appearance of the barouche-landau (or landau barouche) can be
traced in the society columns of the *Morning Post*. On 5 January
1804 it was noted that:

Mr Buxton, the celebrated whip has just launched a new fangled
machine, a kind of nondescript. It is described by the inventor to
be the due medium between a landau and a barouche; but all who
have seen it say it more resembles a fish-cart or a music caravan.[41]

Mr Buxton must have been rather a character. In December 1804 he
was reported to have sold his set of four matched black horses and
to be driving a team made up of a black, a bay, a grey and a brown.

Mr Buxton was not alone – the Hon. Colonel Vaughan's new carriage was described as 'an elegant light landau, barouche fashion'[42]
built by Messrs Godsal, Baxter and Macklew of Long Acre.

The barouche-landau seems to have become associated with
the newly rich. It is mentioned (seven times) as the carriage of
Mrs Elton's brother-in-law, Mr Suckling. When Walter Scott's
novels became successful it was reported by Elizabeth Grant of
Rothiemurchus that 'a few acres began to be added to the recent
purchase of the old tower of Abbotsford, and Mrs Scott set up a
carriage, a barouche landau built in London, which from the time
she got it she was seldom out of.'[43] In fact, the truth was very different. Scott could not find for his wife, who had been ill, a little low
phaeton 'such as with a very quiet horse she may be able to drive
with her own fair hands'[44] for 30 guineas (harness included). He
wrote to enlist the help of the bibliophile Richard Heber in London
who, after much trouble, found a second-hand carriage 'built last
year at an established house in Long Acre'[45] and previously the
property of an elderly gentleman. With harness worth 6 guineas
it cost Scott £34–4–6 shipped to Scotland – less than the cost of a
gig. Charlotte Scott did drive it a lot. Her fond husband thought
she was the best lady whip in Edinburgh. One can see how envy
embroidered the facts.[46]

The number of horses pulling one's carriage made a difference
to the speed and comfort of the journey – no need to walk up hills
to spare the horses. Driving four was expensive for the reasons
noted previously. Sir Walter Elliot wants to know if the Crofts
travel with four horses. For the rich there was the added difficulty
that the duty on four-wheeled carriages and on horses would esca-
late as the numbers of each increased.

But some could still keep up the standards of a former age. Edward Vernon (later Harcourt) (1757–1847) was made Archbishop of York in 1807. He has been described as an exemplary prelate, an eloquent speaker and generous benefactor of his dioceses. He was the husband of one wife, the father of sixteen children and was remembered as the last Archbishop of York to be driven in a coach-and-six.

One economy was not to have carriage horses of one's own. In *Pride and Prejudice* the Hursts have no horses to their carriage and Mr Bennet's horses are often needed on the farm. In *Emma* The Crown keeps two post horses 'for the convenience of the neighbourhood'. In *The Watsons* even Osborne Castle has to order horses for two carriages to go to the ball.

In the winter months particularly, having a carriage in which to go out, especially at night, was a valued comfort. The Watsons do not have a closed carriage in which to go to balls and make do in daytime with an old chair drawn rather slowly by an old mare. Jane Austen had to decline invitations to dine in the winter months which were not fit for her donkey cart. Mary Musgrove complains that it is very uncomfortable not having a carriage of one's own – but then she complains about many things. Sir Thomas Bertram insists, against Mrs Norris' protestations, on Fanny and Edmund taking his carriage to dine with the Grants. Even the nervous Mr Woodhouse goes out at night in his carriage in the snow under the care of his coachman, James. Marianne Dashwood's idea of a proper establishment included 'a carriage, perhaps two'.

Not having a carriage could lead to social isolation unless, like Miss Bates, friends would send their carriages for you or, like Mrs Long in *Pride and Prejudice*, one came in a hack chaise. It is this well-understood aspect of gentle life that makes Fanny Dashwood's comments so unpleasant: 'they will live so cheap! Their housekeeping will be nothing at all. They will have no carriage, no horses and hardly any servants.'[47] Mrs Dashwood sells her carriage before moving to Barton. For the comfort of her children she would have kept it but the discretion of Elinor prevailed. Fortunately Sir John makes his carriage available to them. Not having a carriage has quite other results in *Pride and Prejudice* when Jane is stranded at

Netherfield by her mother's design.

We have seen that women could have their own carriages – typically when married or a widow, though Miss de Bourgh has a little phaeton and ponies. Sir Walter Elliot approves of Lady Russell's choice of carriage: 'Sir Henry Russell's widow, indeed, has no honours to distinguish her arms, but still, it is a handsome equipage.'[48] After marriage Anne Elliot has a 'very pretty landaulette'.[49] Mrs Gardiner hopes to drive right round Pemberley Park one day with Elizabeth in 'a low phaeton, with a nice little pair of ponies'.[50]

Just as with the Heywood's carriage in *Sanditon*, in real life not all carriages were new and glossy. The ever-practical Sydney Smith recorded that:

> it was suggested that a carriage was much wanted in the establishment; after diligently searching, I discovered in the back settlements of a York coachmaker an ancient green chariot, supposed to have been the earliest invention of the kind. I brought it home in triumph to my admiring family. Being somewhat dilapidated, the village tailor lined it, the village blacksmith repaired it; nay, (but for Mrs Sydney's earnest entreaties) we believe the village painter would have exercised his genius upon the exterior; it escaped this danger however, and the result was wonderful. Each year added to its charms: it grew younger and younger; a new wheel, a new spring; I christened it the *Immortal*; it was known all over the neighbourhood; the village boys cheered it, and the village dogs barked at it.[51]

Chapter 11

Single Gentlewomen

IT HAS BEEN ESTIMATED that between 7 and 10 per cent of women did not marry in the early nineteenth century. Like widows, spinsters had more legal rights than married women but often less independence. Jane Austen, famously remarked that 'Single Women have a dreadful propensity for being poor'.[1] Her own circumstances are well known.

To understand the position of unmarried and poor women we must know about the insults to which 'old maids' were generally subject, the family pressures upon them and the limited range of activities by which a gentlewoman might support herself – chiefly in education. Female education emphasized the acquisition of accomplishments. Such education was widely available so that eventually both the accomplishments and those thought capable of teaching them came to be poorly regarded.

The position of a poor single gentlewoman was not pleasant. In 1785 William Hayley described the stereotype as follows:

> it is probable, that after having passed the sprightly years of youth in the comfortable mansion of an opulent father, she is reduced to the shelter of some contracted lodging in a country town, attended by a single female servant, and with difficulty living on the interest of two or three thousand pounds, reluctantly, and perhaps

221

irregularly, paid to her by an avaricious or extravagant brother, who considers such payment as a heavy incumbrance on his paternal estate. Such is the condition in which the unmarried daughters of English gentlemen are too frequently found.[2]

Often spinsters did not live on their own but stayed at home – unpaid – looking after the elderly or being a nurse to an extended family. Jane Austen's sister Cassandra looked after their mother and helped Elizabeth with her many confinements at Godmersham.

In the novels Miss Bates is one such lady. Emma would never have been a poor old maid but could have found herself trapped by her selfish, hypochondriac father. Fanny Price was a subservient poor relative and even Anne Elliot is summoned to look after her sister Mary and her children.

Whether seen by men as a threat to male dominance, or by women as a threat to their husbands, spinsters were resented and often abused. The abuse and ridicule directed at 'old maids' betrays a set of values which the modern reader finds offensive.

It does explain, however, the willingness of Charlotte Lucas to marry Mr Collins, whom she knows to be neither sensible nor agreeable. His society is irksome and his attachment to her must be imaginary. Her parents can give her little fortune but married to Mr Collins she will one day be mistress of Longbourn. Her brothers are 'relieved from their apprehension of [her] ... dying an old maid'.[3] Of Charlotte Lucas we are told:

> Without thinking highly either of men or of matrimony, marriage had always been her object; it was the only honourable provision for a well-educated young woman of small fortune, and however uncertain of giving happiness, must be their pleasantest preservative from want. This preservative she had now obtained; and at the age of twenty-seven, without having ever been handsome, she felt all the good luck of it.[4]

One remembers that the youthful Marianne Dashwood felt that 'a woman of seven and twenty ... can never hope to feel or inspire affection again'[5] and that at twenty-nine Elizabeth Elliot is approaching the years of danger.

Emma Watson thinks differently:

> To be so bent on marriage, to pursue a man merely for the sake of situation, is a sort of thing that shocks me; I cannot understand it. Poverty is a great evil; but to a woman of education and feeling it ought not, it cannot be the greatest. I would rather be a teacher at a school (and I can think of nothing worse) than marry a man I did not like.[6]

The precarious position of women also explains another life path, more a last resort than a choice, which we see in the novels – that of becoming a mistress. At the end of *Persuasion* Mrs Clay is established in London under the protection of Mr Elliot. In *Pride and Prejudice* Lydia elopes with Wickham with no thought of marriage. In *Sense and Sensibility* Colonel Brandon's sister-in-law Eliza had an insufficient allowance after her divorce and thus sank 'deeper in a life of sin'. In *Lady Susan* Lady Vernon seems to have this course in mind when she writes: 'I am not an advocate for the prevailing fashion of acquiring a perfect knowledge of all Languages, Arts and Sciences. It is throwing time away; to be mistress of French, Italian, & German, Music, Singing, Drawing, etc. will gain a Woman some applause, but will not add one Lover to her list.'[7]

Charlotte Lucas was twenty-seven when she married. How old was a spinster or old maid depended on the age of the speaker, according to William Hayley:

> The misses of twenty considered all their unmarried friends, who had passed their thirtieth year, as absolute Old Maids. Those of thirty supposed the æra [era] to commence at about forty-five and some ladies of fifty convinced me how differently they thought upon the subject, by calling others, about three or four years younger than themselves, by the infantine appellation of girls, from whence I presumed they would advance the æra I speak of to the age of sixty at least.[8]

We are told that:

> To support such a change of situation, with that chearfulness [*sic*] and content which several of these fair sufferers possess, requires a noble firmness, or rather dignity of mind, a quality which many illustrious men have failed to exhibit in a similar reverse, and which ought therefore to be doubly honourable in these its more delicate possessors, particularly when we add, that the mortifications of their narrow fortune must be considerably embittered by their disappointment in the great object of female hope. Without the minutest breach of delicacy, we may justly suppose, that it is the natural wish and expectation of every amiable girl, to settle happily in marriage and that the failure of this expectation, from whatever causes it may arise, must be inevitably attended by many unpleasant, and many depressive sensations.[9]

There were, of course, exceptions – single women who did not succumb to the conventional plight. But we know about them only because they were so unusual. One was recorded as a lengthy footnote in *The State of the Poor* (1797):

> Sarah Spencer was the daughter of a gentleman in Sussex; her brother having once been High Sheriff of the county. But, her family possessing only a competent landed estate, and being neither engaged, nor in circumstances to engage, in any lucrative profession, like too many others in this age of universal commerce, insensibly dwindled to nothing; and though she had been well, and genteely, educated; and with such views as are common to people in her sphere of life, yet, on the demise of her father, she found her whole fortune did not amount to quite £300. Her sister Mary, a woman of perhaps not inferior goodness of heart, though certainly of very inferior abilities, was left in a similar predicament ... living in an age and country, in which well-educated women not born to fortunes are peculiarly forlorn: with no habit of exertion, nor even of a rigid frugality; they soon found, that, being thus unable to work, and ashamed to beg, they had no prospect but that of pining to death in helpless and hopeless penury ... at

a loss what else to do, they took a farm; and, without ceasing to be gentlewomen, commenced farmers … much to their credit and advantage.[10]

They were not popular at first and:

long experienced little else than discourtesies and opposition in their neighbourhood. The more active of them was called *Captain Sally*, and her sister her *Man Mary*. With the Gentry around them this was not the case: by these they were visited and respected as they deserved to be; and not seldom, in one and the same day, have they divided their hours in helping to fill the dung-cart and receiving company of the highest rank and distinction.[11]

The Spencer sisters were an unusual example of female enterprise and activity. In the sciences there were some rare women who earned modest amounts from their work. Caroline Herschel (1750–1848) worked with her brother but also discovered eight comets herself (at a time when less than thirty were known) and was awarded a pension of £50 by George III in 1787. She was jointly the first female member of the Royal Astronomical Society with Mary Somerville (1780–1872), the married daughter of an admiral, and an astronomer and mathematician. Mary's translation of Laplace, published as *The Mechanism of the Heavens*, made her famous. She was awarded a pension of £300 a year by the government in 1835. We may note that, ten years later, a Welsh woman Jemima Nicholas was also awarded a pension of £50 when she, armed only with a pitchfork, captured twelve French soldiers, and marched them to captivity in Fishguard Church.

But for every example of an exceptional woman who overcame prejudice, there are countless others who did not. One was the professional landscape painter Harriot Gouldsmith (1786–1863), who wrote in her memoirs:

The authoress of these pages, in one particular instance heard the highest praise bestowed upon a picture publicly exhibited, but she had the mortification afterwards to understand the commendation was in great measure retracted when the picture was understood to be the production of a female.[12]

In general, the supply of rather useless young women was growing. With increased prosperity and social mobility many women were optimistically educated for an elevated style of life. Clara Reeve commented on the fate of women educated above their fortunes:

> What numbers of young ladies of this stamp are turned out into the world to seek their fortunes; boasting of their good education, ignorant of everything useful, disdaining to match with their equals, aspiring to their superiors, with little or no fortune, unable or unwilling to work for themselves. Perhaps one in ten thousand of these may make her fortune, all the rest conclude they shall do the same; and thus they go on practising the air and graces of a fine lady till youth is past, and then discover, in after life, that they have been acting a part above them, without means to support it.[13]

For those who were single and poor, life was difficult. There were few activities in which a gentlewoman could engage without threatening her social position. Even taking in lodgers was an unfavourable social indicator. Gentlewomen could not engage in the activities open to women of other classes: dealing in second-hand clothes, pawnbroking, inn-keeping, running grocery shops, tea-dealing, bookselling, dealing in china and glass, for example. But what of women not over-burdened by notions of gentility? One possibility was a milliner's business, 'a haven for widows and orphans of shopkeepers in other trades, a rather genteel occupation for those with little capital but some knowledge of shop keeping'.[14]

Men had far more scope to engage in trade without sacrificing their gentle status. Sarah Ellis, writing in 1839, observed that:

> It is a curious anomaly in the structure of modern society, that gentlemen may employ their hours of business in almost any degrading occupation, and, if they have but the means of support-ing a respectable establishment at home, may be gentlemen still; while, if a lady does but touch any article, no matter how delicate,

in the way of trade, she loses caste, and ceases to be a lady.[15]

Concepts of gentility governed what most girls were taught. Even if a gentlewoman had wanted to engage in a trade, her education would have been a handicap. There were some exceptions. Jane Marcet's *Conversations on Chemistry, Intended More Especially for the Female Sex*, published in 1805 and her later *Conversations on Political Economy* (1816) were popular in England and in America.

There is evidence that during the first half of the nineteenth century the range of possibilities shrank. Clara Reeve commented even in 1785:

> It is a melancholy consideration, to think of the numbers of young women who are turned loose upon the world, over educated; without means to support themselves, and disqualified to earn their living. There are very few trades for women; the men have usurped two-thirds of those that used to belong to them; the remainder are overstocked.[16]

The opportunities for most women were limited. Sarah Ellis wrote:

> The only field at present open for what is considered lady-like employment, is that of educating the young; and hence the number of accomplished young women, too refined for common useful-ness, whose claims to public attention as governesses tend so much to reduce the value of their services in that important sphere.[17]

This is the background to a consideration of the plight of Jane Fairfax. Her situation in *Emma* does not seem enviable. Its apparent misery is in contrast to the newly married felicity of Mrs Weston, formerly Emma's governess. The talented daughter of an army officer, Jane is clearly a lady, but she is poor with a fortune of only £300. She has been living with the shadow of this future as a governess while enjoying 'all the rational pleasures of an elegant society' with the Campbells.

Resisting the vulgar Mrs Elton's offers of help to find her a post as a governess, Jane Fairfax says, 'There are places in town, offices, where inquiry would soon produce something – Offices for the sale – not quite of human flesh – but of human intellect.' Mrs Elton thinks she is referring to the slave trade. Jane corrects her; 'governess-trade ... was all that I had in view; widely different certainly as to the guilt of those who carry it on; but as to the greater misery of the victims, I do not know where it lies.'[18] Later she seems to be destined to look after the three little girls of a Mrs Smallridge, whose intimacy with Mrs Elton's sister at Maple Grove is possibly not much of a recommendation.

In the novels most governesses are ghostly shadows. In *Mansfield Park* there is Miss Lee to whom, according to Mrs Norris, it would be just the same 'whether she has three girls to teach, or only two – there can be no difference'. (Jane Austen would have known this to be untrue.) Lady Bertram took no interest in the education of her daughters. Miss Lee might be inferred to have had difficult pupils in the Bertram girls, who were admirably taught 'in everything but disposition'.[19] Fanny thought of her fondly. Miss Lee was astonished initially at Fanny's ignorance but taught her French and encouraged her. The fragility of a governess' position is indicated by the casual way in which is discussed the possibility that Miss Lee might suddenly lose her job if Fanny, then fifteen, goes to live with Mrs Norris.

There is the other, nameless governess in *Mansfield Park*, mentioned only because of taking the part of cottager's wife, a 'most trivial, paltry, insignificant part', in the private theatricals at Ecclesford. In *Persuasion* Anne Elliot calls on her old governess in Bath and thereby learns of the plight of her old friend Mrs Smith. And in *Pride and Prejudice* there is Miss Annesley, Georgiana Darcy's paid companion, 'a genteel, agreeable-looking woman, whose endeavour to introduce some kind of discourse, proved her to be more truly well-bred than either [Miss Bingley or Mrs Hurst]'.[20]

Jane Austen knew about the life of a single woman working as a governess or companion. Her 'excellent kind friend' Anne Sharpe was a governess at Godmersham. Jane wrote to Cassandra:

Pray say everything kind for us to Miss Sharpe, who could not regret the shortness of our meeting in Canterbury more than we did. I hope she returned to Godmersham as much pleased with Mrs Knight's beauty and Miss Mille's judicious remarks as those ladies respectively were with hers.[21]

(Le Faye, D. (ed.), *Jane Austen's Letters*, 4th edition (OUP, 2011). Reproduced by permission of Oxford University Press.)

Miss Sharpe's poor health prevented her continuing as a governess and she became for a while a companion to a Miss Bailey, an invalid. Jane knew of Miss Sharpe's tribulations, writing to Cassandra, 'She is born, poor thing! to struggle with Evil – & her continuing with Miss B is I hope a proof that Matters are not always so very bad between them, as her letters sometimes represent.'[22] Later Miss Sharpe was governess to the Pilkington family. Ten people were sent presentation copies of *Emma*: the Prince Regent, his librarian, the Countess of Morley, six of Jane Austen's relatives and Miss Sharpe. One of Jane Austen's last letters, written in May 1817, was to 'my dearest Anne'.[23]

A governess had relatively few opportunities to meet marriageable men. Jane Austen joked to Cassandra that 'a Widower with 3 children has no right to look higher than his daughter's governess'.[24] In 1808 one of their acquaintances, a Mr Robert Sloper, married a lady called Anne Prade, who had been the governess to his five illegitimate half-brothers and sisters.[25] The mild Miss Taylor, Emma's governess for sixteen years, is thought by Mr Knightley fit to be a wife to Mr Weston but not to be a governess for the clever, dominating Emma.

Aristocratic families had long employed gentlemen and gentlewomen. Such employees could be treated as gentle without threatening the social position of their employers. In the late eighteenth century the middle classes started to employ governesses in increasing numbers. Here the social relationship was more complex. A governess might be employed to educate the children of a newly rich family to whom she was in some senses socially superior. Without economic capital, a governess relied on her social and cultural capital to survive. This would have been the position of Jane Fairfax in Mrs Smallridge's family.

The market for governesses, and the great variety in pay, was described in *The Complete Servant* of 1825 as follows:

> As many mothers have an aversion to public education for their daughters, the system of private instruction, by a respectable and well-educated female, is very generally adopted, in many families of moderate fortune, and in all of rank and opulence. Hence there is a constant demand for females of genteel manners, and finished education, at salaries which vary according to qualifications, and number and age of pupils, between £25 and £120 per annum, and often improved, on certain great length of service, by some provision for life.
>
> Teachers in seminaries, half-boarders, educated for the purpose, and the unsettled daughters of respectable families of moderate fortune, who have received a finished education, are usually selected for this important duty; and the engagement is made either through an advertisement in the newspapers, or by agents who arrange between the parties for a moderate fee. But, in general, families apply to the governesses of public seminaries, who have young women in training for these employments.[26]

The book goes on to identify the qualities required of a governess which were, in the following order: good temper and good manners; a command of English and the ability to write a graceful letter; some knowledge of French and Italian; the ability to play the piano, and perhaps the harp or guitar; the ability to dance elegantly; a knowledge of arithmetic, needlework, geography, science, some philosophy, elegant literature, drawing, religion and morals. The same book goes on to emphasize the social isolation of a governess. She:

> will entitle herself to live on a footing with a family, when there are no special parties; and she must possess good sense enough not to intrude on that domestic privacy, and personal independence, which, without offence, is often desirable. Her own apartment, or that of her pupils, ought to be at once the scene of her pleasure and amusement, and if she mingles with the parties of the families, she

must, of course, not make herself too familiar with the domestic servants.[27]

The book is rather optimistic about arrangements for the retirement of the governess. It hopes that:

conducting herself with propriety, and identifying herself with the growing minds and affections of her pupils, she may secure their personal friendship to the end of their mutual lives, and if their moral feelings are not blunted, she may calculate on their gratitude in her old age, or if she survive them in their last will.[28]

The reality could be horribly different. Elizabeth Grant of Rothiemurchus remembered a governess who came to look after her and her brother in 1803–4, 'a young timid girl, a Miss Gardiner, quite new to her business, who was always in a fright lest neither we nor herself were doing right, and whom we soon tyrannised over properly.' She went on 'Poor Miss Gardiner! She was neither reasoning nor reasonable, too young for her situation, without sufficient mind, or heart, or experience for it, a mere school-girl'. The Grant children were not well behaved. When the governess was concentrating on writing a letter, Elizabeth and her brother William 'tied her by her dress and her feet to the legs of the chair and the table, so that as she rose from her engrossing composition, the crash that ensued was astounding, the fright and even pain not small.'[29]

So what was the education that a governess was hoped to impart? Maria and Richard Edgeworth wrote in their *Essays on Practical Education*:

Accomplishments, it seems, are valuable, as being the objects of universal admiration. Some accomplishments have another species of value, as they are tickets of admission to fashionable company. Accomplishments have another, and a higher species of value, as they are supposed to increase a young lady's chance of a prize in the matrimonial lottery. Accomplishments have also, a value as resources against *ennui*, as they afford continual amusement and innocent occupation.[30]

231

They continued:

> A young lady, they say, is nobody, and nothing, without accomplishments; they are as necessary to her as a fortune; they are indeed considered as part of her fortune, and sometimes are even found to supply the place of it. Next to beauty, they are the best tickets of admission into society which she can produce; and everybody knows, that on the company she keeps depends the chance of a young woman's settling advantageously in the world.[31]

The conservative-minded regretted the spread of accomplishments. Clara Reeve, writing in 1792, had one of her characters remark:

> Every rank and degree of people, bring up their children in a way above their situation and circumstances; they step over their proper place, and seat themselves upon a higher form. – they assume an air of consequence; and the children of farmers, artificers and mechanics, all come into the world as gentry. – They send them to the same schools with the first gentry in the county, and they fancy themselves their equals.[32]

The Edgeworths went on to point out that ambitious mothers should not:

> forget that everybody now makes the same reflections; that parents are, and have been for some years, speculating in the same line; consequently, the market is likely to be overstocked, and of course, the value of the commodities must fall. Every young lady (and every young woman is now a young lady) has some pretensions to accomplishments. She draws a little; or she plays a little; or she speaks French a little. Even the blue-board boarding schools, ridiculed by Miss Allscrip in the Heiress, profess to perfect young ladies in some or all of these necessary parts of education. Stop at any good inn on the London roads, and you will probably find that the landlady's daughter can show you some of her own framed drawings, can play a tune upon her spinnet, or support a dialogue in French of a reasonable length, in the customary questions and answers.[33]

We see this process in *Persuasion*. Henrietta and Louisa Musgrove are the daughters of a couple 'not much educated, and not at all elegant' but they have been to school in Exeter where they acquired 'the usual stock of accomplishments, and were now like thousands of other young ladies, living to be fashionable, happy and merry'.[34]

In *Sanditon* we encounter the two Miss Beauforts:

> they were very accomplished and very Ignorant, their time being divided between such pursuits as might attract admiration, and those Labours and Expedients of dexterous Ingenuity, by which they could dress in a style much beyond what they ought to have afforded; they were some of the first in every change of fashion. And the object of all was to captivate some Man of much better fortune than their own.[35]

They would have been nothing at Brighton, but could not move at Sanditon without notice.

Some accomplishments were less elevated. Tears were regarded as evidence of exquisite sensibility. A girl called Sophy Streatfield, a member of Dr Johnson's circle, was known for being able to cry at will while looking lovely. She was much admired by men.

Inevitably the once-rare became devalued. In *Pride and Prejudice* Charles Bingley says, 'I am sure I never heard a young lady spoken of for the first time, without being informed that she was very accomplished.'[36]

The Edgeworths noted the same thing:

> Accomplishments have lost much of that value which they acquired from opinion, since they have become common. They are now so common, that they cannot be considered as the distinguishing characteristics of even a gentlewoman's education. The higher classes in life, and those individuals who aim at distinction, now establish another species of monopoly, and secure to themselves a certain set of expensive masters in music, drawing, dancing, etc. They endeavour to believe, and to make others believe, that no one can be well educated without having served an apprenticeship of so many lessons under some of these privileged masters.[37]

We see evidence of this trend to greater sophistication when Lady Catherine de Bourgh tells Elizabeth that, 'Your mother should have taken you to town every spring for the benefit of masters'.[38] Colonel Campbell procured such masters for Jane Fairfax. Not all pupils benefited as much as Jane. The day that dismissed the music-master was one of the happiest of Catherine Morland's life. The Edgeworths went on to make an important point: 'In a wealthy mercantile nation there is nothing, which can be bought for money, that will long continue to be an envied distinction.'[39] Miss Bingley is herself an example of this – her fortune having been made in trade – and exactly confirms that comment of the Edgeworths. She says an accomplished woman:

> must have a thorough knowledge of music, singing, drawing, dancing and the modern languages, to deserve the word; and besides all this, she must possess a certain something in her air and manner of walking, the tone of her voice, her address and expression, or the word will be but half-deserved.[40]

Since foreign languages were thought to be a suitable subject for the young to study, poor English gentlewomen faced competition from similarly poverty-stricken French *emigrées* of good family. Not all the competition was from French gentlewomen. Maria and Richard Edgeworth wrote in their *Essays on Practical Education*:

> Some years ago, an opera-dancer at Lyons, whose charms were upon the wane, applied to an English gentleman for a recommendation to some of his friends in England, as a governess for young ladies. 'Do you doubt,' said the lady (observing that the gentleman was somewhat confounded by the easy assurance of her request), 'do you doubt my capability? Do I not speak good Parisian French? Have I any provincial accent? I will undertake to teach the language grammatically. And for music and dancing, without vanity, may I not pretend to teach them to any young person?' The lady's excellence in all these particulars was unquestionable. She was beyond dispute a highly accomplished woman. Pressed by her forcible interrogatories, the gentleman was compelled to hint that

an English mother of a family might be inconveniently inquisi-
tive about the private history of a person who was to educate her
daughters. 'Oh,' said the lady, 'I can change my name; and at my
age nobody will make farther inquiries.'[41]

If this seems far-fetched we might remember that Jane Austen's
headmistress at the Abbey School in Reading was a Mme La
Tournelle whose real name was Sarah Hackitt.

Education by a governess might often be superior to that by
a school. In 1789 Agnes Porter travelled by stage coach from
Wincanton to London with 'a Miss from Sherbourne school who,
as soon as we were seated, informed us where she had been educated, and assured us that Sherbourne was the very first place in
the world for female accomplishments'. Induced to sing by another
passenger, the girl then asked Miss Porter: 'Shinty vue [*chantez-
vous*], Madame?' Miss Porter wrote:

> I told her that I should understand her better if she spoke English.
> 'La, Ma'am, how I pity you! What, not speak French? I would not
> give up that accomplishment for the world' ... When the young
> woman and I were by ourselves I told her in French that, as I sup-
> posed our fellow travellers did not understand that language, I
> thought it better to decline the pleasure of answering her in French.
> She looked a little serious, and replied in English 'Ma'am, I am not
> so far in the French phrases.'[42]

In *Persuasion* Anne Elliot's proficiency in Italian – translating 'at
sight these inverted, transposed curtailed Italian lines into clear,
comprehensible elegant English' must have been acquired at the
school in Bath which she attended unhappily for three years after
her mother's death. On the other hand, Elinor Dashwood sees at
Mrs Jennings' house in London in what had been Charlotte's
bedroom a 'landscape in coloured silks of her performance, in
proof of her having spent seven years at a great school in town to
some effect'.[43] A more modest school is that run by Mrs Goddard in
Highbury, 'where a reasonable quantity of accomplishments were
sold at a reasonable price'.[44] It is clear that Jane Austen objected to

schools 'which professed, in long sentences of refined nonsense, to combine liberal acquirements with elegant morality, upon new principles and new systems – and where young ladies for enormous pay might be screwed out of health and into vanity'.[45]

Jane Austen may not have had very happy memories of her time at Mrs Cawley's school, where she fell gravely ill, but probably thought more fondly of Mrs La Tournelle's school in Reading. There are indications in her letters, too, that Jane Austen did not think very highly of schoolmistresses in general.

But even their supporters admitted that not all governesses were competent. A writer in *Fraser's Magazine* commented:

> Candour compels the acknowledgement, that while the respectable and meritorious are grievously underpaid, there are but too many in our profession who would be overpaid *at any price* … Is it not monstrous that while a lady will not give her dress to be made to anyone but a first-rate dress-maker, she will give her children to be educated by a second or third-rate governess? That she will commit their training for this world and the next to a woman whose only qualification for the task is, that she had a twelvemonth's apprenticeship in an inferior boarding school, or – that her father failed last week.[46]

The treatment governesses received varied. Agnes Porter, who was the daughter of the Reverend Francis Porter, Vicar of Wroughton in Wiltshire, was well and kindly treated by Lord Ilchester's family, better treatment than she received from subsequent employers. Maria Edgeworth described an ideal relationship which Agnes seems to have achieved:

> It is the interest of parents to treat the person who educates their children with that perfect equality and kindness which will conciliate her affection, and which will at the same time preserve her influence and authority over her pupils. And it is with pleasure we observe, that the style of behaviour to governesses, in well-bred families, is much changed within these few years. A governess is no longer treated as an upper servant, or as an intermediate being

between a servant and a gentlewoman; she is now treated as the friend and companion of the family, and she must, consequently, have warm and permanent interest in its prosperity: she becomes attached to her pupils from gratitude to their parents, from sympathy, from generosity, as well as from the strict sense of duty.[47]

A governess was always liable to slights. Agnes Porter recorded in her journal in October 1802:

Half an hour at Dr Hunt's. When I rose to come away Mrs Pryce, who sat next me and who is of a most obliging temper, offered to assist me with my cloak. Her husband made her a sign of disapprobation, and in some confusion she dropt the string and pretended to have her attention called another way. This little incident dwelt on my mind more, perhaps, than it merited. Perhaps after my departure he might hear something said to my advantage, for the next morning, on calling here, his address to me was very polite, but I had not forgotten and answered it with a very reserved silent curtesy. I watched Mrs Pryce's movements, to assist her with her cloak, and on his eyeing us I said, half smiling, half serious, 'Hail the small courtesies of life, for smooth do they make the road of it'. I looked up at Mr Pryce – he cast his eyes down – I had *my* revenge.[48]

The ambiguous position of a governess is evident from the next entry in her journal, in which Miss Porter records receiving letters from Lady Ilchester (for whom she had worked), Lady Charlotte Strangways (a former pupil) and Lady Sheffield.

We know that governesses were not well paid. The Edgeworths commented, optimistically, that the profession of governess should be better paid:

A profession we call it, for it should be considered as such; as an honourable profession, which a gentlewoman might follow without losing any degree of the estimation in which she is held by what is called the world. There is no employment, at present, by which a gentlewoman can maintain herself without losing something of that respect, something of that rank in society, which neither female fortitude nor male philosophy willingly foregoes. The liberal professions are open to men of small fortunes; by presenting one similar resource to women, we should give a strong motive for their moral and intellectual improvement.[49]

Miss Weeton as governess in the Pedder family in Ambleside in 1809 was paid 30 guineas. Mary Wollstonecraft was paid £40 a year to be governess to Lord Kingsborough's family at Mitchelstown in County Cork in the 1780s. Both were quite well paid. Customary wages were about £20–£30 a year with lodging. But a governess had to pay for her clothes – as much as half her wage. Some governesses were paid more, perhaps as much as £100, if they had particular accomplishments, but it was very rare.

The Edgeworths' proposal of £300 a year was a fantasy:

To educate the daughters of the nobility Three hundred a year, for twelve or fourteen years, the space of time which a preceptress must probably employ in the education of a young lady, would be a suitable compensation for her care. With this provision she would be enabled, after her pupil's education was completed, either to settle in a family of her own, or she would in the decline of life be happily independent, secure from the temptation of marrying for money.[50]

In *Emma* the bleak outlook is evident in Miss Bates's efforts to be cheerful about Jane's future with Selina Suckling, 'a life of pleasure' and a huge salary, which we and Emma know might have been £30 a year. Miss Bates says all this to Emma whose own income would have been about £1,500 or so. The fates of Jane and Emma seem set to be very different.

It was almost impossible for a governess to save for the future. They relied on the largesse of their kinder employers. In the case of Agnes Porter, Lord Ilchester made her an annual payment of £30 after she had left the family but the income disappeared at his death in 1802.[51] He had left a codicil leaving her 100 guineas a year for life but there was doubt about its validity and it seemed as if it could not be paid until his heir came of age in 1808.

Poverty in old age or in sickness faced most governesses. An Asylum for Aged Governesses was opened by the Duke of Cambridge in 1849. A writer in *Fraser's Magazine* in 1848 noted that:

> governesses can rarely provide for old age or contingencies. But why? Because the emolument received by governesses (however superior) is not sufficient to enable a person, required to keep up the appearance of a gentlewoman, to do so ... The profession of a private governess is the only profession which offers no premium to distinguished abilities, and we see the results, unhappily, every day.[52]

This was the fate from which Jane Fairfax consented to be rescued by the rather moderate Frank Churchill. It is, in an extreme form, the fate that threatens most of Jane Austen's heroines. Fanny Price is similarly genteel but destitute. Neither the Dashwood sisters, Elizabeth Bennet, Catherine Morland nor Anne Elliot are threatened with such poverty, but all face a more or less grim future without marriage. Only Emma, both handsome and rich, could afford not to marry.

Statistical Appendix

CONTENTS

A contemporary estimate of the United Kingdom and Ireland in 1811[1]

	Heads of families	Total persons
The Royal Family, the Lords Spiritual and Temporal, the Great Officers of State, and all above the degree of a Baronet, with their families	576	2,880
Baronets, Knights, Country Gentlemen, and others having large incomes, with their families	46,861	234,305
Dignified Clergy, Persons holding considerable employments in the State, elevated situations in Law, eminent Practitioners in Physic, considerable Merchants, Manufacturers upon a large scale, and Bankers of the first order, with their families	12,200	61,000
Persons holding inferior situations in the Church and State, respectable Clergymen of different persuasions, Practitioners in Law and Physic, Teachers of Youth, of the superior order, respectable Freeholders, Ship Owners, Merchants and Manufacturers of the second class, Warehousemen and respectable Shopkeepers, Artists, respectable Builders, Mechanics, and Persons living on moderate incomes, with their families	233,650	1,168,230
Lesser Freeholders, Shopkeepers of the second order, Innkeepers, Publicans and Persons engaged in miscellaneous occupations, or living on moderate incomes, with their families	564,799	2,798,475
Working Mechanics, Artisans, Handicrafts, Agricultural Labourers, and others, who subsist by labour in various employments, with their families	2,126,095	8,792,800
Menial Servants		1,279,923
Paupers, and their families, Vagrants, Gipsies, Rogues, vagabonds, and idle disorderly persons, supported by criminal delinquency	387,100	1,828,170

To which should be added the army and navy:

	Heads of families	Total persons
Officers of the Army, Navy, and Marines, including all officers on half-pay and superannuated, with their families	10,500	69,000
Non-commissioned Officers in the Army, Navy, and Marines, Soldiers, Seamen, and Marines, including Pensioners of the Army, Navy, etc., and their families	120,000	862,000

A contemporary estimate of the incomes of the richer part of society in 1812[2]

	Number of families	Average annual income of each family (£)	Aggregate income of that class (£)
The Royal Family (extended)	12	41,750	501,000
Peers	516	10,000	5,160,000
Bishops	48	5,010	240,480
Baronets	861	3,510	3,022,110
Eminent merchants, bankers, etc.	3,500	2,600	9,100,000
Knights and Esquires	11,000	2,000	22,000,000
Persons in higher Civil Offices	3,500	980	3,430,000
Lesser merchants trading by sea, including brokers, etc.	22,800	805	18,354,000
Persons employing capital in building & repairing ships	500	804	402,000
Manufacturers employing capital	44,000	804	35,376,000
Principal Warehousemen, selling by wholesale	900	804	723,600
Gentlemen & Ladies living on incomes	35,000	800	28,000,000
Eminent Clergymen	1,500	720	1,080,000
Ship Owners letting ships for freight	8,750	600	5,250,000
Persons educating youth in Universities and chief schools	874	600	524,400
People keeping Houses for Lunatics	70	500	35,000
Judges, barristers, attorneys, clerks, etc.	19,000	400	7,600,000
Physicians, surgeons, apothecaries, etc.	18,000	300	5,400,000
Persons employing professional skill & capital as Engineers, Surveyors, Master Builders of Houses, etc.	8,700	300	2,610,000

Retail price inflation and deflation (1790–1819)[3]

Year	%	Year	%	Year	%
1790	2.88	1800	21.69	1810	2.26
1791	-0.65	1801	5.98	1811	-2.21
1792	-1.22	1802	-14.68	1812	8.94
1793	3.8	1803	-2.23	1813	2.08
1794	2.1	1804	3.77	1814	-6.72
1795	11.2	1805	8.44	1815	-5.56
1796	5.08	1806	0.06	1816	-3.24
1797	-5.06	1807	1.9	1817	4.54
1798	-1.62	1808	2.05	1818	0.29
1799	7.14	1809	7.48	1819	-3.76

In the thirty-year period of 1790–1819 inflation in the United Kingdom averaged 1.58 per cent. However, the period was very volatile and the average figure includes an annual inflation figure of 21.69 per cent (1800) and an annual deflation figure of -14.68 per cent (1802).

Annual average yield on 3 per cent Consols (1790–1817)[4]

Year	Price [£. s. d.]	Yield %
1790	76 7/8	3.90
1791	83 3/4	3.58
1792	90	3.33
1793	75 3/4	3.96
1794	68 3/16	4.40
1795	66 3/8	4.52
1796	62 1/2	4.80
1797	50 13/16	5.90
1798	50 1/2	5.94
1799	59 3/16	5.07
1800	63 11/16	4.71
1801	61	4.92
1802	70 15/16	4.23
1803	60 1/8	4.99
1804	56 5/8	5.30
1805	59 1/2	5.04
1806	61 5/8	4.87
1807	61	4.92
1808	65 15/16	4.55
1809	66 13/16	4.49
1810	67 1/8	4.47
1811	64 1/4	4.67
1812	59	5.08
1813	61	4.92
1814	61	4.92
1815	67	4.48
1816	59 3/4	5.02
1817	73 3/16	4.10

The pay and allowances of naval officers in November 1814[5]

Rank	Net Annual Pay* £. s. d.	Income Tax** £. s. d.	After tax income £. s. d.
Captain of 1st Rate (837 men)	802–0–2	80–4–0	721–16–2
Captain of 6th Rate (135 men)	284–7–9	28–8–9	255–19–0
Commander of sloop etc. (<121 men)	272–19–7	27–5–11	245–13–4
Commander of sloop etc. (<75 men)	250–2–11	25–0–3	225–2–8
Lieutenant in Flagship	128–4–5	11–14–11	116–9–6
Lieutenant in other ships	112–4–2	10–7–8	100–15–0

*Net Annual Pay is shown after deduction of three pence per pound for the Widows' Fund, a shilling per month to the Chatham Chest and sixpence per month to the Royal Hospital at Greenwich.

**Income tax at 10% on incomes over £150, graded to nil for incomes under £50.

The pay of admirals was complicated but, broadly, a rear-admiral might have a gross income of £823 and the admiral and commander-in-chief perhaps £2,857.[6]

The half-pay of naval officers (1814)[6]

When a naval officer was not at sea he received so-called 'half-pay' at a daily rate as follows:

Rank	Before 1814	After 1814
Admiral of the Fleet	£3–0–0	£3–3–0
Admiral	£2–0–0	£2–2–0
Vice-Admiral	£1–10–0	£1–12–0
Rear-Admiral	£1–2–6	£1–5–0
Captain	From 7/- to 12/-	From 10/6 to 14/9
Commander	6/6	From 8/6 to 10/6
Lieutenant	From 4/- to 5/-	From 5/- to 7/-

Midshipmen received no half-pay at all.

Among captains the most senior 100 received the highest amount, the next 150 an intermediate figure, and all the rest the lowest. Among lieutenants, the top 300 received the maximum, the next 700 a middling sum, and the great remainder – some 3,000 – received the minimum. For lieutenants, their half-pay was substantially more than half their full pay which was 6 s. a day – indeed, for the top 300 half-pay was more.

The cost of a horse (1827)[7]

	£.	s.	d.
Oats – Three quarterns per day, making 5 ½ pecks per week	0	4	6
Hay – About 1½ truss at 3s. per truss, or £4 4s. per load	0	4	6
Straw – One truss per week	0	1	6
Food, per week	0	10	6
Forty-six weeks, in the stable, at 10s. 6d	24	3	0
Six weeks grass, in the Spring, at 5s	1	10	0
Food, per annum	25	13	0
Shoeing, Farriery, and incidental Expenses	1	18	3
Duty (for one Horse)	1	8	9
Annual Loss, or Wear & Tear of the Horse, 10% on its value, say £25	2	10	0
Expense of the Horse, exclusive of the Groom and Stable Rent	31	10	0
Occasional Groom, 46 weeks, at 3s. 3d. per week, and Duty 10s	7	18	0
Stable-Rent, 1s. per week	2	18	0
Total Costs	**£42**	**6**	**0**

The cost of carriages (1827)[8]

A Chaise, Tilbury, Gig, or other Carriage, with less than four wheels, drawn by one horse:

	£.	s.	d.
Duty	3	6	0
Repairs, and Wear and Tear of the Wheels and Carriage	6	2	0
Repairs, and Wear and Tear of the Harness, & other Expenses	2	12	0
Total	**12**	**0**	**0**

A Curricle, or other Carriage, with less than four wheels, and drawn by two or more horses:

	£.	s.	d.
Duty	4	10	0
Repairs, and Wear and Tear of the Carriage & Harness, etc.	10	10	0
Total	**15**	**0**	**0**

A Coach, Chariot, Phaeton, or other Carriage, with four wheels:

	£.	s.	d.
Duty	6	0	0
Repairs, and Wear and Tear of the Carriage	26	0	0
Repairs, and Wear and Tear of the Harness, etc.	4	0	0
Whips, Brushes, Oil, and other Incidental Expenses	4	0	0
Total	**40**	**0**	**0**

The duty on horses for riding or drawing carriages (1827)[9]

No. of horses	Duty per horse £. s. d.	Duty per annum £. s. d.
1	1 8 9	1 8 9
2	2 7 3	4 14 6
3	2 12 3	7 16 9
4	2 15 0	11 0 0
5	2 15 9	13 18 9
6	2 18 0	17 8 0
7	2 19 9	20 18 3
8	2 19 9	23 18 0
9	3 0 9	27 6 9
10	3 3 6	31 15 0
11	3 3 6	34 18 6
12	3 3 6	38 2 0
13	3 3 9	41 8 9
14	3 3 9	44 12 6
15	3 3 9	47 16 3
16	3 3 9	51 0 0
17	3 4 0	54 8 0

Duty on carriage with four wheels

No. of carriages	Duty per carriage £. s. d.	Duty per annum £. s. d.
1	6 0 0	6 0 0
2	6 10 0	13 0 0
3	7 0 0	21 0 0
4	7 10 0	30 0 0
5	7 17 6	39 7 6
6	8 4 0	49 4 0
7	8 10 0	59 10 0
8	8 16 0	70 8 0
9	9 1 0	81 13 6

The Bingleys' Servants

If we assume that Mr and Mrs Bingley had an income of £5,000 per year, we can estimate the number and type of servants they might have had, as well as their wages.[10]

	Wages	Livery	Duty			Total		
Female Servants	£	£	£.	s.	d.	£.	s.	d.
Housekeeper	26							
Lady's Maid	21							
Nurse	20							
Cook	20							
Housemaid	18 18s							
Under Housemaid	14							
Laundry Maid	12 12s							
Kitchen Maid	10							
Still Room Maid	10							
Male Servants								
Butler	50		3	16	6	53	16	6
Valet	29	15	3	16	6	47	16	6
Footman	27	16	3	16	6	46	16	6
Under Footman	20	15	3	16	6	38	16	6
Coachman	33	21	3	16	6	57	16	6
Groom	27	16	3	16	6	46	16	6
Second Groom	24	14	3	16	6	41	16	6
Under Groom	21	12	3	16	6	36	16	6
Assistant	26		3	16	6	29	16	6
Gardener	27		3	16	6	30	16	6
Second Gardener	26		3	16	6	29	16	6
Under Gardener	25		3	16	6	28	16	6
Totals	**£487-10-0**	**£109-0-0**	**£45-18-0**			**£642-8-0**		

Mrs Bingley's housekeeping

Here is an estimate of what Mrs Bingley's housekeeping might have been.

The family consisting of Mr & Mrs Bingley and three children, with an establishment of thirteen male and nine female servants (in all twenty-seven persons):

	£.	s.	d.
Bread and Flour: for twenty-seven persons (1s each)	1	7	0
Butter: 1lb each (or 27 lb) at 1s	1	7	0
Butcher's meat: 1 lb per day each, or 189 lb at 7d per lb	5	10	3
Fish, poultry, etc., at 9s 3d a day	3	4	9
Beer or ale: 2 quarts each, per day, or 94½ gallons, at 8d	3	3	0
Other liquors: 1s per day	3	17	0
Cheese: ¾ lb per week each, or 20½ lb at 10½d.	0	18	0
Garden-produce: gardener's wages and duty	0	16	0
Grocery of all kinds (except tea and sugar): 1s each	1	7	0
Sugar: 1 lb each per week (or 27 lb) at 10d per lb	1	2	6
Tea, coffee, etc., (servants finding their own)	0	14	0
Milk and eggs, produce of four cows, and the poultry (9d each)	1	0	3
Total for provisions, weekly (being £1,265 11s per annum)	24	6	9
Coals and wood: for 20 fires (average 2s 6d per week, for each fire)	2	10	0
Candles, gas and oil	2	2	0
Soap, starch, blue, etc., for washing (4s a day)	1	8	0
Sundries for cleaning, scouring, etc. (4s a day)	1	8	0
Extra for entertainments, per annum	100	0	0
Medicine, medical assistance, etc., per annum	50	0	0
Total housekeeping	**£1,800 per annum**		

Endnotes

Foreword

1 Extract from 'Letter to Byron', in Auden, W.H. and MacNeice, L. (1937), *Letters from Iceland*. London: Faber & Faber.

Preface

1 Mullan, J. (2012), *What Matters in Jane Austen?* London: Bloomsbury.

2 *Sense and Sensibility*, Chapter 5.

3 Letter to Cassandra, dated 1–2 October 1808, in Le Faye, D. (2011), *Jane Austen's Letters*, 4th edition. Oxford: Oxford University Press, p.147.

4 Southey, R. (1807c), *Letters from England, by Don Manuel Alvarez Espriella*. London: Longman, Hurst, Rees and Orme. Vol. III, pp.70–2.

5 Southey, R. (1807b), *Letters from England, by Don Manuel Alvarez Espriella*. London: Longman, Hurst, Rees and Orme. Vol. II, p.145.

6 Ibid, pp.116–7.

7 Ibid, p.141.

8 Le Faye, D. (2002), *Jane Austen's 'Outlandish Cousin', The Life and Letters of Eliza de Feuillide*. London: British Library, p.113.

9 Southey (1807c), pp.119–20.

10 See for example, Officer, L.H. and Williamson, S.H., *Five Ways to Compute the Relative Value of a UK Pound Amount, 1270 to Present*, Measuring Worth (2015). www.measuringworth.com/ukcompare/ (accessed June 2015).

11 A Retail Price Index, expressed with 2010 being equal to 100, shows the figure in 1800 to have been 1.588 and the figure in 2014 to be 114.51. That is a multiplier of 72.11. See Clark, G., 'What Were the British Earnings and Prices Then? (New Series),' Measuring Worth, 2015. www.measuringworth.com/ukearncpi (accessed June 2015).

12 His net income would have been £4,500. Multiplied by 72.11, in 2014 this gives us a net income of £324,500, which would be equivalent to a gross income of about

£540,000 (using modern tax rates averaging roughly 40 per cent).

13 The average annual earnings figure in 1800 was £23.58 and in 2014 it was £25,028.60, giving a multiplier of 1061.4. See Clark, G., 'What Were the British Earnings and Prices Then? (New Series),' Measuring Worth, 2015. www.measuringworth.com/ukearncpi.

14 *Emma*, Chapter 49.

CHAPTER 1 SOCIAL CHANGE

1 Colquhoun, P. (1814), *A Treatise on the Wealth, Power and Resources of the British Empire*, first edition, pp.106–7.

2 Ibid, pp.43 and 35.

3 Ibid, p.42.

4 Ibid, p.29.

5 Colquhoun, P. (1815), *A Treatise on the Wealth, Power, and Resources of the British Empire*, second edition, pp.46–7.

6 Ibid, p.68.

7 Southey, R. (1807b), *Letters from England, by Don Manuel Alvarez Espriella*. London: Longman, Hurst, Rees and Orme. Vol. II, p.118.

8 Southey, R. (1807c), *Letters from England, by Don Manuel Alvarez Espriella*. London: Longman, Hurst, Rees and Orme. Vol. III, p.135.

9 *Emma*, Chapter 36.

10 Entry for 4 July 1781, in Andrews, C.B. (ed.) (1934), *The Torrington Diaries*. London: Eyre & Spottiswoode, Vol.1, pp.48–9.

11 Southey (1807b), p.158.

12 Bisset, J. (1800), *A Poetic Survey round Birmingham with a Brief Description of the Different Curiosities of the Place, intended as a Guide to Strangers*, p.29. James Bisset (c. 1762–1832) was born in Perth, and made money as a maker of ornamental goods and medals and as an art-dealer. He established a museum and picture gallery in 1808 in New Street, Birmingham – the city's first. He may be seen wearing a tall hat in a painting known as 'John Freeth and his Circle or Birmingham Men of the last Century' by Johannes Eckstein (Birmingham Museums and Art Gallery). See also Davidoff, L. and Hall, C. (1987), *Family Fortunes: Men and Women of the English Middle Class 1780–1850*, pp.416–20.

13 Dewey, C. (1991), *The Passing of Barchester*. London: Hambledon Continuum, pp.131–4.

14 See Slothouber, L., 'Bingley's Four or Five Thousand and Other Fortunes from the North', *Persuasions*, 35, pp.50–63.

15 *The Gentleman's Magazine* (1792), Vol. 62, p.770.

16 *The Gentleman's Magazine* (1843), Vol. 173, pp.656–7.

17 *Emma*, Chapter 25.

18 *Mansfield Park*, Chapter 27.

19   Ibid, Chapter 13.

20   *Pride and Prejudice*, Chapter 25.

21   *Northanger Abbey*, Chapter 22.

22   Letter written by Jane Austen, dated 9–10 January 1796, in Le Faye, D. (2011), *Jane Austen's Letters*, 4th edition. Oxford: Oxford University Press, p.2.

23   Thompson, F.M.L. (2001), *Gentrification and the Enterprise Culture: Britain 1780–1980*. Oxford: Oxford University Press, p.99. Reproduced by permission of Oxford University Press.

24   *Emma*, Chapter 32.

25   Le Faye, D. (2011), *Jane Austen's Letters*, 4th edition. Oxford: Oxford University Press.

26   *Pride and Prejudice*, Chapter 34.

27   *Pride and Prejudice*, Chapter 58.

28   *Pride and Prejudice*, Chapter 56.

29   *Persuasion*, Chapter 3.

30   *Persuasion*, Chapter 3.

31   *The Gentleman's Magazine*, 6 July 1810, p.14.

32   Ibid, p. 14.

33   *The Gentleman's Magazine*, 31 August 1810, p.30.

34   Ibid, p.30.

35   *Emma*, Chapter 2.

36   *Persuasion*, Chapter 9.

37   Rogers, N., 'Money, Land and Lineage: The Big Bourgeoisie of Hanoverian London', *Social History*, Vol. 4 (1979), p.439n.

38   Ibid, p.444.

39   Entry for 9 November 1818 in Rush, R., (1833), *Residence at the Court of London*. London: Richard Bentley, p.330.

40   Entry for 21 Feb 1827 in Henry Reeve (ed.), *The Greville Memoirs*, Vol. 1 (1874), pp.90–1.

41   Southey (1807c), p.122.

42   Letter marked 'Foston' and dated 25 November 1816, in Smith, Nowell C. (ed.) (1953), *The Letters of Sydney Smith*. Oxford: Clarendon Press, pp.269–70.

43   Southey, Robert (1807a), *Letters from England, by Don Manuel Alvarez Espriella*. London: Longman, Hurst, Rees and Orme. Vol. I, pp.169–70.

44   Grant, E. (1911), *Memoirs of a Highland Lady: The Autobiography of Elizabeth Grant of Rothiemurchus*. London: John Murray, pp.360–1.

45   Ibid, pp.360–1.

Chapter 2 Incomes and Taxation

1   Colquhoun, P. (1815), *A Treatise on the Wealth, Power and Resources of the British Empire*, second edition, pp.124–5.

2   Copeland, E., 'What's a Competence? Jane Austen, her sister novelists and the 5%'s', *Modern Language Studies*, Vol. 9, No. 3 (1979), pp.161–8.

3   West, J., (1797), *A Gossip's Story* (London: publisher unknown), pp.39–40; quoted in Copeland, 'What's a Competence? Jane Austen, her sister novelists and the 5%'s' in *Modern Language Studies*, Vol. 9, No. 3 (1979).

4   *Sense and Sensibility*, Chapter 17.

5   Copeland, E. (1995), *Women Writing about Money: Women's Fiction in England, 1790–1820*. Cambridge: Cambridge University Press, p.24.

6   *Mansfield Park*, Chapter 3.

7   Colquhoun (1815), p.65.

8   O'Brien, P.K., 'The Political Economy of British Taxation 1660–1815', *The Economic History Review*, Vol. 41, No. 1 (February 1988), p.2.

9   Slothouber, L., 'Bingley's Four or Five Thousand and Other Fortunes from the North', *Persuasions*, 35 (2013), p.38.

10   *Mansfield Park*, Chapter 9.

11   For Philip Godsal's tax payments, see Ford, J. (2005) *Coachmaker, the Life and Times of Philip Godsal 1747–1826* (Shrewsbury: Quiller), pp.162–6.

12   Beardsley, M. and Bennett, N. (eds) (2007–9), *Gratefull to Providence: The Diary and Accounts of Matthew Flinders, 1775–1802*. Woodbridge: The Lincoln Record Society/Boydell Press, p.204.

13   de Selincourt, Ernest (ed.) (1967), *The Letters of William and Dorothy Wordsworth*, 2nd edition. Oxford: Clarendon Press, Vol. I, p.657.

14   Jackson, T.V., 'British incomes circa 1800', *Economic History Review*, Vol. 52, No. 2 (1999), p.263.

15   *Sense and Sensibility*, Chapter 37.

16   Ford, J. (2005), p.165.

17   Jackson, T.V. (1999), p.274.

18   Letter to Phylly Walter, dated 11 December 1797, in Le Faye, D. (2002), *Jane Austen's 'Outlandish Cousin': The Life and Letters of Eliza de Feuillide*. London: British Library, p.150.

19   Letter to Francis Jeffery, dated 30 January 1806, in Smith, N.C. (ed.) (1953), *The Letters of Sydney Smith*. Oxford: Clarendon Press, pp.111–12.

Chapter 3 Land and Settlements

1   Mingay, G.E. (1963), *English Landed Society in the Eighteenth Century*. London: Routledge & Kegan Paul, p.3.

2   G.E. Mingay (1963), p.273.

3   D'Archenholz, M. (1789), *A Picture of England containing a Description of the Laws, Customs and Manners of England, translated from the French.* London: Edward Jeffery, pp.26–7.

4   Figures quoted in O'Brien, P.K., 'British Incomes and Property in the early nineteenth century', *The Economic History Review*, Vol. 12, No. 2 (1959), pp.255–67.

5   Colquhoun, P. (1815), *A Treatise on the Wealth, Power and Resources of the British Empire*, second edition, p.326.

6   *Mansfield Park*, Chapter 3.

7   Colquhoun (1815), p.327.

8   Ibid, p.386, note F.

9   *Sanditon*, Chapter 7.

10 Habakkuk, J. (1993), *Marriage, Debt and the Estates System.* Oxford: Clarendon Press, p.47.

11 Ibid, p.2.

12 Ward, J.T., 'The Beaumont Family Estates in the Nineteenth Century', *Bulletin of the Institute of Historical Research*, Vol. 35 (1962), pp.169–77.

13 Bonnard, G.A. (ed.) (1966), *Edward Gibbons: Memoirs of My Life.* London: Nelson, p.149.

14 Ibid, p.154.

15 Ibid, p.24.

16 Letter to William Godwin, 24 November 1816, in Jones, F.L. (ed.) (1964), *The Letters of Percy Bysshe Shelley.* Oxford: Oxford University Press, Vol. 1, p.514.

17 Letter to William Godwin, 25 January 1816 in Jones (1964), p.445.

18 See Greene, D., 'The Originals of Pemberley', in *Eighteenth Century Fiction*, Vol. 1 (October 1988), pp.1–23.

19 Spring, D. (1963), *The English Landed Estate in the Nineteenth Century: Its Administration.* Baltimore: Johns Hopkins Press, pp.35–7.

20 Habakkuk (1993), p.356.

21 Spring (1963), p.183. The figures are from 1848.

22 Ibid, p.191. The figures are from 1832.

23 Habakkuk (1993), pp.300–1.

24 Simond, L. (1817), *Journal of a Tour and Residence in Great Britain during the Years 1810 and 1811*, 2nd edition. Edinburgh: Archibald Constable and Company, Vol. 2, pp.75–6.

25 Habakkuk (1993), p.86.

26 Ibid, p.227.

27 Bovill, E.W. (1962), *English Country Life.* London and New York: Oxford University Press, pp.6–9.

28 Letter from Jane Austen, dated 6 June 1811, in Le Faye, D. (ed.) (2011), *Jane Austen's Letters*, 4th edition. Oxford: Oxford University Press, p.201.

29   Slothouber, L. (2015), *Jane Austen: Edward Knight & Chawton: Commerce and Community*. Gaithersburg: Woodpigeon Publishing, pp. 32–3.

30   Sambrook, P. (2003), *A Country House at Work: Three Centuries of Dunham Massey*. London: National Trust Books, p.145.

31   Andrews, C.B. (ed.) (1934–8), *The Torrington Diaries*. London: Eyre & Spottiswoode, Vol.I, p.213.

32   Ibid, Vol.II, p.16.

33   *Persuasion*, Chapter 11.

Chapter 4 Poverty

1   Morton Eden, Sir Frederic (1797), *The State of the Poor*, Vol. 1. London: J. Davis, p.359.

2   *Emma*, Chapter 10.

3   Letter dated 24 December 1798, in Le Faye, D. (ed.) (2011), *Jane Austen's Letters*, 4th edition. Oxford: Oxford University Press, p.32.

4   See Piggott, P., 'Jane Austen's Southampton Piano', in the Collected Reports 1976–1985 of the Jane Austen Society, pp.146–9.

5   *Pride and Prejudice*, Chapter 30.

6   *Emma*, Chapter 10.

7   Morton Eden (1797), Vol. 2, p.137.

8   Ibid, pp.546–7, where the village is spelt 'Rode'.

9   It is estimated that farmworkers probably worked about 300 days each year. Farm work is seasonal with harvest and hay-making being peak times – together lasting about eight weeks. Harvest-time wages were roughly 1.5 times winter wages. Some labourers were temporary, some permanent; some might be men in their prime, others might be women, girls, boys or old men – all of whom were paid much less; some wages were paid with beer, food and even housing, some not. Farm accounts do not often make these things clear. See Clark, G., 'Farm Wages and Living Standards in the Industrial Revolution: England 1670–1869', *The Economic History Review*, Vol. 54, No. 3 (August 2001), pp.477–505.

10   Clark (2001), p.485, Table 4.

11   Ibid, p.496, Table 9.

12   Cozens-Hardy, B. (ed.) (1968), *Mary Hardy's Diary*. Norwich: Norfolk Records Society, p.9.

13   Horrell, S. and Humphries, J., 'Women's Labour Force Participation 1790–1865', in *Economic History Review*, Vol. 48, No. 1 (1995), p.102, Table 2.

14   See, for example, Burnette, J., 'An Investigation of the Female–Male Wage Gap during the Industrial Revolution in Britain', *Economic History Review*, Vol. 50, No. 2 (1997), pp.257–81, and particularly Table 1, pp.258–9.

15   Burnette (1997), p.265.

16   *Emma*, Chapter 39.

17 Horrell, S. and Humphries, J., 'Families' Living Standards, 1787–1865', *Journal of Economic History*, Vol. 52, No. 4 (1992), p.858n.

18 Snell, K.D.M., 'English Rural Societies and Geographical Marital Endogamy, 1700–1837', *Economic History Review*, Vol. 55, No. 2 (2002), pp.286–7.

19 *Emma*, Chapter 43.

20 Officer, L.H. and Williamson, S.H., 'Annual Inflation Rates in the United States, 1775–2013, and United Kingdom, 1265–2013', Measuring Worth. URL: www.measuringworth.com/uscompare (accessed 2013).

21 Morton Eden (1797), Vol. 3, Appendix XIII, p.cccli.

22 General Report on Enclosures, drawn up by order of the Board of Agriculture (1808). London: McMillan printers, Appendix IV, pp.152–3.

23 Morton Eden (1797), Vol. 1, p.xviii.

24 Ibid, p.xviii.

25 General Report on Enclosures, drawn up by order of the Board of Agriculture (1808). Appendix III, p.149.

26 Ibid, Appendix V, p.166.

27 Southey, R. (1807a), *Letters from England, by Don Manuel Alvarez Espriella*. London: Longman, Hurst, Rees and Orme. Vol. I, p.30.

28 General Report on Enclosures, drawn up by order of the Board of Agriculture (1808). Appendix IV, p.159.

29 Shaw-Taylor, L., 'Labourers, Cows, Common Rights and Parliamentary Enclosure, 1760–1810', *Past & Present*, Vol. 171 (2001), pp.95–126.

30 Howitt, W. (1844), *The Rural Life of England*, 3rd edition. London: Longman, Brown, Green and Longmans, p.175.

31 Warner, Rev. Richard (1802), *Excursions from Bath*, being Vol. IV of the Topographical Works of the Rev. Richard Warner. Bath: R. Crutwell & Son, p.7.

32 Ibid, p.7.

CHAPTER 5 SERVANTS

1 *Pride and Prejudice*, Chapter 55.

2 Le Faye, D. (ed.) (2011), *Jane Austen's Letters*, 4th edition. Oxford: Oxford University Press, p.97.

3 Cozens-Hardy, B. (ed.) (1968), *Mary Hardy's Diary*. Norwich: Norfolk Records Society, p.113.

4 Adams, S. and Adams, S. (1825), *The Complete Servant, being a Practical Guide to the Peculiar Duties and Business of all Descriptions of Servants from the Housekeeper to the Servant of all Work, and from the Land Steward to the Footboy*. London: Knight and Lacey, pp.iv–v.

5 *Persuasion*, Chapter 17.

6 Simond, L. (1817), *Journal of a Tour and Residence in Great Britain during the Years 1810 and 1811*, 2nd edition. Edinburgh: Archibald Constable and Company, p.140.

7   Le Faye (2011), p.69.

8   See Steedman, C. (2007), *Master and Servant, Love and Labour in the English Industrial Age*. Cambridge: Cambridge University Press.

9   *Mansfield Park*, Chapter 38.

10   Letter to Mrs James Austen, in Austen-Leigh, R.A. (ed.) (1942), *Austen Papers 1704–1856*. Privately printed, p.266.

11   *Emma*, Chapter 52.

12   *Persuasion*, Chapter 6.

13   *Sense and Sensibility*, Chapter 49.

14   Le Faye, D. (2004), *Jane Austen: A Family Record*, 2nd edition. Cambridge: Cambridge University Press, p. 72.

15   *Sense and Sensibility*, Chapter 2.

16   *Mansfield Park*, Chapter 3.

17   *Sense and Sensibility*, Chapter 30.

18   Adams, S. and Adams, S. (1825), *The Complete Servant, being a Practical Guide to the Peculiar Duties and Business of all Descriptions of Servants from the Housekeeper to the Servant of all Work, and from the Land Steward to the Footboy*. London: Knight and Lacey, p.10.

19   *Mansfield Park*, Chapter 10.

20   Adams and Adams (1825), pp.51–2.

21   Ibid, pp. 152

22   Sambrook, P. (2003), *A Country House at Work: Three Centuries of Dunham Massey*. London: National Trust Books, pp.28–9.

23   Adams and Adams (1825), p.236.

24   Ibid, p. 254

25   Le Faye (2011), p.303.

26   Adams and Adams (1825), p.195

27   Le Faye (2011), p.282.

28   Cozens-Hardy (1968), pp.31 and 70.

29   Adams and Adams (1825), p.294.

30   Ibid, p.341.

31   Ibid, pp.340–1.

32   Boykin, Edward (1957), *Victoria, Albert and Mrs Stevenson*. London: F. Muller, p.23.

33   Entry for 7 July 1827, in Broughton, Lord (1910), *Recollections of a Long Life*. London: John Murray, Vol. 3, p.207.

34   Adams and Adams (1825), p.342.

35   Entry for 20 August 1788, in Andrews, C.B. (ed.) (1934–8), *The Torrington Diaries*. London: Eyre & Spottiswoode, Vol.I, p.362.

36   Sambrook (2003), pp.121–2.

37   Holland, Lady (1855), *A Memoir of the Reverend Sydney Smith by his Daughter*. London: Longman, Brown, Green and Longmans, p.160.

38   Adams and Adams (1825), p.364.

39   Climenson, E.J. (ed.) (1899), *Passages from the Diaries of Mrs Philip Lybbe Powys of Hardwick House, Oxon. 1756–1808*. London: Longmans, Green, p.222.

40   Grant, E. (1911), *Memoirs of a Highland Lady: The Autobiography of Elizabeth Grant of Rothiemurchus*. London: John Murray, p.158.

41   Adams and Adams (1825), p.372.

42   See the *Journal of Aeronautical History*, Paper 2011/6 by J.A.D. Ackroyd. I am grateful to Melissa Stourton and to Vivian Bairstow for information about the ingenious Sir George. There are various versions of this story but it seems that the most likely servant was John Appleby, a groom.

43   Andrews (1934–8), Vol. I, p.53.

44   Simond (1817), p.139.

45   Wise, D. (ed.) (1987), *Diary of William Tayler*, Footman 1837. London: The St Marylebone Society, p.19.

46   Climenson (1899), pp.217–19.

47   Cadogan v. Cadogan, the Lady and the Parson 1777–1794, in Stone, L. (1993), *Broken Lives, Separation and Divorce in England 1660–1857*. Oxford: Oxford University Press, pp.270–79.

48   Boykin (1957), pp.18–19.

49   Adams and Adams (1825), p.417.

50   See Murray, V. (1998), *High Society*. London: Viking, p.68.

51   Le Faye (2011), p.290.

52   Nimrod [Apperley, C.J.] (1927), *My Life and Times*, edited by E.D. Cuming. Edinburgh: William Blackwood and Sons, pp.13–14.

53   Moore, D. Langley (1974), *Lord Byron Accounts Rendered*. London: John Murray, Appendix 3, pp.464–5; Le Faye (2011), p.563.

54   *Mansfield Park*, Chapter 8.

55   Moore (1974), Appendix 4, pp.471–4.

56   Marchand, L.A. (ed.) (1973–82), *Byron's Letters and Journals*. London: John Murray, Vol. 1, 1798–1810, p.181.

57   Marchand (1973–82), Vol. 2, p.85.

58   Marchand (1973–82), Vol. 6, p.43.

59   Holland (1855), p.164.

60   Anonymous (1825), *The Duties of a Lady's Maid, with Directions for Conduct and Numerous Receipts for the Toilette*. London: James Bulcock, pp.48–9.

61   Quoted in Adkins, R. and L.A. (2013), *Eavesdropping on Jane Austen's England*. London: Little, Brown.

62   See the online edition of *Dictionary of National Biography* (2011). Oxford: Oxford University Press. (www.oxforddnb.com/)

Chapter 6 Investment and Speculation

1   Anonymous (1818), *The London Guide and Stranger's Safeguard Against the Cheats, Swindlers, and Pickpockets*, 1st edition. London, p.3.

2   Colquhoun, P. (1797), *A Treatise on the Police of the Metropolis, explaining the Various Crimes and Misdemeanors which at the Present are felt as a Pressure upon the Community; and suggesting Remedies for their Prevention.* London: C. Dilly, p.107.

3   Ibid, p.108.

4   Southey, R. (1807b), *Letters from England, by Don Manuel Alvarez Espriella.* London: Longman, Hurst, Rees and Orme, Vol. II, p.121.

5   Craig, S., 'Northanger Abbey: Money in the Bank', *Persuasions* (2010), Vol. 32.

6   *Northanger Abbey*, Chapter 26.

7   Southey, R. (1807a), *Letters from England, by Don Manuel Alvarez Espriella.* London: Longman, Hurst, Rees and Orme, Vol. I, pp.248–9

8   Caroline Austen, in Le Faye, D. (ed.) (1986), *Reminiscences of Caroline Austen.* Exeter: The Jane Austen Society, p.27.

9   Russell, G., 'Faro's Daughters: Female Gamesters, Politics and the Discourse of Finance in 1790s Britain', *Eighteenth Century Studies*, Vol. 33, No. 4 (Summer 2000), pp.481–504.

10   *Pride and Prejudice*, Chapter 15.

11   Edmond Hoyle (1817), *The New Hoyle.* London: G. Walker, p.199.

12   Ibid, p.199.

13   For what follows see Grant, G.L. (2001), *English State Lotteries 1694–1826.* London: Geoffrey L. Grant.

14   The Repository of Arts, Literature & Fashions, etc, The Second Series. Vol. VI, No. xxxii (August 1818). Advertisement.

15   Letter to Cassandra, dated Thursday 20 May 1813, in Le Faye, D. (ed.) (2011), *Jane Austen's Letters*, 4th edition. Oxford: Oxford University Press, p.219.

16   Ashton, J. (1893), *A History of English Lotteries.* London: The Leadenhall Press, pp.118–19.

17   A young man won the diamond which was sold at Christie's on 10 May 1802 for 9,500 guineas. It subsequently came into the hands of Rundell and Bridge, the jewellers, who were said to have sold it to an Egyptian Pasha for £30,000. See Ashton (1893), p.129.

18   Thomas Trotter (1808), *View of the Nervous Temperament, Being a Practical Inquiry Into the Increasing Prevalence, Prevention, and Treatment of Those Diseases Commonly Called Nervous, etc.*, 2nd edition. Troy, NY: Wright, Goodenow & Stockwell, p.160.

19   Ashton (1893), p.161.

20   Somerville, T. (1861), *My Own Life and Times 1741–1814.* Edinburgh: Edmonston & Douglas, p.201.

21   Ibid, p.202.

22   Ibid, pp.201–5.

23 *Sanditon*, Chapter 2.

24 Ibid, Chapter 2.

25 Walton, J.K. (1983), *The English Seaside Resort: A Social History, 1750–1914.* Leicester: Leicester University Press, p.106.

26 Ibid, p.112.

27 Feltham, J. (1813), *A Guide to All the Watering and Sea-bathing Places for 1813 with a Description of the Lakes, a Sketch of a Tour in Wales, and Itineraries.* London: Longman, Hurst, Rees, Orme and Brown, p.276.

28 Cope, S.R., 'The Goldsmids and the Development of the London Money Market during the Napoleonic Wars', *Economica*, New Series, Vol. 9, No. 34 (1942), p.189.

29 Hales, S. (1796), *The Bank Mirror or a Guide to the Funds in which is Given a Clear and Full Explanation of the Process of Buying and Selling Stock, etc.* London: S. Hales, p.22.

30 Ibid, p.44.

31 Ibid, p.46.

32 See W. Toone, *The Chronological Historian, Or, A Record of Public Events: Historical, Political, Biographical, Literary, Domestic and Miscellaneous; Principally Illustrative of the Ecclesiastical, Civil, Naval and Military History of Great Britain and Its Dependencies, from the Invasion of Julius Cæsar to the Present Time,* 1826, Vol. 2, p.438. A newspaper editor, Daniel Stuart, was suspected of being the forger.

33 See *The Morning Chronicle*, Monday, 13 September 1813.

34 *The Morning Chronicle*, Thursday 5 May 1803.

35 Abraham Goldsmid, in partnership with his brother Benjamin, was the first specialist bill-broker and their firm therefore might be termed the first London discount house. Though very successful at first, both were subject to depression and both committed suicide. See Cope (1942), pp.180–206.

36 *The Morning Chronicle*, Thursday 5 May 1803.

37 *The Morning Post*, Tuesday, 5 August 1806.

38 *The Morning Post*, Thursday 10 March 1814.

39 Hales (1796), p.16.

40 *Persuasion*, Chapter 24.

41 *Sense and Sensibility*, Chapter 33.

42 *Lady Susan*, Letter 5.

43 See Cope, S.R., 'The Original Security Bank', *Economica*, Vol. 13, No. 49 (1946), pp.50–5.

44 Joplin, T. (1826), *Views on the Subject of Corn and Currency.* London: Baldwin, Cradock and Joy, p.47.

45 Letter dated 17 July 1803, in de Selincourt, E. (ed.) (1967), *The Letters of William and Dorothy Wordsworth*, 2nd edition. Oxford: Clarendon Press, Vol. I, p.398.

46 Wright, J.F., 'British Government Borrowing in Wartime 1750–1815', *Economic History Review*, New Series, Vol. 52, No. 2 (1999), p.355.

47 Simond (1817), p.238.

48 Green, D.R. and Owens, A., 'Gentlewomanly Capitalism? Spinsters, Widows and Wealth Holdings in England and Wales, *c.*1800–1860', *Economic History Review*, Vol. 56, No. 3 (2003), p.518, Table 3.

49 Anonymous (1827b), *A Legacy of Affection, Advice, and Instruction, from a Retired Governess, to the Present Pupils of an Establishment for Female Education which She Conducted upwards of Forty Years.* London: Sir Richard Phillips and Co., p.300.

50 *Sense and Sensibility*, Chapter 33.

51 Beardsley, M. and Bennett, N. (eds) (2009), *Gratefull to Providence, The Diary and Accounts of Matthew Flinders, 1775–1802*, pp.164 and 186.

52 Trotter, T. (1808), p.268. I am grateful to Hazel Jones for this reference.

53 *Sanditon*, Chapter 2.

54 Hales (1796), p.27.

55 Gayer, A.D. *et al.*, 'British Share Prices, 1811–1850', *The Review of Economics and Statistics*, Vol. 22, No. 2 (1940), p.82. The index is a weighted price index and ignores dividends.

56 Letter to Cassandra, dated Tuesday 30 April 1811, in Le Faye (2011), p.192.

57 Arnold, A.J. and McCartney, S., 'Veritable Gold Mines before the Arrival of Railway Competition: but Did Dividends Signal Rates of Return in the English Canal Industry?', *Economic History Review*, Vol. 64, No. 1 (2011), p.215.

58 Ibid, p.219.

59 Morton Eden, Sir Frederic (1797), *The State of the Poor.* London: J. Davis, Vol. 2, p.591.

60 Warner, Reverend R. (1802), *Excursions from Bath, Being Vol. IV of the Topographical Works of the Rev. Richard Warner.* Bath: R. Crutwell & Son, p.16.

61 Southey (1807b), pp.155–6.

62 Beardsley and Bennett (2009), p.212.

63 Binney, J.E.D. (1958), *British Public Finance and Administration, 1774–92.* Oxford: Clarendon Press, p.91.

64 *Sense and Sensibility*, Chapter 6.

65 Berry, M. (1914), *The Berry Papers, Being the Correspondence Hitherto Unpublished of Mary and Agnes Berry*, edited by Lewis Melville. London: John Lane, pp.179–181.

66 Ibid, p.180.

Chapter 7 The Navy

1 Analysis of 5,183 deaths in 1810, in Lewis, M. (1960), *A Social History of the Navy 1793–1815.* London: Allen & Unwin, p.420.

2 Ibid, p.348. Looking only at ships of twenty-eight guns and more in the period 1793–1815, the Royal Navy lost eighty-four ships which were wrecked, seven having foundered and ten which were burned or blown up – all without any enemy intervention. Britain's enemies lost a total of 377 ships.

3 Ibid, p.31.

4   It is thought that the grave of Captain Flinders is under platform fifteen at Euston Station in London.

5   Lewis, Michael A. (ed.) (1953), *A Narrative of My Professional Adventures (1790–1839) by Sir William Henry Dillon, KCH, Vice Admiral of the Red*. London: Navy Records Society, Vol. 93, p.237.

6   Ibid, p.84.

7   *Persuasion*, Chapter 7.

8   *Mansfield Park*, Chapter 31.

9   Dickinson, H.W. (2007), *Educating the Royal Navy*. London: Routledge, p.16.

10   *Mansfield Park*, Chapter 11.

11   Thursfield, Rear-Admiral H.G. (ed.) (1951), *Some Account of the Writer's Situation as a Chaplain in the British Navy by Edward Mangin MA*, in *Five Naval Journals 1789–1817*. London: Navy Records Society, pp.7–8.

12   Ibid.

13   The Regulations of 1790 laid down a tariff for swearing: commissioned officers paid one shilling for each offence, and warrant officers six pence, with men to wear a wooden collar or some other shameful badge of distinction. Few captains paid any attention and the order disappeared in 1806, but Gambier enforced them, weighting the collar with two thirty-two-pound shots. See Lewis, Michael A. (1953), *A Narrative of My Professional Adventures (1790–1839) by Sir William Henry Dillon, KCH, Vice Admiral of the Red*. London: Navy Records Society, Vol. 93, pp.97–104.

14   Thursfield (1951), p.10.

15   Ibid.

16   Vesey Hamilton, Admiral Sir Richard (ed.) (1903), *Letters and Papers of Admiral of the Fleet Sir Thomas Byam Martin, GCB*, Vol. 1. London: Navy Records Society, pp.56–60.

17   *Mansfield Park*, Chapter 24.

18   Le Faye, D. (2004), *Jane Austen: A Family Record*, 2nd edition. Cambridge: Cambridge University Press, p.56.

19   Dickinson (2007), p.33.

20   Lewis (1953), pp.148–9.

21   *Persuasion*, Chapter 25.

22   Letter dated 28 January 1805, in Austen-Leigh, R.A. (ed.) (1942), *Austen Papers 1704–1856*. Privately printed, p.234.

23   At the Battle of Santo Domingo on 6 February 1806 Sir John Duckworth's six ships of the line defeated five French ships, including the 130-gun *Imperial*. His force had taken many prizes before then so we may imagine that Wentworth might have spent quite a lot.

24   Trotter, T. (1808), *View of the Nervous Temperament, Being a Practical Inquiry into the Increasing Prevalence, Prevention, and Treatment of Those Diseases Commonly Called Nervous, etc.* Troy, NY: Wright, Goodenow & Stockwell, p.15.

25   Taylor, S. (2012), *Commander: The Life and Exploits of Britain's Greatest Frigate Captain*. London: Faber & Faber, pp.79–80.

26   Erskine, D. (ed.) (1954) *Augustus Hervey's Journal*. London: William Kimber, p 163.

27   Watson, G. (1827), *A Narrative of the Adventures of a Greenwich Pensioner, Written by Himself*. Newcastle: R.T. Edgar (printer), p. 89.

28   Ibid, p.89.

29   Ibid, p.89.

30   *Persuasion*, Chapter 4.

31   Le Faye, D. (2002), *Jane Austen's 'Outlandish Cousin', The Life and Letters of Eliza de Feuillide*. London: The British Library, p.118.

32   *Persuasion*, Chapter 11.

33   See Lincoln, M. (2007), *Naval Wives and Mistresses*. London: National Maritime Museum, p.32.

34   *Persuasion*, Chapter 4.

35   See *Caledonian Mercury* of Monday, 28 September 1812.

36   This action is vividly described in the opening pages of Adkins, R. (2006), *The War for All the Oceans*. London: Little, Brown.

37   *Persuasion*, Chapter 8.

38   Letter dated Wednesday 27 May 1801, in Le Faye, D. (ed.) (2011), *Jane Austen's Letters*, 4th edition. Oxford: Oxford University Press, p.95.

39   I am grateful to Roy and Lesley Adkins for this information.

40   See the illuminating account given in Kindred, S.J., 'Charles Austen: Prize Chaser and Prize Taker on the North American Station 1805–1808', *Persuasions*, 28 (2004), pp.188–194 (on which this paragraph is based).

41   Letter dated 18 August 1811, inAusten-Leigh, R.A. (ed.) (1942), *Austen Papers 1704–1856*. Privately printed, p. 249.

42   Letter dated 20 March 1812, in Austen-Leigh (1942), pp.251–2.

43   See Kaplan, D., 'Domesticity at Sea: the Example of Charles and Fanny Austen', *Persuasions*, Vol. 14 (2004), pp.113–21.

44   Vesey Hamilton (1903), pp.90–1.

45   *Naval Chronicle*, Vol. 5 (1801), pp.256–7.

46   Ibid, pp.256–7.

47   Hill, J.R. (1998), *The Prizes of War*. Stroud: Sutton, p.181.

48   *Persuasion*, Chapter 8.

49   *Persuasion*, Chapter 3.

50   Blane, G. (1785), *Observations on the Diseases Incident to Seamen*. London: John Murray, p. 211.

51   *Persuasion*, Chapter 18.

52   *Naval Chronicle* (1801), pp.254–5.

53   Hill (1998), p.177.

54   It was still smaller than the greatest capture of all, when the *Active* and the *Favourite* took the Spanish frigate *Hermione* in 1762, where a seaman's share was

£485. Captains Sawyer and Pownoll got about £65,000 each. Both men had been courting sisters, the daughters of a Lisbon merchant, whom they were now rich enough to marry.

55   Hill (1998), p.65.

56   Lloyd, C. (ed.) (1953), *The Keith Papers*. London: Navy Records Society, p. 218.

57   Rodger, N.A.M. (2004), *The Command of the Ocean*. London: Allen Lane, p.524.

58   *Naval Chronicle* (1806) Vol. 15, p.269.

59   Lewis (1953), p.328.

60   See Hilton, J.D., 'An Admiral and his Money: Vice Admiral Cuthbert Collingwood', *The Mariner's Mirror*, Vol. 95, No. 3 (2009), pp.296–300.

61   Southam, B.C. (2000), *Jane Austen and the Navy*. London: Hambledon Press, p.34–5.

62   Letter dated 14 October 1803, in Nicolas, Sir N.H. (1845), *The Dispatches and Letters of Vice Admiral Lord Viscount Nelson, with notes by Sir Nicholas Harris Nicolas*, Vol. 5. London: Henry Colburn, p.245.

63   Navy Records Society, *Recollections of James Anthony Gardner*, Vol. 31 (1906).

64   See Consalvo, C., 'Prospects and Promotion of British Naval Officers 1793–1815', *The Mariner's Mirror*, Vol. 91, No. 2 (2005).

65   *Mansfield Park*, Chapter 36.

66   Ibid, Chapter 38.

67   *Naval Chronicle*, Vol. 97, pp.153–4.

68   Letter dated 17 Jan 1801 to Lady Hamilton, in Pettigrew, T.J. (1849), *Memoirs of the Life of Vice-Admiral Lord Viscount Nelson, KB, Duke of Bronte*. London: T. and W. Boone, Vol. 1, pp.136.

69   Ibid, p.410.

70   Hibbert, C. (1994), *Nelson: A Personal History*. London: Viking, p.245.

71   *Persuasion*, Chapter 8.

72   Southam (2000), p.52.

73   *Persuasion*, Chapter 24.

74   *Mansfield Park*, Chapter 6.

75   Ibid, Chapter 6.

CHAPTER 8 THE CHURCH

1   Entry for 4 July 1789, in Andrews, C.B. (ed.) (1934–8), *The Torrington Diaries*. London: Eyre & Spottiswoode, Vol.II, p.130.

2   Southey, R. (1807b), *Letters from England, by Don Manuel Alvarez Espriella*. London: Longman, Hurst, Rees and Orme, Vol.II, p.344.

3   Simond, L. (1817), *Journal of a Tour and Residence in Great Britain during the Years 1810 and 1811*, 2nd edition. Edinburgh: Archibald Constable and Company, pp.156–7.

4   Grant, E. (1911), *Memoirs of a Highland Lady: The Autobiography of Elizabeth Grant of Rothiemurchus*. London: John Murray, p.366

5   Holland, Lady, (1855), *A Memoir of the Reverend Sydney Smith by his Daughter.*
     London: Longman, Brown, Green and Longmans, p.25.

6   *Dean and Chapter Act Book, 1768–1802*, Vol. 5, p.231 verso, quoted in Trueman,
     B.E.S., 'Corporate Estate Management: Guy's Hospital Agricultural Estates 1726–
     1815', *Agricultural History Review*, Vol. 28, No. 1 (1980), p.31.

7   Christie, O.F. (ed.) (1966), *The Diary of the Rev. William Jones, 1777–1821.* London:
     Brentano's, p.155.

8   Southey (1807a), p.42.

9   Holland (1855), p.43.

10   Simond (1817), pp.174–5.

11   *Mansfield Park*, Chapter 48.

12   *Sense and Sensibility*, Chapter 38.

13   Quoted in Le Faye, D. (ed.) (2004), *Jane Austen: A Family Record*, 2nd edition.
     Cambridge: Cambridge University Press, p.235.

14   *Persuasion*, Chapter 9.

15   Wade, J. (1831), *The Extraordinary Black Book.* London: Effingham Wilson, p.20 – a
     not-wholly-reliable exposition of abuses in Church and State by John Wade (1788–
     1875), a Benthamite radical.

16   *Mansfield Park*, Chapter 3.

17   Ibid, Chapter 3.

18   Smith, S., 'Letter on the Curates' Salary Bill', *Edinburgh Review*, No. XXV, Art. II
     (1808), p.28.

19   See for several summary biographies Brown, C.K.F. (1953), *A History of the English
     Clergy, 1800–1900.* London: Faith Press, pp.80–111.

20   Ibid, p.80.

21   Colquhoun, P. (1815), *A Treatise on the Wealth, Power and Resources of the British
     Empire*, 2nd edition. London: Joseph Mawman, p.124, Table 4.

22   Evans, E.J. (1976), *The Contentious Tithe: The Tithe Problem and English Agriculture,
     1750–1850.* London and Boston, Mass.: Routledge & Kegan Paul, p.2.

23   The Bishop of Durham did not lose his palatinate until 1836.

24   The Right Reverend John Moore's (1730–1805) eldest son by his second mar-
     riage was Reverend George Moore (1771–1845), who married (as his second wife)
     Harriet Mary Bridges, one of Sir Brook Bridge's thirteen children. One of her
     sisters, Elizabeth, married Edward Austen Knight (see Le Faye, D. (ed.) (2011), *Jane
     Austen's Letters*, 4th edition. Oxford: Oxford University Press).

25   Evans (1976), p.5.

26   Wade (1831), p.24.

27   *Mansfield Park*, Chapter 11.

28   Dewey, C. (1991), *The Passing of Barchester.* London: Hambledon Press, p.144.

29   Christie (1966), p.191.

30   *The Loiterer*, No. 21, Saturday 20 June 1789.

31 *Pride and Prejudice*, Chapter 60.

32 Letter dated August 1802, in Smith, Nowell C. (ed.) (1953), *The Letters of Sydney Smith*. Oxford: Clarendon Press, p. 73.

33 Pearson, H. (1934), *The Smith of Smiths*. London: Hamish Hamiliton, p.127.

34 Southey, R. (1807a), p.212

35 Ibid, p.212

36 *Mansfield Park*, Chapter 25.

37 *Mansfield Park*, Chapter 9.

38 *Mansfield Park*, Chapter 11.

39 *Mansfield Park*, Chapter 9.

40 Holland (1855), p.41.

41 Southey (1807a), p 219.

42 *Mansfield Park*, Chapter 34.

43 Letter dated Monday 11 December 1815, in Le Faye (2011), p.319.

44 Grant (1911), pp.131–2.

45 *The Loiterer*, No. 8, Saturday 21 March 1789.

46 Ibid.

47 Southey (1807b), *Letters from England, by Don Manuel Alvarez Espriella*. London: Longman, Hurst, Rees and Orme, Vol. II, pp.291–2.

48 *The Loiterer*, No. 8, Saturday 21 March 1789.

49 Virgin, P. (1989), *The Church in an Age of Negligence: Ecclesiastical Structure and Problems of Church Reform 1700–1840*. Cambridge: James Clarke, p.282, Table XI.

50 *The Loiterer*, No. 12, Saturday 18 April 1789.

51 Virgin (1989), p.284, Table XIII.

52 *The Loiterer*, No. 21, Saturday 20 June 1789.

53 *Persuasion*, Chapter 9.

54 Tindal Hart, A. (1970) *The Curate's Lot, The Story of the Unbeneficed English Clergy*. London: J. Baker, p.103.

55 Virgin (1989), p.295, Table XX.

56 Holland (1855), p.11.

57 Somerville, T. (1861), *My Own Life and Times 1741–1814*. Edinburgh: Edmonston & Douglas, p.282.

58 Holland (1855), p.11.

59 Brown (1953), p 19.

60 Collins, I. (1994), *Jane Austen and the Clergy*. London: Hambledon Press, p.29.

61 Tindal Hart (1970), p.127.

62 Evans (1976), p.9.

63 Plumptre, A. (1798), *The Rector's Son*. London: Lee and Hurst.

64 Christie (1966), p.94.

65 Ibid, p.174.

66 He also became fatter. Having kept a coffin in his study for many years, he used it as a cupboard – in death he proved too large for it.

67 Smith, S. (1808), pp.25–6.

68 Evans (1976), p.3.

69 Brown (1953), p.15n.

70 *The Loiterer*, No. 21, Saturday 20 June 1789.

71 Christie (1966), p.148.

72 Fendell, C.P. and Crutchley, E.A. (eds) (1933), *The Diary of Benjamin Newton, Rector of Wath, 1816–18*. Cambridge: Cambridge University Press, p.43.

73 Ibid, p.48.

74 Quoted in Tindal Hart (1970), p.130.

75 Tindal Hart (1970), p.115.

76 Evans (1976), p.4.

77 Holland (1855), p.144.

78 For what follows, see Outhwaite, R.B. (1997), *Scandal in the Church*. London: Hambledon Press.

79 Colquhoun (1807b), p.124, Table 4.

80 *Sense and Sensibility*, Chapter 50.

81 Collins (1994), pp.86–9.

82 Ibid, pp.28–9.

83 Letter dated 27–8 December 1808, in Le Faye (2011), p.167.

84 O'Brien, P.K., 'British Incomes and Property in the Early Nineteenth Century', *Economic History Review*, Vol. 12, No. 2 (1959), p.266.

85 *Catherine, or the Bower*.

86 Collins (1994), p.51.

87 Morton Eden, Sir Frederick (1797), *The State of the Poor*. London: J. Davis, Vol. 1, p.ix.

88 Ibid, p.xii.

89 Evans (1976), p.7.

90 Christie (1966), p.147.

91 Ibid, p.187.

92 Evans (1976), p.33.

93 Virgin (1989), p.270, Table I.

94 Evans (1976), p.31.

95 See Kaplan, D., 'Henry Austen and John Rawston Papillon', *Jane Austen Society Report* (1987).

96 Pearson (1934), p.132.

97   Smith (1953), p.166.

98   Huxley, V. (2013), *Jane Austen and Adlestrop*. Gloucestershire: Windrush Publishing, pp.66–8.

99   *Mansfield Park*, Chapter 25.

100   Ibid, Chapter 25.

101   Ibid, Chapter 25.

102   *Northanger Abbey*, Chapter 26.

103   *Mansfield Park*, Chapter 25.

104   Ibid, Chapter 25.

105   *Northanger Abbey*, Chapter 26.

106   See Wilson, R.G. and Mackley, A.L., 'How Much Did the English Country House Cost to Build, 1660–1880?', in *Economic History Review*, Vol. 52, No. 3 (1999).

107   Huxley (2013), p.21.

108   *Mansfield Park*, Chapter 6.

109   Virgin (1989), p.280, Table ix.

CHAPTER 9 SHOPPING

1   Williams, C. (trnsl.)(1933), *Sophie in London, 1786, Being the Diary of Sophie von La Roche*. London: Jonathan Cape, p.87.

2   Ibid, p.141.

3   Ibid, p.111.

4   Ibid, p.132.

5   Southey, R. (1807a), *Letters from England, by Don Manuel Alvarez Espriella*. London: Longman, Hurst, Rees and Orme, Vol. I, p 83.

6   Grant, E. (1911), *Memoirs of a Highland Lady: The Autobiography of Elizabeth Grant of Rothiemurchus*. London: John Murray.

7   Rush, R. (1833), *Residence at the Court of London*. London: Richard Bentley, p.51 (7 January 1818).

8   Mui, H.C. and Mui, L.H. (1989), *Shops and Shopkeeping in Eighteenth-Century England*, extracted from Tables on pp.67–9.

9   Williams (1933), p.83. Mrs Lybbe Powys also liked Colchester in 1781 calling it 'an exceeding pretty town full of good houses'.

10   See Stobart, J., 'Shopping Streets as Social Space: Leisure, Consumerism and Improvement in an Eighteenth-Century Town', *Urban History*, Vol. 25, No, 1 (1998).

11   *Northanger Abbey*, Chapter 2.

12   *Emma*, Chapter 24.

13   *Sanditon*, Chapter 4.

14   Mui and Mui (1989), pp.77–81.

15   Ibid, p.100.

16   Letter to Cassandra, dated 27 October 1798, in Le Faye, D. (ed.) (2011), *Jane Austen's Letters*, 4th edition. Oxford: Oxford University Press, p.18.

17   See Mitchell, I., 'The Changing Role of Fairs in the Long Eighteenth Century: Evidence from the North Midlands', *Economic History Review*, Vol. 60, No. 3 (2007), pp.545–73.

18   Ibid, p.561.

19   Howitt, W. (1844), *The Rural Life of England*, 3rd edition. London: Longman, Brown, Green and Longmans, pp.497–8.

20   Letter to Anna Lefroy, dated Friday 29 September 1815, in Le Faye (2011), p.302.

21   Letter to Caroline Austen, dated Sunday 21 April 1816, in Le Faye (2011), p.328.

22   Letter to Cassandra, dated Saturday 25 September 1813, in Le Faye (2011), p.240.

23   Jane Austen, *A Collection of Letters, third letter.*

24   Southey (1807a), pp.120–1.

25   *The Lady's Magazine*, April 1800, pp. 171–76.

26   Southey (1807a), p.119.

27   McKendrick, N., Brewer, J. and Plumb, J.H. (1982), *The Birth of a Consumer Society: The Commercialization of Eighteenth-Century England.* London: Europa, p.29.

28   Letter to Anna Lefroy [?], possibly dated December 1814, in Le Faye (2011), p.300 and note p.445.

29   Letter to Cassandra, dated 26 November 1815, in Le Faye (2011), p.313.

30   Letter to Cassandra, dated Thursday 18 April 1811, in Le Faye (2011), p.187.

31   Letter to Cassandra, dated Thursday 16 September 1813, in Le Faye, D. (ed.) (2011), *Jane Austen's Letters*, 4th edition. Oxford: Oxford University Press, p.233. Reproduced by permission of Oxford University Press.

32   Le Faye, D., 'The Austens and their Wedgwood Ware', *Jane Austen Society Report* (2005), pp.12–13.

33   For what follows see McKendrick, N., 'Josiah Wedgwood and the Commercialization of Potteries', in McKendrick, Brewer and Plumb (1982), pp.100–145.

34   Ibid, p.112.

35   Williams (1933), p.122.

36   See McKendrick, N., 'Josiah Wedgwood and the Commercialization of Potteries', in McKendrick, Brewer and Plumb (1982), p.113.

37   Hazlitt, W. (1830), *The Conversations of James Northcote Esq. RA.* London: Henry Colbourn and Richard, Conversation No. 19, p.264.

38   McKendrick, Brewer and Plumb (1982), pp.61–2.

39   *Pride and Prejudice*, Chapter 39.

40   Roberts, W. (ed.) (1834), *Memoirs of the Life and Correspondence of Mrs Hannah More.* London: R.B. Seeley and W. Burnside, Vol. I, pp.64–5.

41   Letter to Cassandra, dated Sunday 2 June 1799, in Le Faye (2011), p.44.

42   *Pride and Prejudice*, Chapter 47.

43   *Mansfield Park*, Chapter 40.

44   Ibid, Chapter 40.

45   See Copeland, E. (1995). *Women Writing about Money – Women's Fiction in England 1790–1820*. Cambridge: Cambridge University Press, p.89 onwards.

46   *Sense and Sensibility*, Chapter 33.

47   Ibid, Chapter 17.

48   Byrde, P. (1999), *Jane Austen Fashion*. Ludlow: Excellent Press, p.66.

49   Stobart, J. (2011), 'Gentlemen and Shopkeepers: Supplying the Country House in Eighteenth-century England', *Economic History Review*, Vol. 64, No. 3, p.888.

50   Ibid, p.896.

51   *Pride and Prejudice*, Chapter 31.

52   Ibid, Chapter 8.

53   Howitt, W. (1838), *The Rural Life of England*, Vol. I. London: Longman, Brown, Green and Longmans, p.31.

54   Marchand, J. (ed.) (1995), *A Frenchman in England 1784, being the Mélanges sur l'Angleterre of Francois de la Rochefoucauld*. London: Caliban, pp.28–30. Rochefoucauld (1765–1848) was the son of the Duc de Liancourt. Under Louis XVIII he was made a field marshal and a duke, before succeeding his father as Duc de Rochefoucauld.

55   Ibid, p.30.

56   Ibid, p.31.

57   Bovill, E.W. (1962), *English Country Life*. Oxford and New York: Oxford University Press, p.109.

58   Alexander, L. (1808), *Memoirs of the Life and Commercial Connections, Public and Private, of the late Benj. Goldsmid, Esq. of Roehampton*. London: the author, pp.97–9.

59   Holland, Lady (1855), *A Memoir of the Reverend Sydney Smith by his Daughter*, Vol. I. London: Longman, Brown, Green and Longmans, p.335.

60   Berg, M. (2005), *Luxury and Pleasure in Eighteenth-Century Britain*. Oxford: Oxford University Press, p.238.

61   Ibid, p.241.

62   Letter to Cassandra, dated Thursday 6 June 1811, in Le Faye (2011), p.202.

63   Slothouber, 'Elegance and Simplicity: Jane Austen and Wedgwood', *Persuasions*, 31, pp.163–72.

64   Sparrow, J., (1963), *Independent Essays*. London: Faber & Faber, pp.88–96.

CHAPTER 10 CARRIAGES

1   Howitt, W. (1838), *The Rural Life of England*, Vol. I. London: Longman, Brown, Green and Longmans, p.110.

2   Le Faye, D. (2004), *A Family Record*, 2nd edition. Cambridge: Cambridge University Press, p.106. A neighbouring squire, not knowing the Austen crest, reported that

'Mr Austen had put a coronet on his carriage because of his son's being married to a French Countess.' On 31 December 1797 Henry married Eliza de Feuillide.

3   Letter to James-Edward Austen, dated 9 July 1816, in Le Faye, D. (ed.) (2011), *Jane Austen's Letters*, 4th edition. Oxford: Oxford University Press, p.330..

4   Letter dated 24 January 1817, in Le Faye (2011), p.94–5.

5   Letter dated 26–7 May 1801, in Le Faye (2011), p.341.

6   Letter dated 20 May 1813, in Le Faye (2011), p.219.

7   Letter dated 24 May 1813, in Le Faye (2011), p.222.

8   *The Memoirs of Mr. Clifford: an Unfinished Tale.*

9   Felton, W. (1794), *A Treatise on Carriages*, Vol. 2. London, the author, pp.114–15.

10   Letter dated 24 January 1813, in Le Faye (2011).

11   *Persuasion*, Chapter 10.

12   *Sense and Sensibility*, Chapter 19.

13   *Northanger Abbey*, Chapter 7.

14   Anonymous (1827a), *A New System of Practical Domestic Economy Founded on Modern Discoveries and the Private Communications of Persons of Experience*. London: Henry Colbourn, p.461.

15   Ibid, p.458.

16   *Northanger Abbey*, Chapter 11.

17   *Sanditon*, Chapter 7.

18   Jones, H. (2014), *Jane Austen's Journeys*. London: Robert Hale, p.84.

19   *Northanger Abbey*, Chapter 20.

20   Ibid, Chapter 20.

21   *Morning Post*, 29 December 1804.

22   Ibid.

23   Climenson, Emily J. (ed.) (1899), *Passages from the Diaries of Mrs Philip Lybbe Powys of Hardwick House, Oxon. 1756–1808*. London: Longmans, Green, p. 210.

24   Felton, W., (1794), *A Treatise on Carriages*, Vol.II. London: the author.

25   Ibid, table on p.13.

26   *Sanditon*, Chapter 2.

27   Felton (1794), p.24.

28   *Persuasion*, Chapter 5.

29   *Morning Chronicle*, 22 September 1817.

30   Williams, C. (transl.) (1933), *Sophie in London, 1786, being the Diary of Sophie von La Roche*. London: Jonathan Cape, p. 158.

31   Wood, L. (1990), 'Furniture for Lord Delaval: metropolitan and provincial', *Furniture History*, Vol. 26, p.201.

32   *The Three Sisters*, Letter 1.

33   Felton (1794), p.i.

34 *Morning Post*, 29 December 1804.

35 It has been a long-lasting fashion to which may be attributed the colour of Pop Larkin's Rolls Royce in *The Darling Buds of May*.

36 Trotter, Thomas (1808), *View of the Nervous Temperament, being a Practical Inquiry Into the Increasing Prevalence, Prevention, and Treatment of Those Diseases Commonly Called Nervous, etc.* Troy, NY: Wright, Goodenow & Stockwell.

37 Only after 1815 was the qualification of an apothecary made more formal. Keats served a five-year apprenticeship from 1810 as a surgeon-apothecary. In 1815 the new Apothecaries Act required six months' training in a hospital before a candidate could present himself before the Court of Examiners of the Society of Apothecaries and become licenced, as Keats did. A further six months would be required before being able to apply for membership of the Royal College of Surgeons.

38 Gittings, R. (1968), *John Keats*. London: Heinemann, pp.63–4.

39 Holland, Lady (1855), *A Memoir of the Reverend Sydney Smith by his Daughter*. London: Longman, Brown, Green and Longmans, pp.168–9.

40 *Sense and Sensibility*, Chapter 3.

41 *Morning Post*, Friday 5 January 1804.

42 *Morning Post*, Friday 20 January 1804.

43 Grant, E. (1911), *Memoirs of a Highland Lady: The Autobiography of Elizabeth Grant of Rothiemurchus*. London: John Murray.

44 See letter of 5 May 1800, in Grierson, H.J.C. (ed.) (1932–7), *The Letters of Sir Walter Scott*. London: Constable & Co.

45 Partington, W. (1932), *Sir Walter's Post-Bag*. London: John Murray, pp.10–11.

46 Lockhart, J.G. (1837), *Memoirs of the Life of Sir Walter Scott*, Vol. III. Paris: Baudry's European Library, p.251.

47 *Sense and Sensibility*, Chapter 2.

48 *Persuasion*, Chapter 17.

49 Ibid, Chapter 24.

50 *Pride and Prejudice*, Chapter 24.

51 Holland (1855), p.161.

CHAPTER 11 SINGLE GENTLEWOMEN

1 Letter to Fanny Knight, 13 March 1817, in Le Faye, Deirdre (ed.) (2011), *Jane Austen's Letters*, 4th edition. Oxford: Oxford University Press, p.347.

2 William Hayley (1785), *A Philosophical, Historical, and Moral Essay on Old Maids, by a Friend to the Sisterhood*. London: T. Cadell, p.7.

3 *Pride and Prejudice*, Chapter 22.

4 Ibid, Chapter 22.

5 *Sense and Sensibility*, Chapter 8.

6 *The Watsons*, part one.

7   *Lady Susan*, Letter 7.

8   Hayley (1785), p.3.

9   Hayley (1785), pp.7–8.

10 Morton Eden, Sir Frederic (1797), *The State of the Poor*, Vol. I. London: J. Davis, p.626.

11 Ibid, p.626.

12 See Heleniak, K.M., 'Money and Marketing problems. The Plight of Harriet Gouldsmith (1786–1863), *The British Art Journal*, Vol. 6, No. 3 (2005).

13 Reeve, C. (1792), *Plans of Education; with Remarks on the Systems of Other Writers, in a Series of Letters between Mrs Darnford and her Friends*. London: T. Hookam and J. Carpenter, pp.61–2.

14 Mui, H.C. and Mui, L.H. (1989), *Shops and Shopkeeping in the Eighteenth Century*. Kingston: McGill–Queen's University Press, p.58.

15 Ellis, Sarah (1839), *The Women of England: Their Social Duties and Domestic Habits*. London: Fisher and Son, p.323–4.

16 Reeve (1792), p.119.

17 Ellis (1839).

18 *Emma*, Chapter 35.

19 *Mansfield Park*, Chapter 2.

20 *Pride and Prejudice*, Chapter 45.

21 Le Faye (2011), p.117.

22 Letter dated 30 January 1809, in Le Faye (2011), p.180.

23 It is ironic that poor Miss Sharpe's copy of *Emma*, inscribed 'With the author's compliments' by a publisher's clerk, was sold at auction in 2008 for £180,000 and reportedly then to a private collector for £325,000.

24 Letter dated 20 February 1807, in Le Faye (2011), p.129.

25 Letter dated 9 December 1808, in Le Faye (2011), p.164 and note p.572.

26 Adams, S. and Adams, S. (1825), *The Complete Servant, being a Practical Guide to the Peculiar Duties and Business of all Descriptions of Servants from the Housekeeper to the Servant of all Work, and from the Land Steward to the Footboy*. London: Knight and Lacey, pp.272–6.

27 Ibid, p.274.

28 Ibid, p.275.

29 Grant E. (1911), *Memoirs of a Highland Lady: The Autobiography of Elizabeth Grant of Rothiemurchus*. London: John Murray.

30 Edgeworth, M. and Edgeworth, R.L. (1815), *Essays on Practical Education*, Vol. 2, p.174.

31 Ibid, pp.178–9.

32 Reeve (1792), pp.60–61.

33 Edgeworth and Edgeworth (1815), p.183.

34 *Persuasion*, Chapter 5.

35 *Sanditon*, Chapter 11.

36 *Pride and Prejudice*, Chapter 8.

37 Edgeworth and Edgeworth (1815), p.386.

38 *Pride and Prejudice*, Chapter 29.

39 Edgeworth and Edgeworth (1815), p.184.

40 *Pride and Prejudice*, Chapter 8.

41 Edgeworth and Edgeworth (1815), p.170–1.

42 Letter from Agnes Porter to Lady Mary Fox Strangways, dated 21 December 1789, in Martin, J. (ed.) (1998), *A Governess in the Age of Jane Austen: The Journals and Letters of Agnes Porter.* London: Hambledon, p.82.

43 *Sense and Sensibility*, Chapter 26.

44 *Emma*, Chapter 3.

45 Ibid, Chapter 3.

46 Lewis, S., 'On the Social Position of Governesses', *Fraser's Magazine* (April 1848), p.413.

47 Edgeworth and Edgeworth (1815), p.209.

48 Diary entry, dated 21 October 1802, of Agnes Porter, in Martin (1998), p.216.

49 Edgeworth and Edgeworth (1815), p.209.

50 Ibid, p.210–11.

51 Martin (1998), p.217.

52 Lewis (1848), p.412.

Statistical Appendix

1 Colquhoun, P. (1815), *A Treatise on the Wealth, Power and Resources of the British Empire, second edition.* London: Joseph Mawman, pp.106–7.

2 Colquhoun (1815), pp.124–5.

3 Officer, L.H. and Williamson, S.H., 'Annual Inflation Rates in the United States, 1775–2013, and United Kingdom, 1265–2013', *Measuring Worth*, 2013. URL: www. measuringworth.com/uscompare/ (accessed June 2015).

4 Homer, S. and Sylla, R. (eds) (2005), *A History of Interest rates*, 4th edition. Hoboken, NJ: John Wiley, pp.158 and 192.

5 Based on Steel's List of the Royal Navy, in Lewis, Michael A. (1960), *A Social History of the Navy 1793–1815*. London: Allen & Unwin, p.308–9.

6 Ibid, p.311.

7 Anonymous (1827a), *A New System of Practical Domestic Economy, founded on Modern Discoveries, and the Private Communications of Persons of Experience.* London: Henry Colburn, p.458.

8   Ibid, p.461.
9   Ibid, p.463.
10   Ibid, pp.448–9.

Bibliography

BOOKS

Abbott, John L. (ed.) (2004), *The Selected Essays of Donald Greene*. Lewisburg: Bucknell University Press.

Adams, Samuel and Adams, Sarah (1825), *The Complete Servant, being a Practical Guide to the Peculiar Duties and Business of all Descriptions of Servants from the Housekeeper to the Servant of all Work, and from the Land Steward to the Footboy*. London: Knight and Lacey.

Adkins, Roy (2006), *The War for all the Oceans*. London: Little, Brown.

—— and Adkins, Lesley (2013), *Eavesdropping on Jane Austen's England*. London: Little, Brown.

Alexander, Levy (1808), *Memoirs of the Life and Commercial Connections, Public and Private, of the late Benj. Goldsmid, Esq. of Roehampton*. London: the author.

Andrews, C.B. (ed.) (1934–8), *The Torrington Diaries*. London: Eyre & Spottiswoode.

Anonymous (1818), *The London Guide and Stranger's Safeguard Against the Cheats, Swindlers, and Pickpockets*, 1st edition. London, p.3.

Anonymous (1825), *The Duties of a Lady's Maid, with Directions for Conduct and Numerous Receipts for the Toilette*. London: James Bulcock.

Anonymous (1827a), *A New System of Practical Domestic Economy, founded on Modern Discoveries, and the Private Communications of Persons of Experience*. London: Henry Colburn.

Anonymous (1827b), *A Legacy of Affection, Advice, and Instruction, from a Retired Governess, to the Present Pupils of an Establishment for Female Education which She Conducted upwards of Forty Years*. London: Sir Richard Phillips and Co.

Ashton, John (1893), *A History of English Lotteries*. London: The Leadenhall Press.

Austen-Leigh, R.A. (ed.) (1942), *Austen Papers 1704–1856*. Privately printed.

Barchas, Janine (2012), *Matters of Fact in Jane Austen*. Baltimore, Ma.: Johns Hopkins University Press.

Beardsley, M. and Bennett, N. (eds) (2007–9), *Gratefull to Providence: The Diary and Accounts of Matthew Flinders, 1775–1802*. Woodbridge: The Lincoln Record Society/Boydell Press.

Berg, Maxine (2005), *Luxury and Pleasure in Eighteenth-Century Britain*. Oxford: Oxford University Press.

Berry, Mary (1914), *The Berry Papers*. London: John Lane.

Binney, J.E.D. (1958), *British Public Finance and Administration, 1774–92*. Oxford: Clarendon Press.

Bisset, J. (1800), *A Poetic Survey round Birmingham with a Brief Description of the Different Curiosities of the Place, intended as a Guide to Strangers*. Birmingham: the author.

Bonnard, G.A. (ed.) (1966), *Edward Gibbons: Memoirs of My Life*. London: Nelson.

Bovill, E.W. (1962), *English Country Life*. London and New York: Oxford University Press.

Boykin, Edward (1957), *Victoria, Albert and Mrs Stevenson*. London: F. Muller.

Broughton, Lord (1909–11), *Recollections of a Long Life*. London: John Murray.

Brown, Francis C.K. (1953), *A History of the English Clergy, 1800–1900*. London: Faith Press.

Byrde, Penelope (2008), *Jane Austen's Fashions: Fashion and Needlework in the Works of Jane Austen*. Bath: Moonrise Press.

Christie, O.F. (ed.) (1966), *The Diary of the Revd. William Jones, 1777–1821*. London: Brentano's.

Climenson. Emily J. (ed.) (1899), *Passages from the Diaries of Mrs Philip Lybbe Powys of Hardwick House, Oxon. 1756–1808*. London: Longmans, Green.

Collins, Irene (1994), *Jane Austen and the Clergy*. London: Hambledon Press.

Colquhoun, Patrick (1797), *A Treatise on the Police of the Metropolis, explaining the Various Crimes and Misdemeanors which at the Present are felt as a Pressure upon the Community; and suggesting Remedies for their Prevention*. London: C. Dilly.

—— (1814), *A Treatise on the Wealth, Power, and Resources of the British Empire*, 1st edition. London: Joseph Mawman.

—— (1815), *A Treatise on the Wealth, Power, and Resources of the British Empire*, 2nd edition. London: Joseph Mawman.

Copeland, Edward (1995), *Women Writing about Money: Women's Fiction in England, 1790–1820*. Cambridge: Cambridge University Press.

Cozens-Hardy, B. (1968), *Mary Hardy's Diary*. Norwich: Norfolk Records Society.

D'Archenholz, M. (1789), *A Picture of England containing a Description of the*

Laws, Customs and Manners of England, translated from the French. London: Edward Jeffery.

Davidoff, L. and Hall, C. (1987), *Family Fortunes: Men and Women of the English Middle Class 1780–1850*. London: Hutchinson.

Dewey, Clive (1991), *The Passing of Barchester*. London: Hambledon Press.

Dickinson, H.W. (2007), *Educating the Royal Navy*. London: Routledge.

Edgeworth, Maria and Edgeworth, Richard L. (1815), *Essays on Practical Education: A New Edition in Two Volumes*. London: R. Hunter.

Ellis, Sarah (1839), *The Women of England: Their Social Duties and Domestic Habits*. London: Fisher and Son.

Erskine, D. (ed.) (1954), *Augustus Hervey's Journal*. London: William Kimber.

Evans, E.J. (1976), *The Contentious Tithe, the Tithe Problem and English Agriculture, 1750–1850*. London and Boston, Mass.: Routledge & Kegan Paul.

Feltham, John (1813), *A Guide to All the Watering and Sea-bathing Places for 1813 with a Description of the Lakes, a Sketch of a Tour in Wales, and Itineraries*. London: Longman, Hurst, Rees, Orme and Brown.

Felton, William (1794), *A Treatise on Carriages*. London: the author.

Fendell, C.P. and Crutchley, E.A. (eds) (1933), *The Diary of Benjamin Newton, Rector of Wath, 1816–18*. Cambridge: Cambridge University Press.

Ford, John (2005), *Coachmaker, the Life and Times of Philip Godsal 1747–1826*. Shrewsbury: Quiller Press.

Gittings, Robert (1968), *John Keats*. London: Heinemann.

Grant, Elizabeth (1911), *Memoirs of a Highland Lady: The Autobiography of Elizabeth Grant of Rothiemurchus*. London: John Murray.

Grant, G.L. (2001), *English State Lotteries 1694–1826*. London: Geoffrey L. Grant.

Grierson, H.J.C. (ed.) (1932–7), *The Letters of Sir Walter Scott*. London: Constable & Co.

Habakkuk, John (1993), *Marriage, Debt and the Estates System*. Oxford: Clarendon Press.

Hales, Charles (1796), *The Bank Mirror or a Guide to the Funds in which is Given, a Clear and Full Explanation of the Process of Buying and Selling Stock, etc.* London: the author.

Hart, Arthur Tindal (1970), *The Curate's Lot: The Story of the Unbeneficed English Clergy*. London: J. Baker.

Hayley, William (1785), *A Philosophical, Historical, and Moral Essay on Old Maids, by a Friend to the Sisterhood*. London: T. Cadell.

Hazlitt, William (1830), *The Conversations of James Northcote Esq. RA*. London: Henry Colburn and Richard Bentley.

Hibbert, Christopher (1994), *Nelson: A Personal History*. London: Viking.

Hill, J.R. (1998), *The Prizes of War*. Stroud: Sutton.

Holland, Lady (1855), *A Memoir of the Reverend Sydney Smith by his Daughter*. London: Longman, Brown, Green and Longmans.

Homer, S. and Sylla, R. (2005), *A History of Interest Rates*, 4th ed. Hoboken, NJ: John Wiley.

Howitt, William (1844), *The Rural Life of England*, 3rd edition. London: Longman, Brown, Green and Longmans.

Hoyle, Edmond (1817), *The New Hoyle*. London: G. Walker.

Huxley, Victoria (2013), *Jane Austen and Adlestrop*. Gloucestershire: Windrush Publishing.

Jones, F.L. (ed.) (1964), *The Letters of Percy Bysshe Shelley*. Oxford: Clarendon Press.

Jones, Hazel (2009), *Jane Austen and Marriage*. London: Continuum.

—— (2014), *Jane Austen's Journeys*. London: Robert Hale.

Joplin, Thomas (1826), *Views on the Subject of Corn and Currency*. London: Baldwin, Cradock and Joy.

Lane, Maggie (1984), *Jane Austen's Family*. London: Robert Hale.

—— (2014), *Growing Older with Jane Austen*. London: Robert Hale.

Le Faye, Deirdre (ed.) (1986), *Reminiscences of Caroline Austen*. Exeter: The Jane Austen Society.

—— (2002), *Jane Austen's 'Outlandish Cousin', The Life and Letters of Eliza de Feuillide*. London: The British Library.

—— (2004), *Jane Austen: A Family Record*, 2nd edition. Cambridge: Cambridge University Press.

—— (2011), *Jane Austen's Letters*, 4th edition. Oxford: Oxford University Press.

Lewis, Michael A. (ed.) (1953), *A Narrative of my Professional Adventures (1790–1839) by Sir William Henry Dillon, KCH, Vice Admiral of the Red*. London: Navy Records Society.

Lewis, Michael (1960), *A Social History of the Navy 1793–1815*. London: Allen & Unwin.

—— (1965), *The Navy in Transition 1814–1864*. London: Hodder and Stoughton.

Lincoln, Margarette (2007), *Naval Wives and Mistresses*. London: National Maritime Museum.

Lloyd, Christopher, (ed.) (1953), *The Keith Papers*. London: Navy Records Society.

McKendrick, N., Brewer J. and Plumb, J.H. (1982), *The Birth of a Consumer Society: The Commercialization of Eighteenth-Century England*. London: Europa.

Marchand, Jean (ed.) (1995), *A Frenchman in England 1784, being the Mélanges sur l'Angleterre of François de la Rochefoucauld*. London: Caliban.

Marchand, Leslie A. (ed.) (1973–82), *Byron's Letters and Journals*, London: John Murray.

Martin, Joanna (ed.) (1998), *A Governess in the Age of Jane Austen: The Journals and Letters of Agnes Porter*. London: Hambledon Press.

Michie, E.B. (2011), *The Vulgar Question of Money*. Baltimore: Johns Hopkins University Press.

Mingay, G.E. (1963), *English Landed Society in the Eighteenth Century*. London: Routledge & Kegan Paul.

Moore, Doris Langley (1974), *Lord Byron's Accounts Rendered*. London: John Murray.

Morton Eden, Sir Frederic (1797), *The State of the Poor*, Vols I–III. London: J. Davis.

Mui, Ho-Cheung and Mui, Lorna H. (1989), *Shops and Shopkeeping in the Eighteenth Century*. Kingston: McGill–Queen's University Press.

Mullan, John (2012), *What Matters in Jane Austen?* London: Bloomsbury.

Murray, Venetia (1998), *High Society*. London: Viking.

Nicolas, Sir N.H. (1845), *The Dispatches and Letters of Vice Admiral Lord Viscount Nelson, with notes by Sir Nicholas Harris Nicolas*, Vol. 5. London: Henry Colburn.

Nimrod [Apperley, Charles James] (1927), *My Life and Times*, edited by E.D. Cuming. Edinburgh: William Blackwood and Sons.

Outhwaite, R.B. (1997), *Scandal in the Church*. London: Hambledon Press.

Pearson, Hesketh (1934), *The Smith of Smiths*. London: Hamish Hamilton.

Pettigrew, Thomas Joseph (1849), *Memoirs of the Life of Vice-Admiral Lord Viscount Nelson, KB, Duke of Bronte, etc.* London: T. and W. Boone.

Reeve, Clara (1792), *Plans of Education; with Remarks on the Systems of Other Writers, in a Series of Letters between Mrs Darnford and her Friends*. London: T. Hookham and J. Carpenter.

Reeve, Henry (ed.) (1874), *Charles Greville: Memoirs*. London: Longmans, Green & Co.

Roberts, William (ed.) (1834), *Memoirs of the Life and Correspondence of Mrs Hannah More*. London: R.B. Seeley and W. Burnside, Vol. I.

Rodger, N.A.M. (2004), *The Command of the Ocean*. London: Allen Lane.

Rush, Richard (1833), *Residence at the Court of London*. London: Richard Bentley.

Sambrook, Pamela (2003), *A Country House at Work: Three Centuries of Dunham Massey*. London: National Trust Books.

de Selincourt, Ernest (ed.) (1967), *The Letters of William and Dorothy Wordsworth*, 2nd edition. Oxford: Clarendon Press, Vol. I.

Simond, Louis (1817), *Journal of a Tour and Residence in Great Britain during the Years 1810 and 1811*, 2nd edition. Edinburgh: Archibald Constable and Company.

Slothouber, Linda (2015), *Jane Austen, Edward Knight and Chawton: Commerce and Community*. Gaithersburg: Woodpigeon Publishing.

Smith, Nowell C. (ed.) (1953), *The Letters of Sydney Smith*. Oxford: Clarendon Press.

Somerville, Thomas (1861), *My Own Life and Times 1741–1814*. Edinburgh: Edmonston & Douglas.

Southam, B.C. (2000), *Jane Austen and the Navy*. London: Hambledon Press.

Southey, Robert (1807a), *Letters from England, by Don Manuel Alvarez Espriella*. London: Longman, Hurst, Rees and Orme, Vol. I.

—— (1807b), *Letters from England, by Don Manuel Alvarez Espriella*. London: Longman, Hurst, Rees and Orme, Vol. II.

—— (1807c), *Letters from England, by Don Manuel Alvarez Espriella*. London: Longman, Hurst, Rees and Orme, Vol. III.

Sparrow, J. (1963), *Independent Essays*. London: Faber and Faber.

Spring, David (1963), *The English Landed Estate in the Nineteenth Century: Its Administration*. Baltimore: Johns Hopkins Press.

Steedman, Carolyn (2007), *Master and Servant, Love and Labour in the English Industrial Age*. Cambridge: Cambridge University Press.

Stone, Lawrence (1993), *Broken Lives, Separation and Divorce in England 1660–1857*. Oxford: Oxford University Press.

Taylor, Stephen (2012), *Commander: The Life and Exploits of Britain's Greatest Frigate Captain*. London: Faber and Faber.

Thursfield, Rear Admiral H.G. (ed.) (1951), *Some Account of the Writer's Situation as a Chaplain in the British Navy by Edward Mangin MA, in Five Naval Journals 1789–1817*. London: Navy Records Society.

Todd, Janet (ed.) (2005), *Jane Austen in Context*. Cambridge: Cambridge University Press.

Tomalin, Claire (1997), *Jane Austen: A Life*. London: Viking.

Toone, W. (1826), *The Chronological Historian, Or, A Record of Public Events: Historical, Political, Biographical, Literary, Domestic and Miscellaneous; Principally Illustrative of the Ecclesiastical, Civil, Naval and Military History of Great Britain and Its Dependencies, from the Invasion of Julius Cæsar to the Present Time*, Vol. 2. London: Longman, Rees, Orme, Brown and Green.

Trotter, Thomas (1812), *View of the Nervous Temperament, being a Practical Inquiry Into the Increasing Prevalence, Prevention, and Treatment of Those Diseases Commonly Called Nervous, etc.* London: Longman, Rees, Orme, Brown and Green.

Vesey Hamilton, Sir Richard (ed.) (1903), *Letters and Papers of Admiral of the Fleet Sir Thomas Byam Martin, GCB*. London: Navy Records Society.

Virgin, P. (1989), *The Church in an Age of Negligence, Ecclesiastical Structure and Problems of Church Reform 1700–1840*. Cambridge: James Clarke.

Wade, John (1831), *The Extraordinary Black Book*. London: Effingham Wilson.

Walton, J.K. (1983), *The English Seaside Resort: A Social History, 1750–1914*. Leicester: Leicester University Press.

Warner, Rev. Richard (1802), *Excursions from Bath, being vol. IV of the Topographical Works of the Rev. Richard Warner*. Bath: R. Crutwell & Son.

Watson, George (1827), *A Narrative of the Adventures of a Greenwich Pensioner, written by himself*. Newcastle: R.T. Edgar (printer).

Williams, Clare (transl.) (1933), *Sophie in London, 1786, being the Diary of Sophie von La Roche*. London: Jonathan Cape (1933).

Wise, Dorothy (ed.) (1987), *Diary of William Tayler, Footman 1837*. London: The St Marylebone Society.

Journals and Periodicals

Ackroyd, J.A.D., *Journal of Aeronautical History*, Paper 2011/6.

Arnold, A.J. and McCartney, S., 'Veritable Gold Mines before the Arrival of Railway Competition: but Did Dividends Signal Rates of Return in the English Canal Industry?', *Economic History Review* (2011), Vol. 64, No. 1.

Burnette, J., 'An Investigation of the Female–male Wage Gap during the Industrial Revolution in Britain', *Economic History Review* (1997), Vol. 50, No. 2.

Clark, G., 'Farm Wages and Living Standards in the Industrial Revolution: England 1670–1869', *Economic History Review* (2001), Vol. 54, No. 3.

Consalvo, Charles, 'Prospects and Promotion of British Naval Officers 1793–1815', *The Mariner's Mirror* (2005), Vol. 91, No. 2.

Cope, S.R., 'The Goldsmids and the Development of the London Money Market during the Napoleonic Wars', *Economica* (1942) Vol. 9, No. 34.

—— 'The Original Security Bank', *Economica* (1946), Vol. 13, No. 49.

Copeland, Edward, 'What's a Competence? Jane Austen, her Sister Novelists and the 5%'s', *Modern Language Studies* (1979), Vol. 9, No. 3.

Craig, Sheryl, 'Northanger Abbey: Money in the Bank', *Persuasions* (2010), Vol. 32.

Gayer, A.D. *et al*, 'British Share Prices, 1811–1850', *The Review of Economics and Statistics* (1940), Vol. 22, No. 2.

Green, D.R. and Owens, A., 'Gentlewomanly Capitalism? Spinsters, Widows and Wealth Holdings in England and Wales, *c.* 1800–1860', *Economic History Review* (2003), Vol. 56, No. 3.

Greene, D., 'The Originals of Pemberley', *Eighteenth Century Fiction*, Vol. 1 (October 1988).

Hilton, J.D., 'An Admiral and his Money: Vice Admiral Cuthbert Collingwood', *The Mariner's Mirror* (2009), Vol. 95, No. 3.

Horrell, S. and Humphries, J., 'Families' Living Standards, 1787–1865', *Journal of Economic History* (1992), Vol. 52, No. 4.

—— 'Women's Labour Force Participation 1790–1865', *Economic History Review* (1995), Vol. 48, No. 1.

Jackson, T.V., 'British Incomes circa 1800', *Economic History Review*, (1999), Vol. 52, No. 2.

Kaplan, D., 'Henry Austen and John Rawston Papillon', *Jane Austen Society Report* (1987).

Kindred, Sheila Johnson, 'Charles Austen: Prize Chaser and Prize Taker on the North American Station 1805–1808', *Persuasions* (2004), No. 26.

Le Faye, Deirdre, 'The Austens and their Wedgwood Ware', *Jane Austen Society Report* (2005).

Lewis, S., 'On the Social Position of Governesses', *Fraser's Magazine*, (April 1848).

Mitchell, I., 'The Changing Role of Fairs in the Long Eighteenth Century: Evidence from the North Midlands', *Economic History Review* (2007), Vol. 60, No. 3, 2007.

Moore Heleniak, Kathryn 'Money and Marketing Problems: The Plight of Harriot Gouldsmith (1786–1863), *The British Art Journal* (2005), Vol. 6, No. 3.

O'Brien, P.K., 'British Incomes and Property in the Early Nineteenth Century', *Economic History Review* (1959), Vol. 12, No. 2.

—— 'The Political Economy of British Taxation 1660–1815', *Economic History Review* (1988), Vol. 41, No. 1.

Rogers, Nicholas, 'Money, Land and Lineage: The Big Bourgeoisie of Hanoverian London', *Social History* (1979), Vol. 4.

Russell, G., 'Faro's Daughters: Female Gamesters, Politics and the Discourse of Finance in 1790s Britain', *Eighteenth Century Studies* (2000), Vol. 33, No. 4.

Shaw-Taylor, L., 'Labourers, Cows, Common Rights and Parliamentary Enclosure, 1760–1810', *Past & Present* (2001), Vol. 171.

Slothouber, Linda, 'Elegance and Simplicity: Jane Austen and Wedgwood', *Persuasions* (2009), No. 31.

—— 'Bingley's Four or Five Thousand, and other Fortunes from the North', *Persuasions* (2013), No. 35.

Snell, K.D.M., 'English Rural Societies and Geographical Marital Endogamy, 1700–1837', *Economic History Review*, (2002), Vol. 55, No. 2.

Solar, P.M., 'Poor Relief and English Economic Development', *Economic History Review*, (1995), Vol. 48, No. 1.

Stobart, J., 'Gentlemen and Shopkeepers: Supplying the Country House in Eighteenth Century England', *Economic History Review* (2011), Vol. 64, No. 3.

—— 'Shopping Streets as Social Space: Leisure, Consumerism and Improvement in an Eighteenth-century Town', *Urban History* (1998), Vol. 25, No. 1.

Trueman, B.E.S., 'Corporate Estate Management: Guy's Hospital Agricultural Estates 1726–1815', *The Agricultural History Review* (1980), Vol. 28, No. 1.

Ward, J.T., 'The Beaumont Family Estates in the Nineteenth Century', *Bulletin of the Institute of Historical Research* (1962), Vol. 35.

Wilson, R. G., and Mackley, A. L., ' How much did the English Country House Cost to Build, 1660–1880?' in *Economic History Review* (1999), Vol. 52, No. 3.

Wood, L., 'Furniture for Lord Delaval: Metropolitan and Provincial', *Furniture History* (1990), Vol. 26.

Wright, J.F., 'British Government Borrowing in Wartime 1750–1815', *Economic History Review* (1999), Vol. 52, No. 2.

ONLINE RESOURCES

Clark, Gregory, '*What Were British Earnings and Prices Then?* (New Series)', Measuring Worth, 2014. URL: http://www.measuringworth.com/uke-arncpi (accessed June 2015).

Officer, Lawrence H. and Williamson, Samuel H., 'Five Ways to Compute the Relative Value of a UK Pound Amount, 1270 to Present', Measuring Worth, 2014. URL: http://www.measuringworth.com/ukcompare/ (accessed June 2015).

INDEX